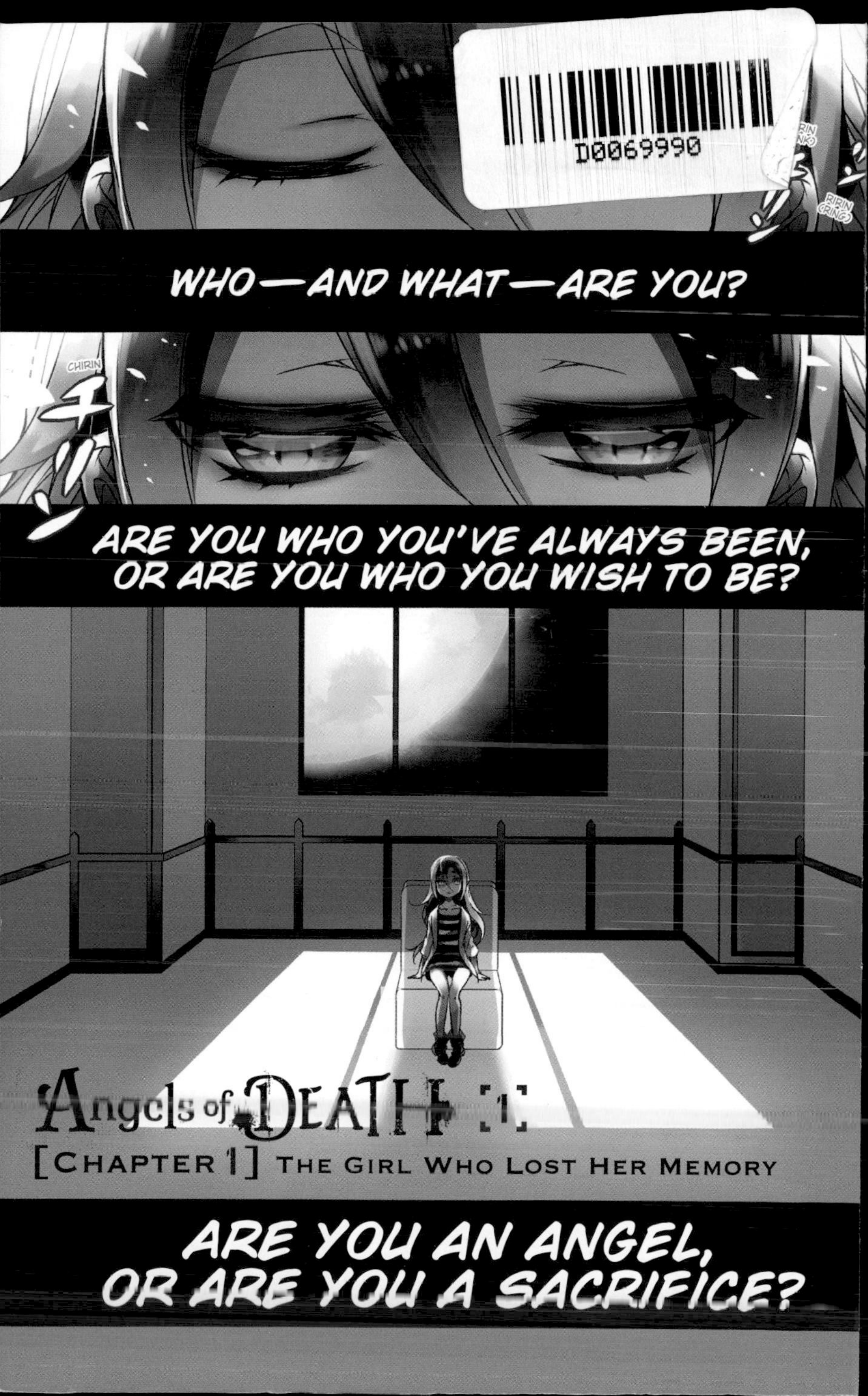
RIRIN (RING)
WHO—AND WHAT—ARE YOU?
CHIRIN
ARE YOU WHO YOU'VE ALWAYS BEEN, OR ARE YOU WHO YOU WISH TO BE?
Angels of DEATH [1]
[CHAPTER 1] THE GIRL WHO LOST HER MEMORY
ARE YOU AN ANGEL, OR ARE YOU A SACRIFICE?

Angels of DEATH [1]

Art by Kudan Naduka
Original Story by Makoto Sanada

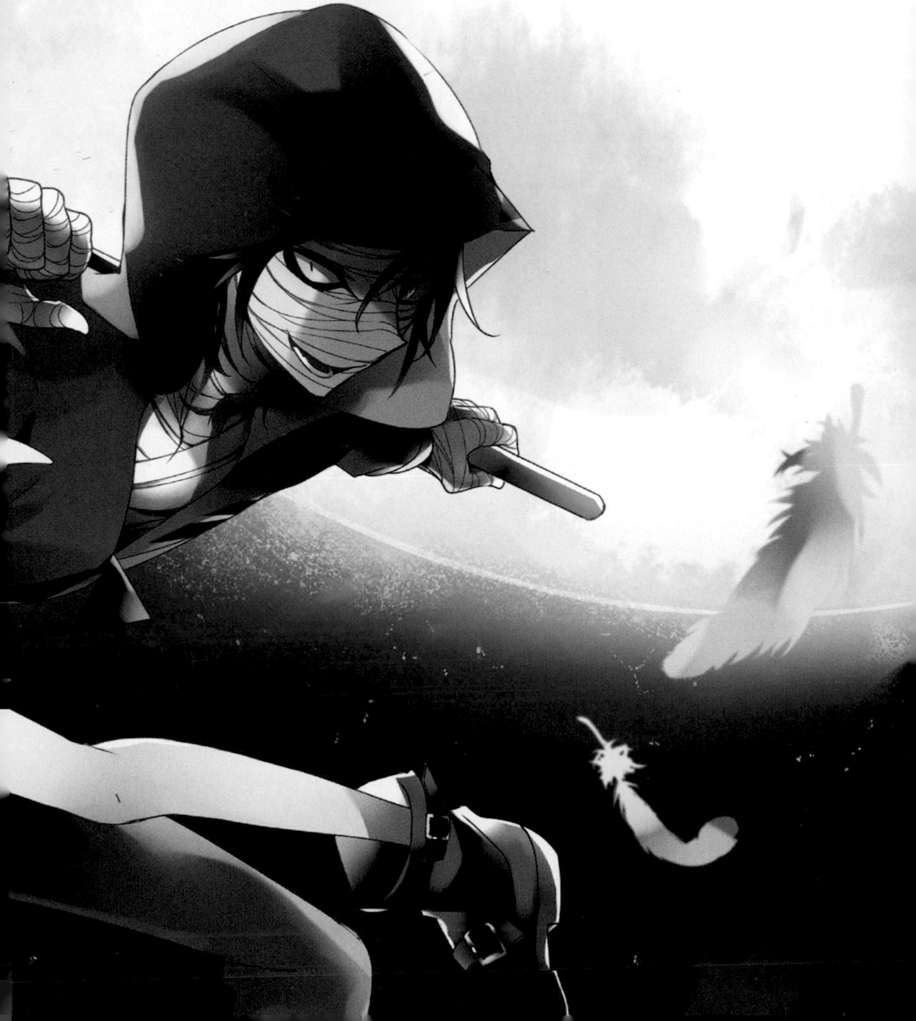

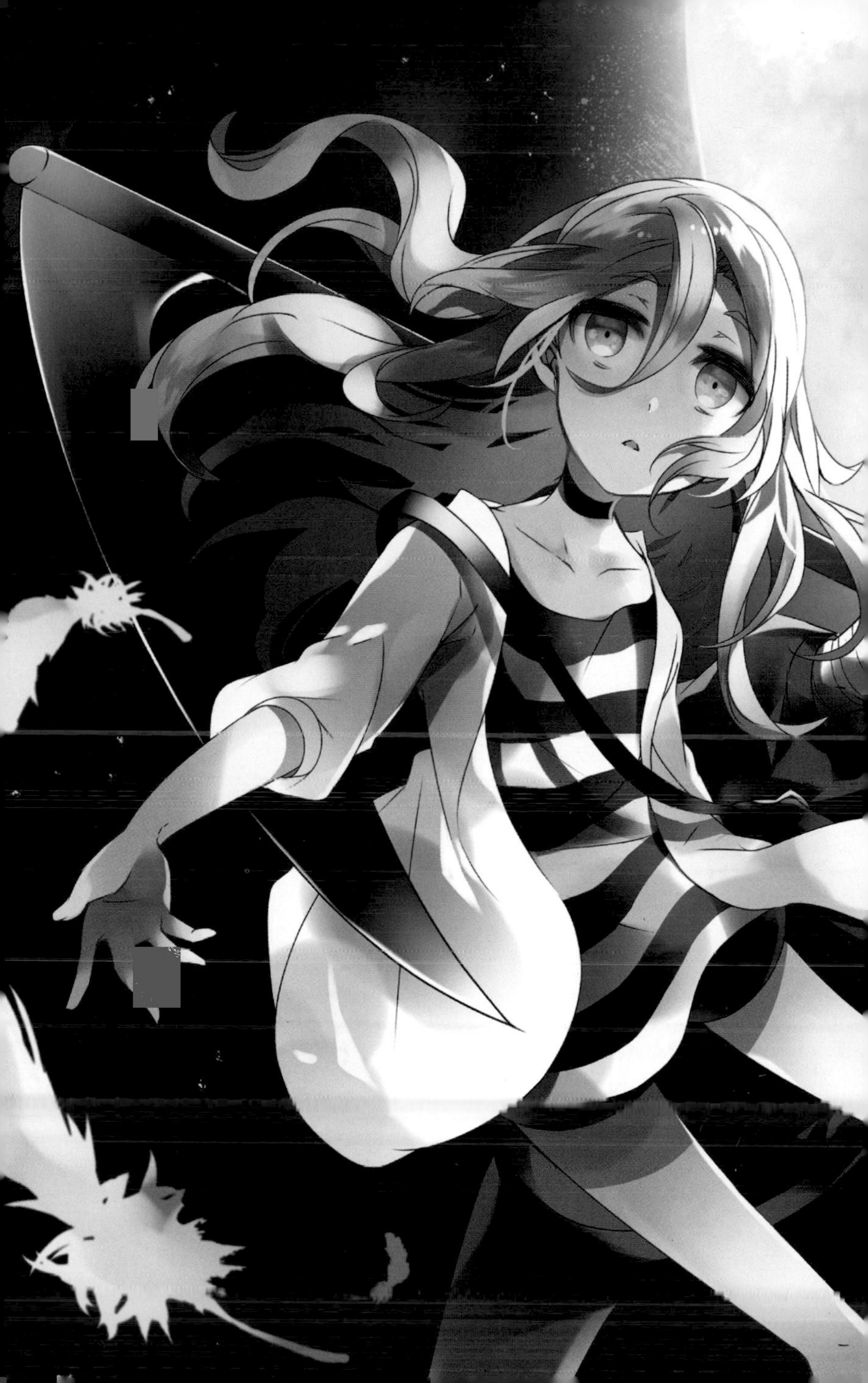

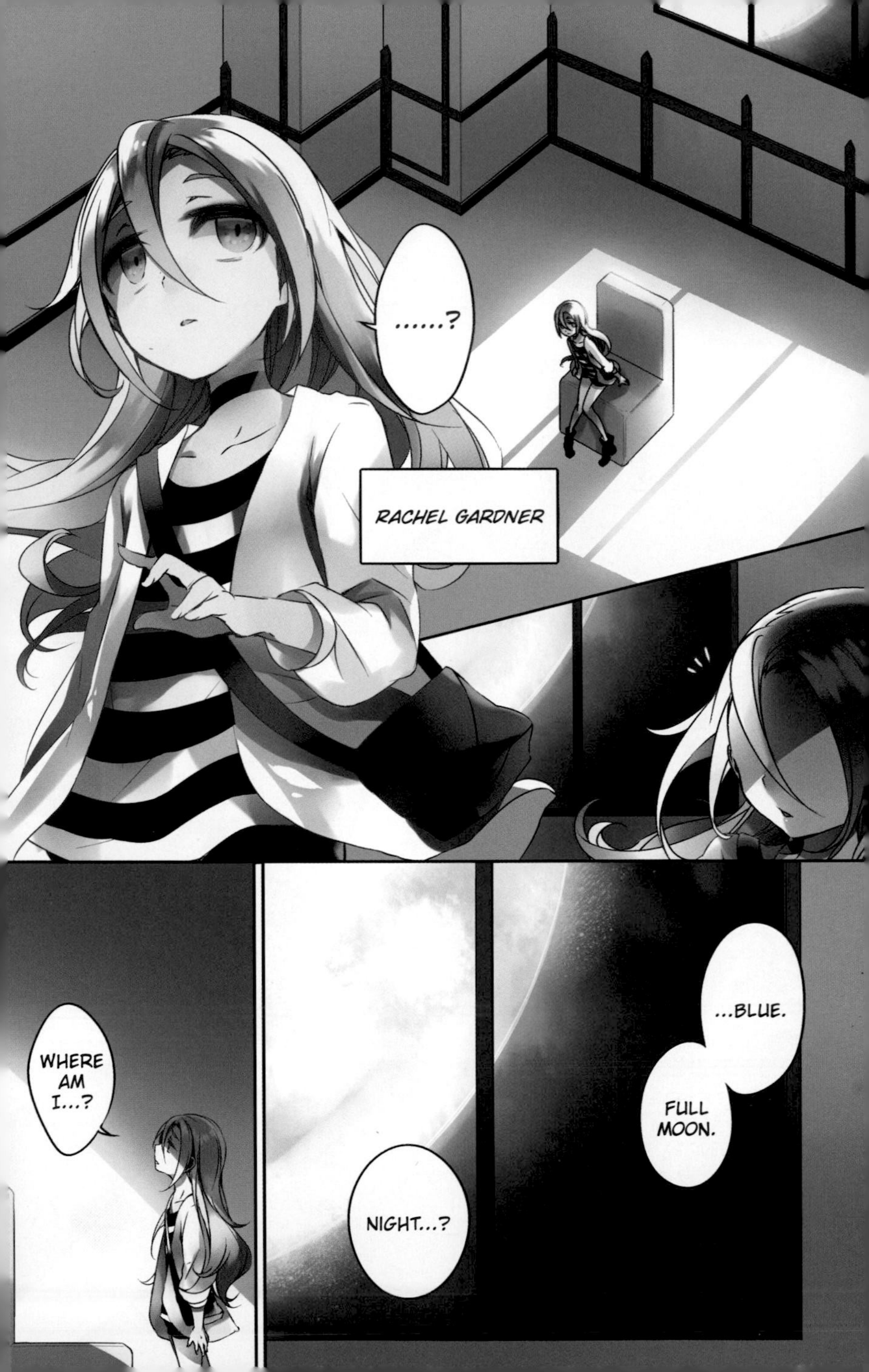

......?
RACHEL GARDNER
...BLUE.
FULL MOON.
NIGHT...?
WHERE AM I...?

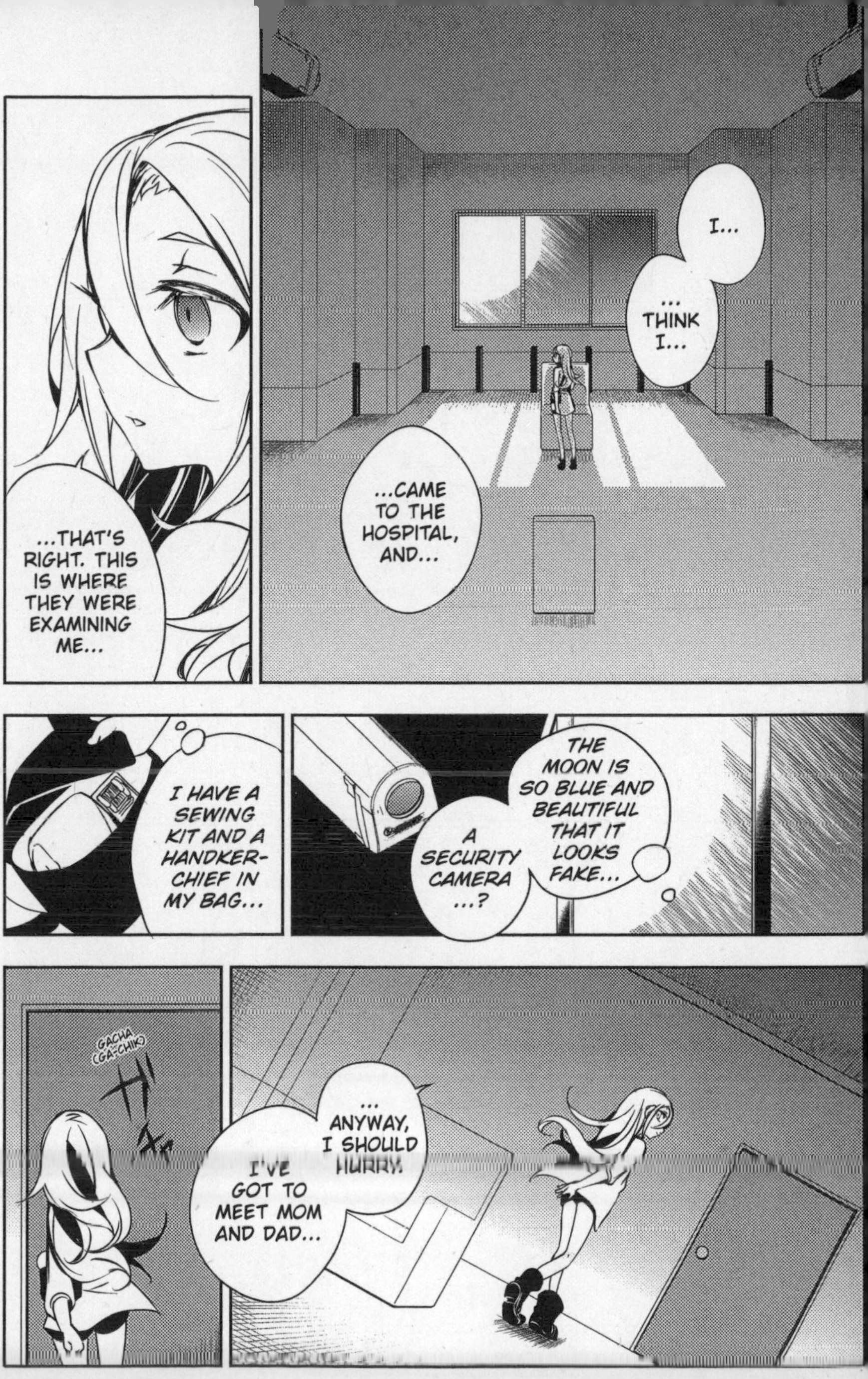
I...
...THINK I...
...CAME TO THE HOSPITAL, AND...
...THAT'S RIGHT. THIS IS WHERE THEY WERE EXAMINING ME...
THE MOON IS SO BLUE AND BEAUTIFUL THAT IT LOOKS FAKE...
A SECURITY CAMERA ...?
I HAVE A SEWING KIT AND A HANDKER-CHIEF IN MY BAG...
...ANYWAY, I SHOULD HURRY.
I'VE GOT TO MEET MOM AND DAD...
GACHA (GA-CHIK)

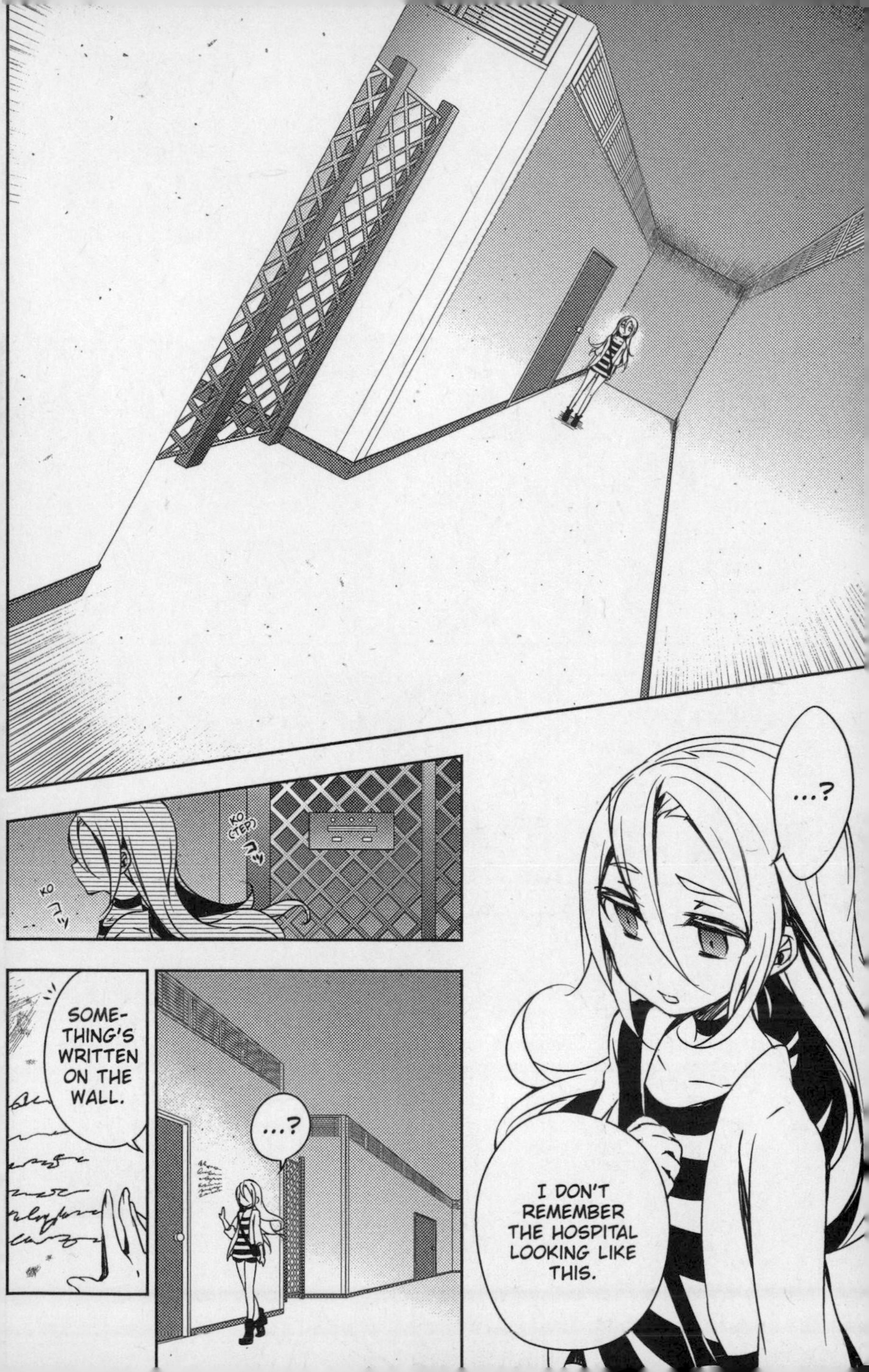
...?
I DON'T REMEMBER THE HOSPITAL LOOKING LIKE THIS.
KO (TEP)
KO
...?
SOME-THING'S WRITTEN ON THE WALL.

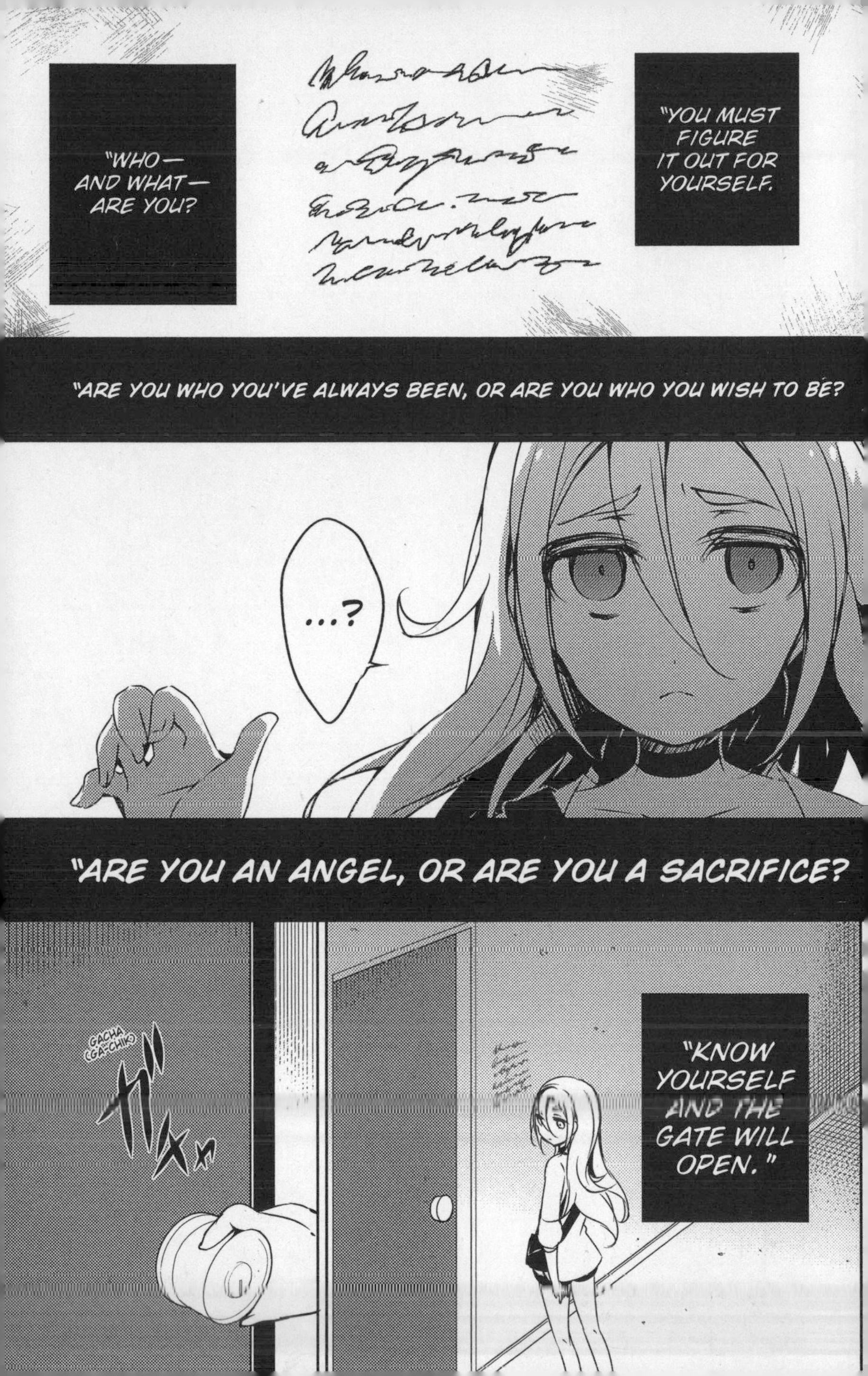
"YOU MUST FIGURE IT OUT FOR YOURSELF.
"WHO— AND WHAT— ARE YOU?
"ARE YOU WHO YOU'VE ALWAYS BEEN, OR ARE YOU WHO YOU WISH TO BE?
...?
"ARE YOU AN ANGEL, OR ARE YOU A SACRIFICE?
"KNOW YOURSELF AND THE GATE WILL OPEN."
GACHA (GA-CHIK)

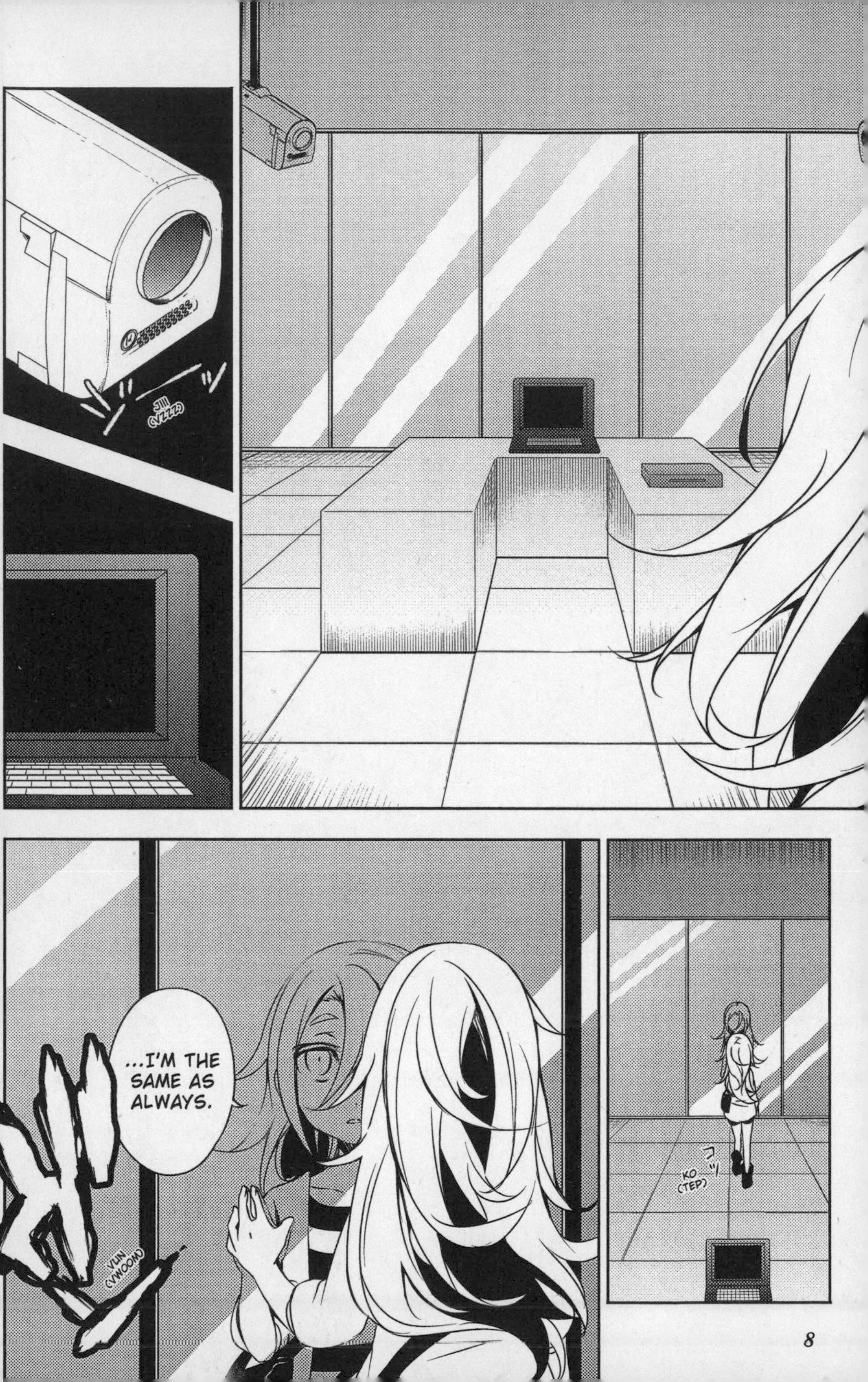
JIII
(VZZZ)
コッ
KO
(TEP)
...I'M THE SAME AS ALWAYS.
VUN
(VWOOM)

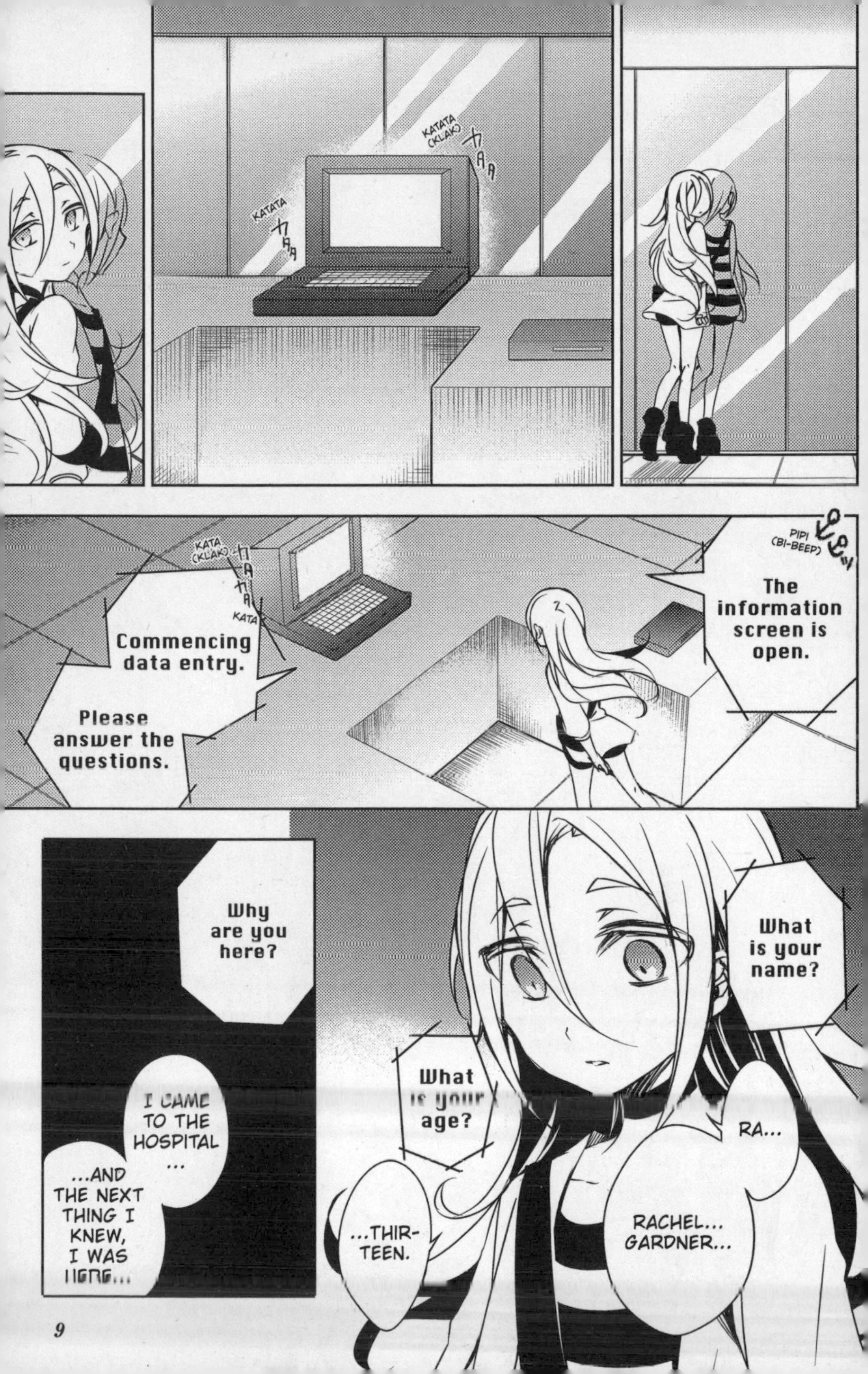
KATATA (KLAK)
KATATA
PIPI (BI-BEEP)
The information screen is open.
KATA (KLAK)
KATA
Commencing data entry.
Please answer the questions.
What is your name?
RA...
RACHEL... GARDNER...
What is your age?
...THIR-TEEN.
Why are you here?
I CAME TO THE HOSPITAL ...
...AND THE NEXT THING I KNEW, I WAS HERE...

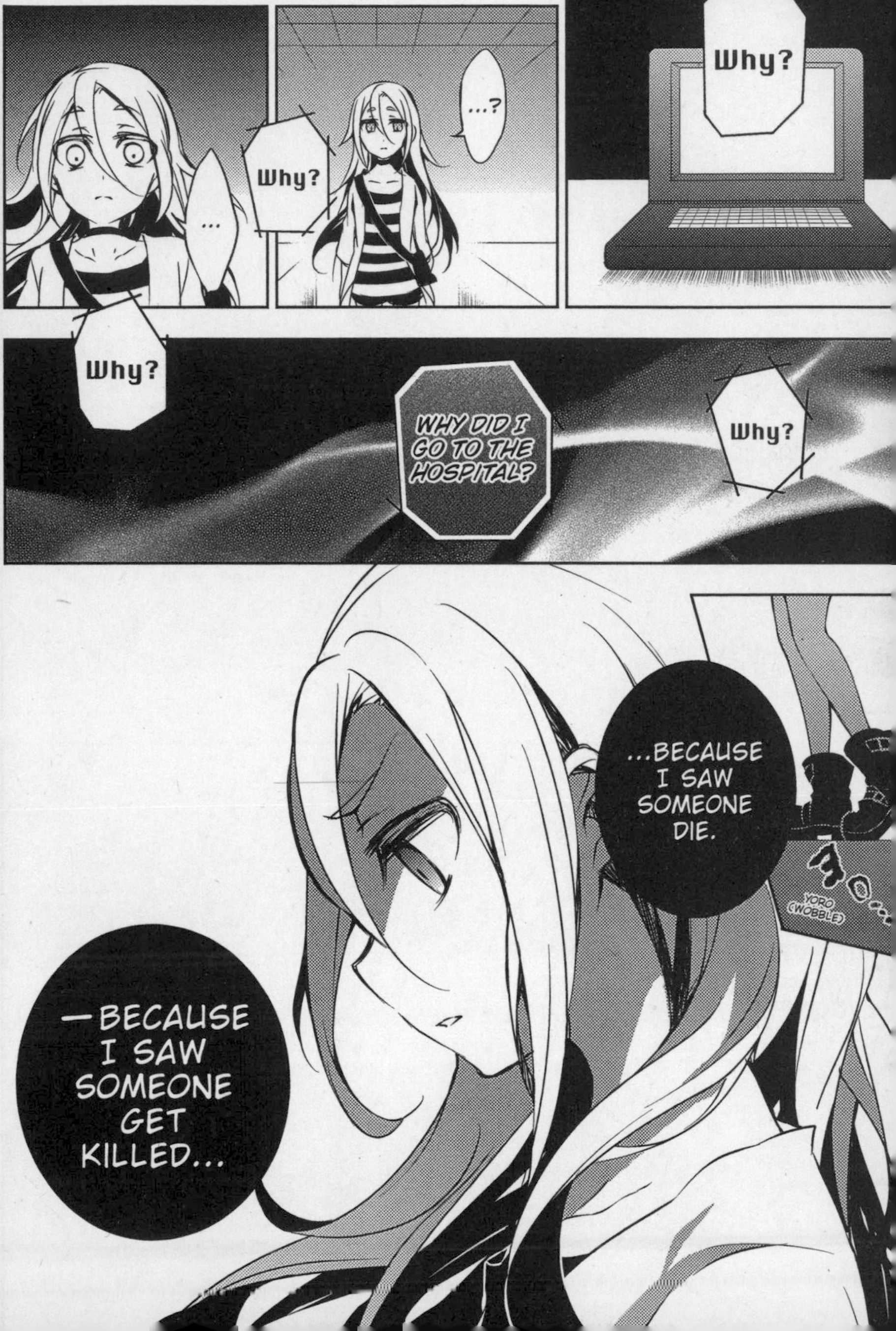
Why?
...?
Why?
...
Why?
WHY DID I GO TO THE HOSPITAL?
Why?
...BECAUSE I SAW SOMEONE DIE.
YORO (WOBBLE)
—BECAUSE I SAW SOMEONE GET KILLED...

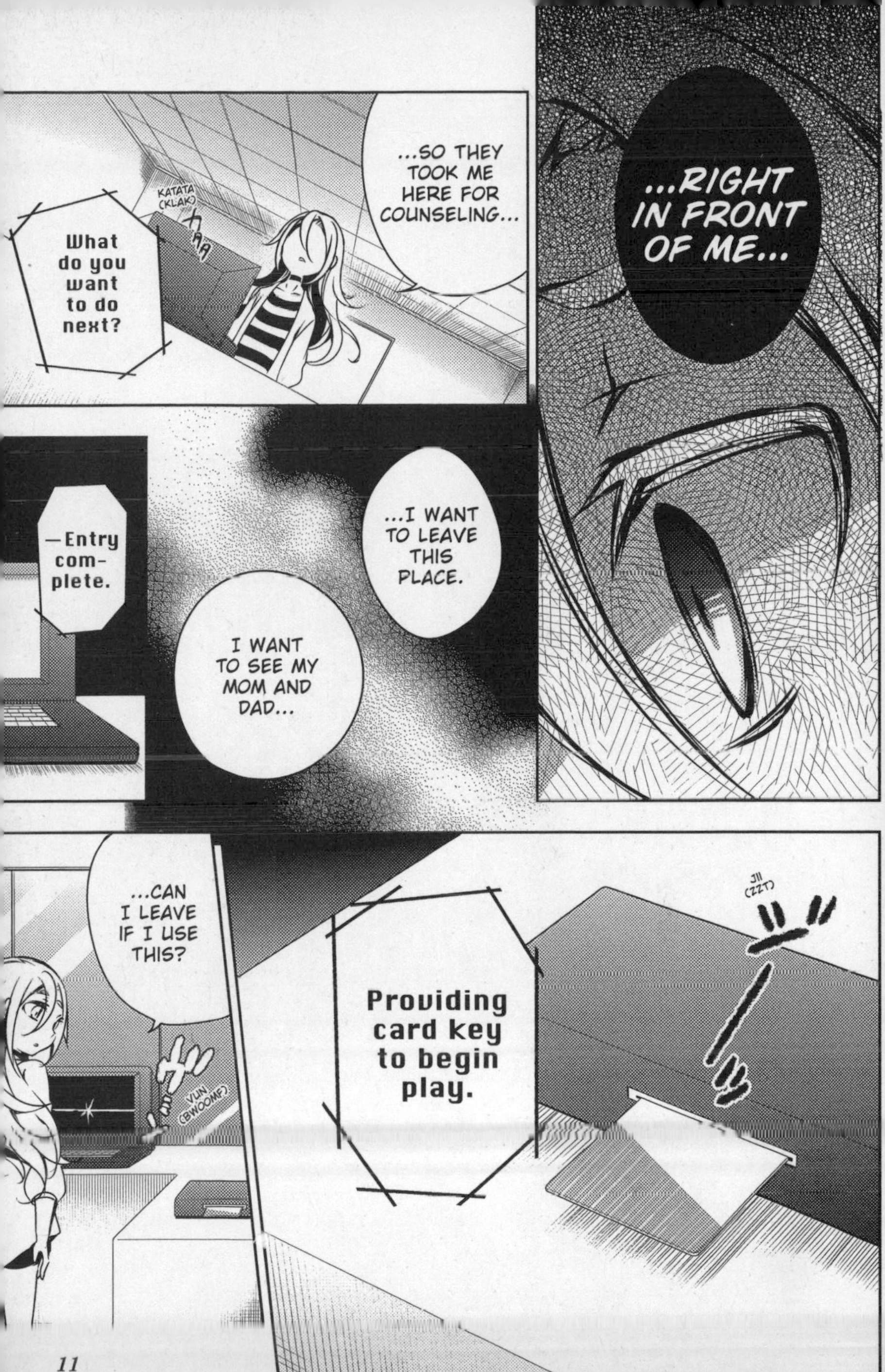
...RIGHT IN FRONT OF ME...
...SO THEY TOOK ME HERE FOR COUNSELING...
KATATA (KLAK)
What do you want to do next?
...I WANT TO LEAVE THIS PLACE.
I WANT TO SEE MY MOM AND DAD...
—Entry complete.
JII (ZZZT)
Providing card key to begin play.
...CAN I LEAVE IF I USE THIS?
VUN (BWOOMF)

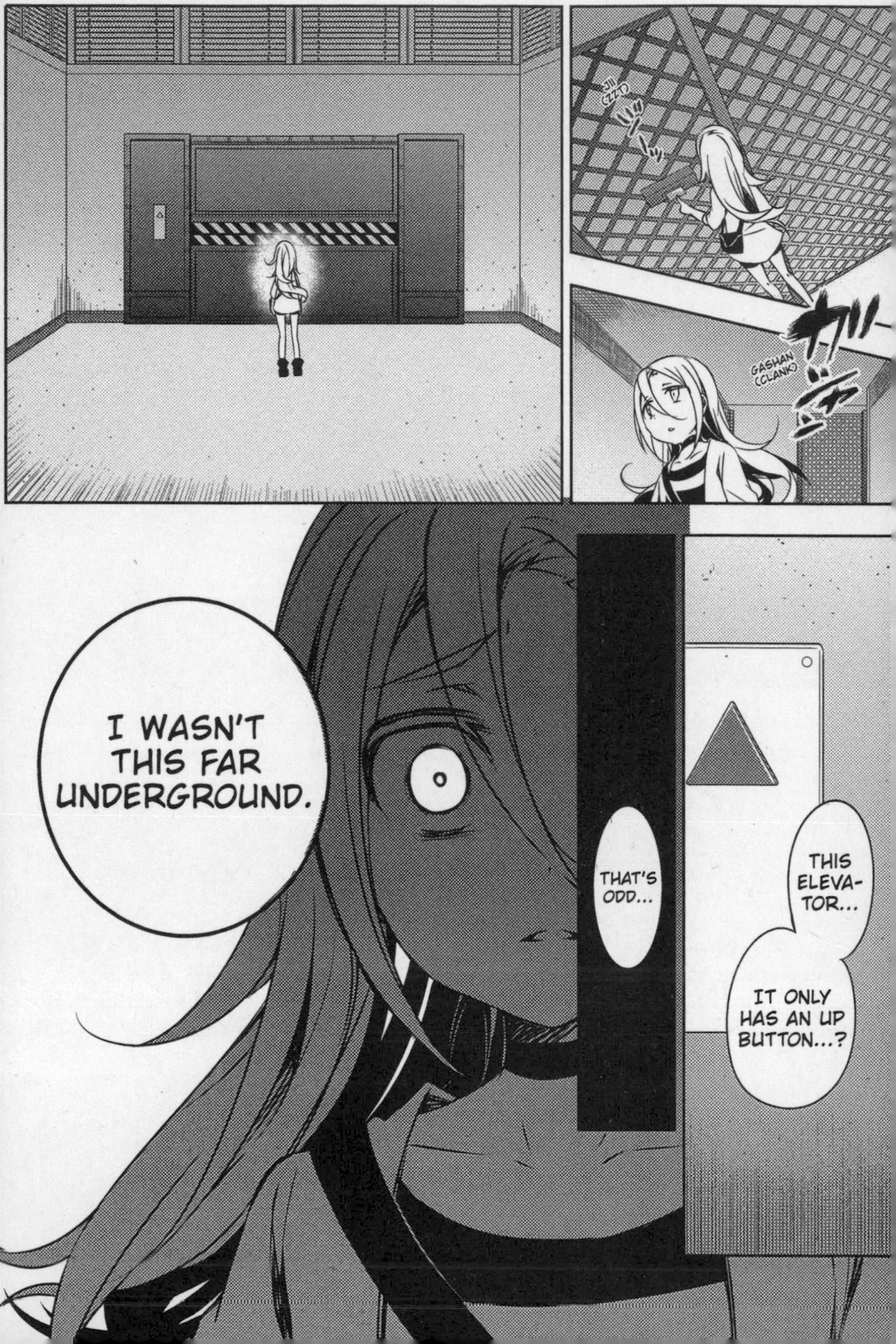
JII (ZZZT)
GASHAN (CLANK)
THIS ELEVATOR...
IT ONLY HAS AN UP BUTTON...?
THAT'S ODD...
I WASN'T THIS FAR UNDERGROUND.

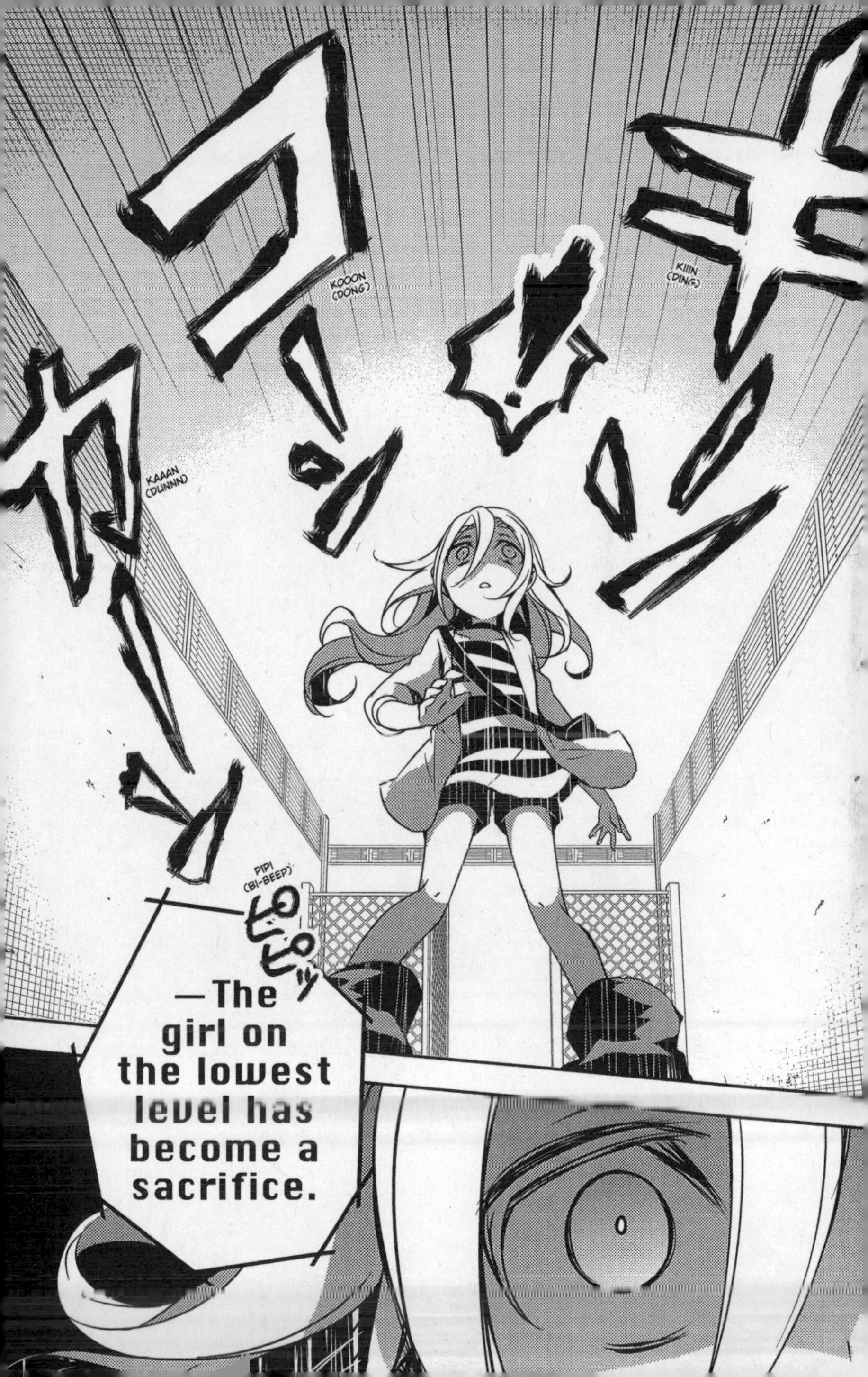
KIIN (DING)
KOOON (DONG)
KAAAN (DUNNN)
PIPI (BI-BEEP)
—The girl on the lowest level has become a sacrifice.

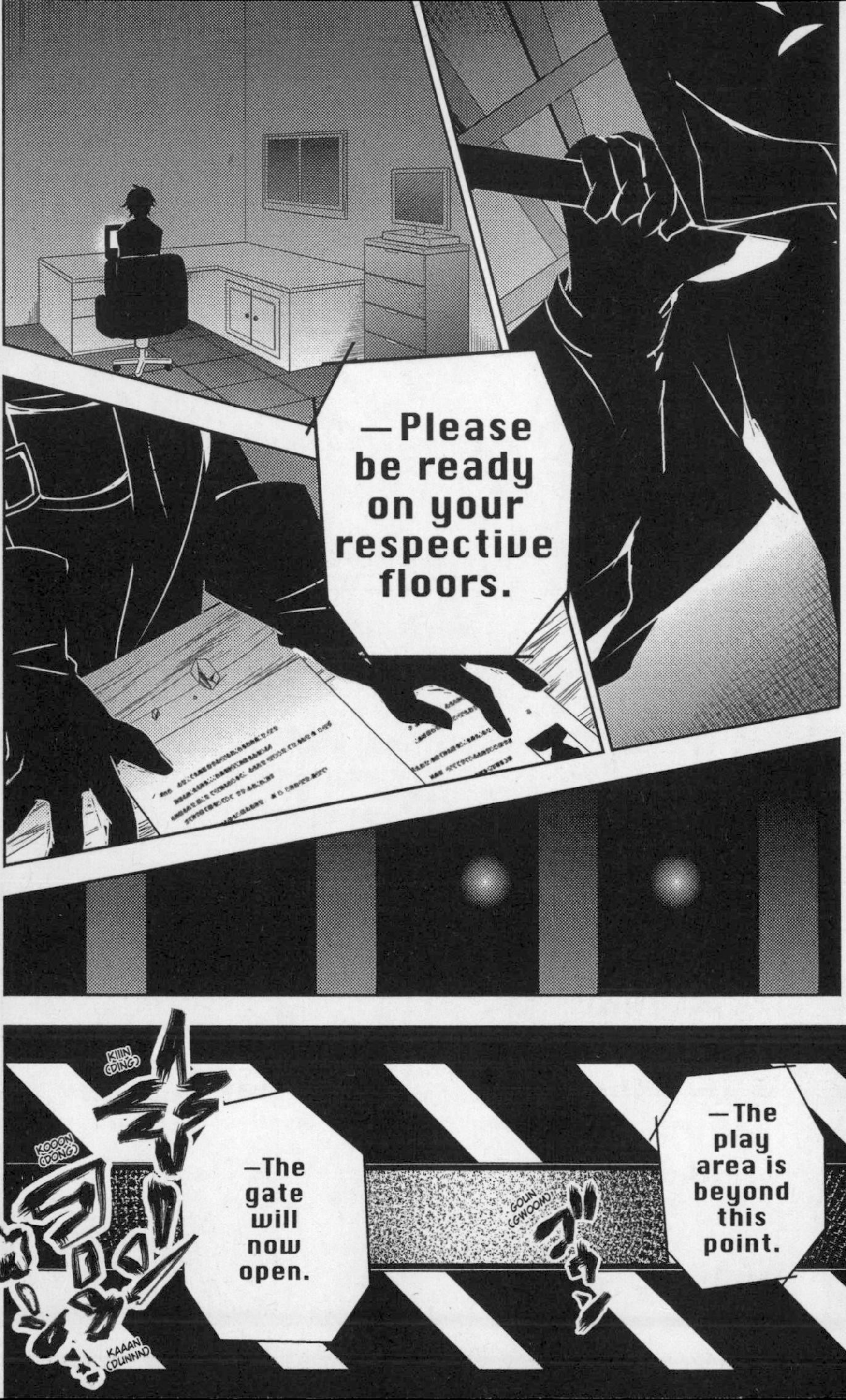
—Please be ready on your respective floors.
—The play area is beyond this point.
GOUN (GWOOM)
—The gate will now open.
KIIIN (DING)
KOOON (DONG)
KAAAN (DUNNN)

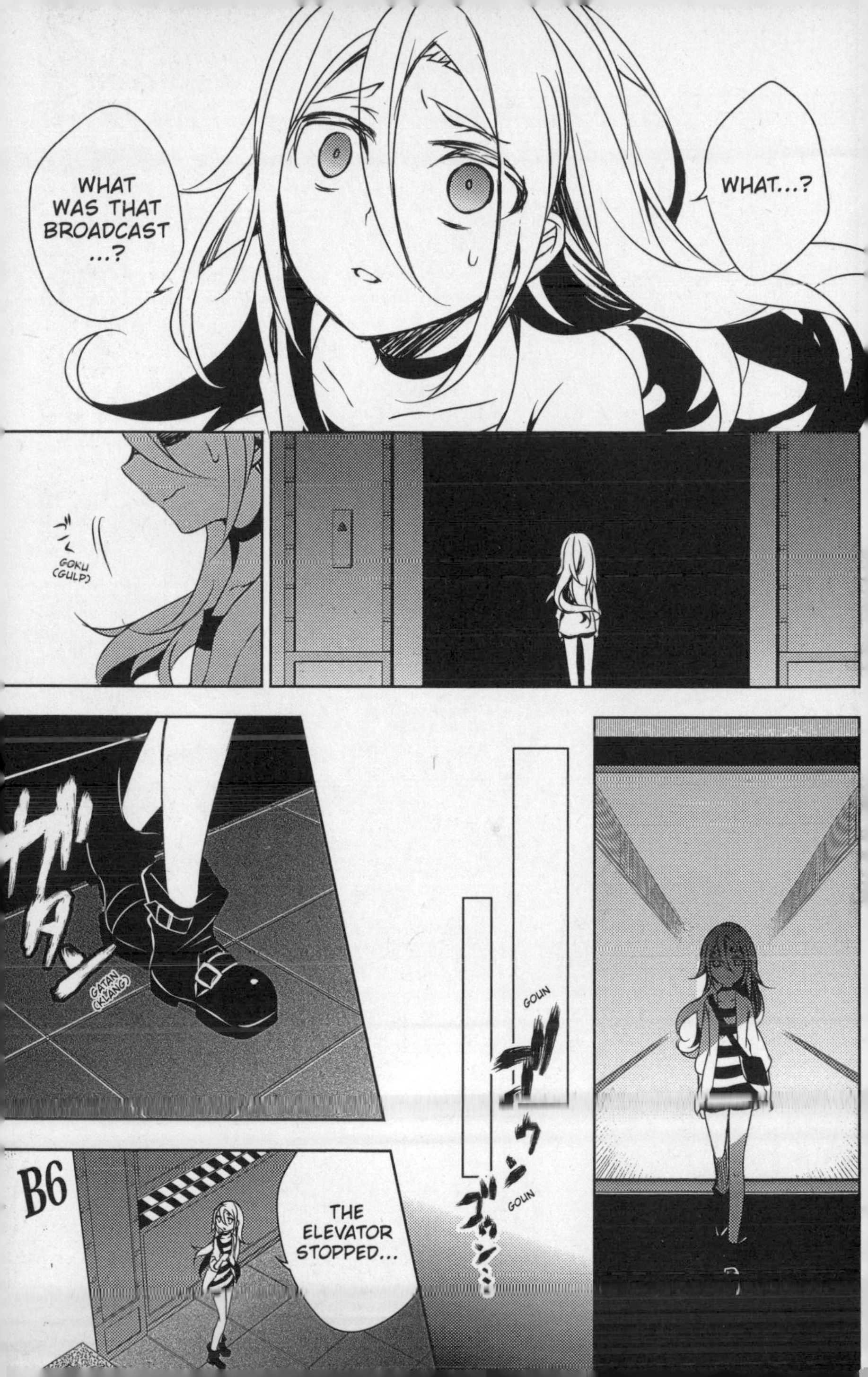
WHAT...?
WHAT WAS THAT BROADCAST ...?
GOKU (GULP)
GOUN
GOUN
GATAN (KLANG)
B6
THE ELEVATOR STOPPED...

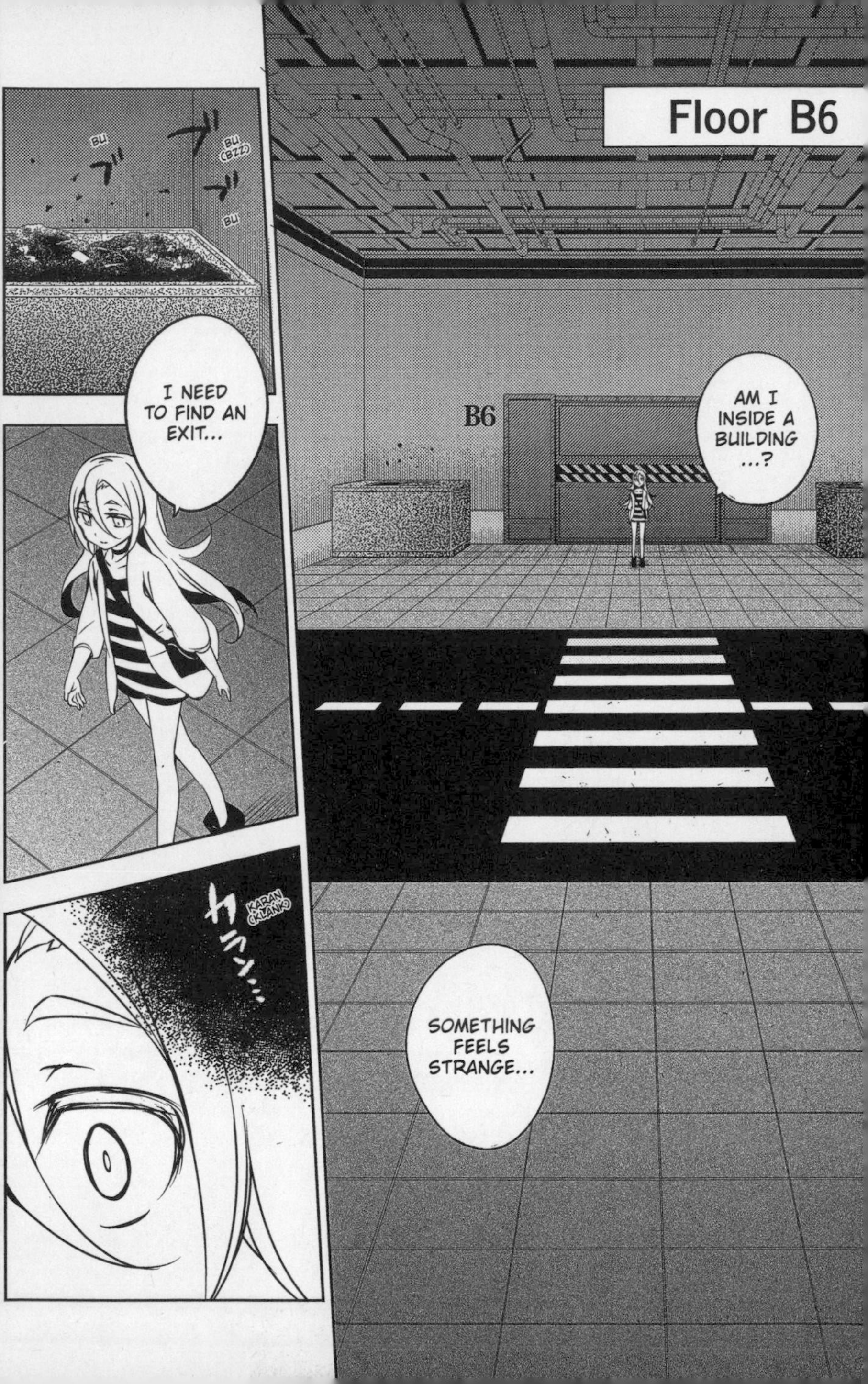
Floor B6
B6
AM I INSIDE A BUILDING ...?
SOMETHING FEELS STRANGE...
BU
BU (BZZZ)
BU
I NEED TO FIND AN EXIT...
KARAN (KLANK)

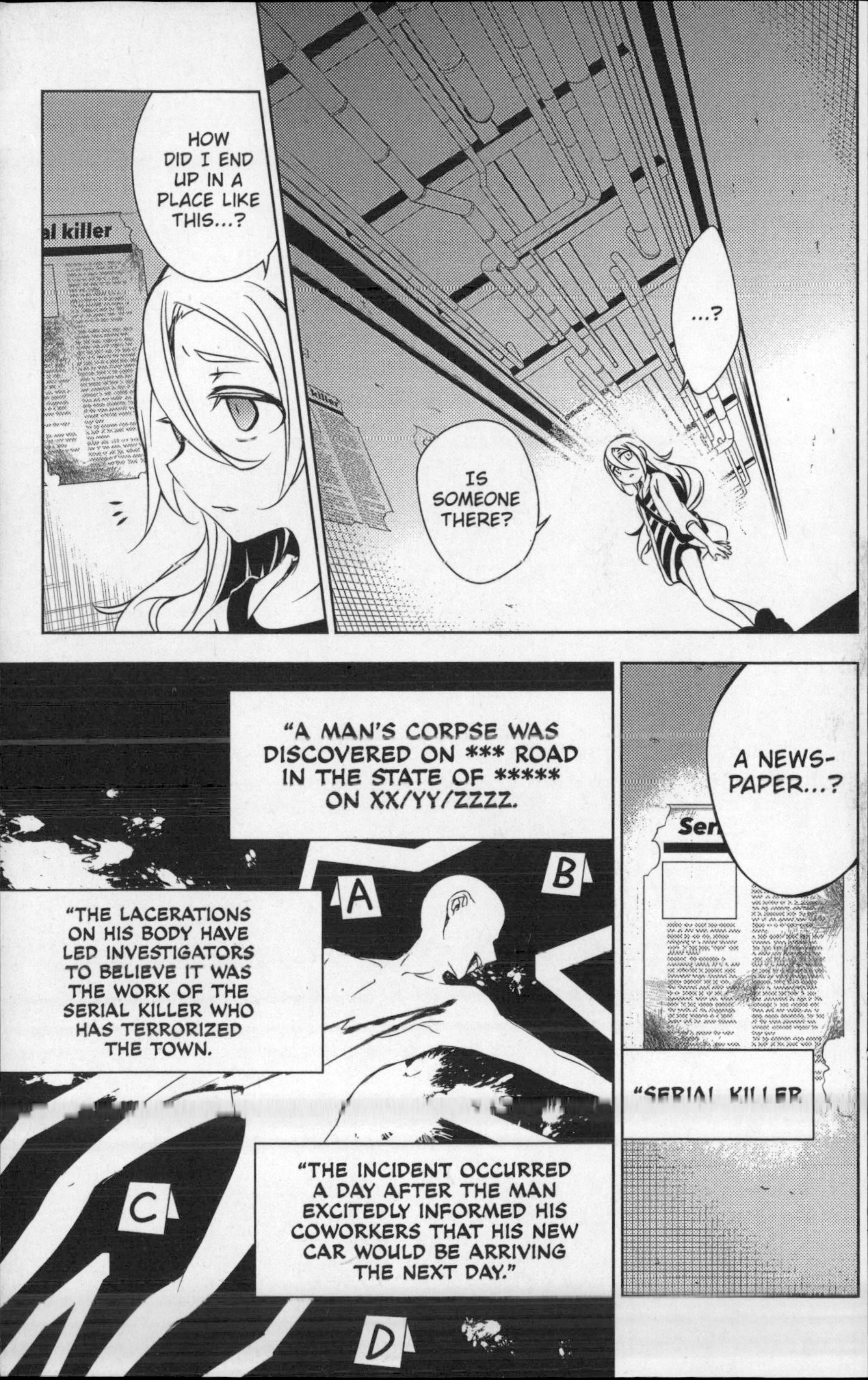
...?
IS SOMEONE THERE?
HOW DID I END UP IN A PLACE LIKE THIS...?
A NEWS-PAPER...?
“SERIAL KILLER
“A MAN'S CORPSE WAS DISCOVERED ON *** ROAD IN THE STATE OF ***** ON XX/YY/ZZZZ.
B
A
“THE LACERATIONS ON HIS BODY HAVE LED INVESTIGATORS TO BELIEVE IT WAS THE WORK OF THE SERIAL KILLER WHO HAS TERRORIZED THE TOWN.
“THE INCIDENT OCCURRED A DAY AFTER THE MAN EXCITEDLY INFORMED HIS COWORKERS THAT HIS NEW CAR WOULD BE ARRIVING THE NEXT DAY.”
C
D

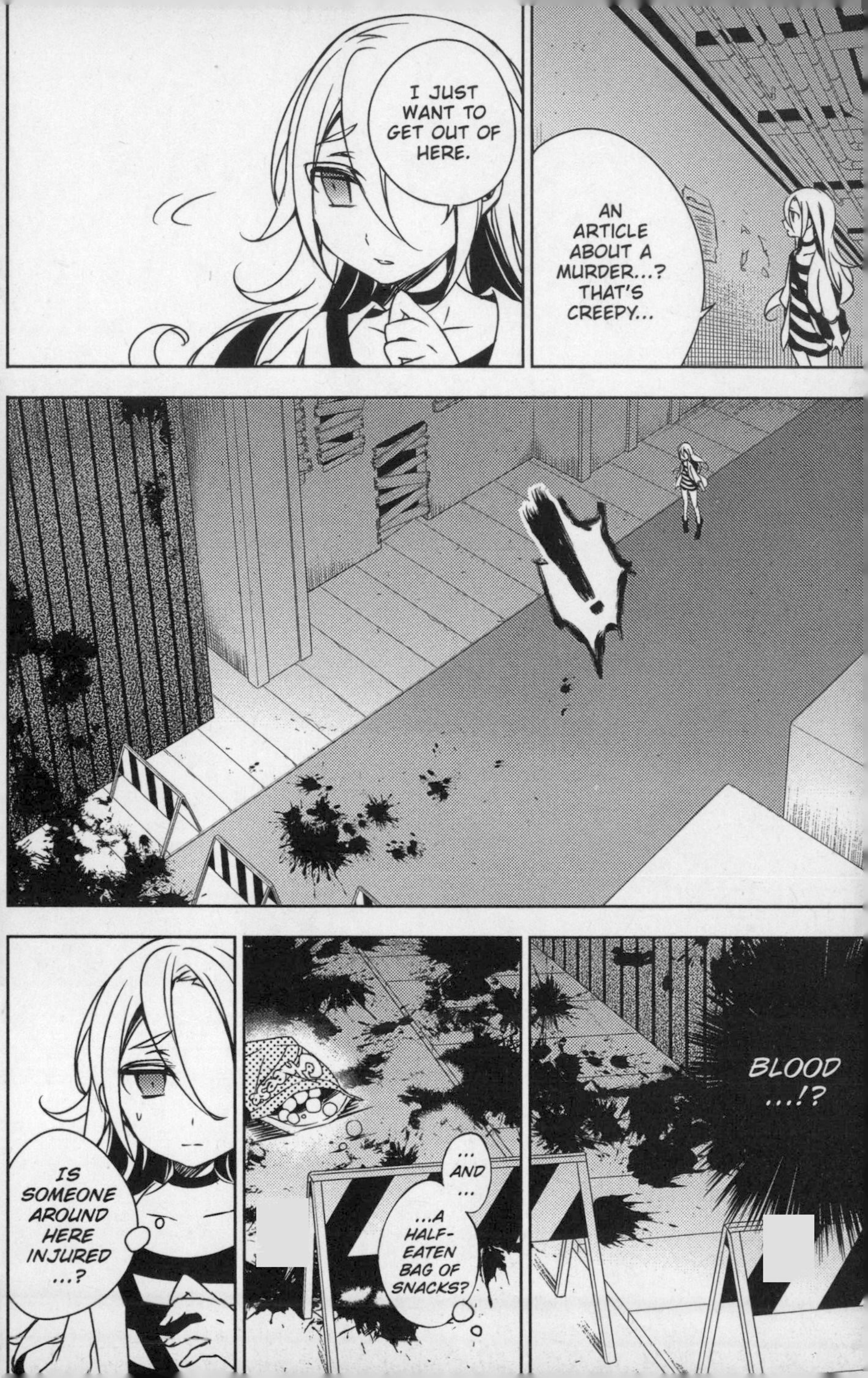
AN ARTICLE ABOUT A MURDER...? THAT'S CREEPY...
I JUST WANT TO GET OUT OF HERE.
!
BLOOD ...!?
...AND...
...A HALF-EATEN BAG OF SNACKS?
IS SOMEONE AROUND HERE INJURED ...?

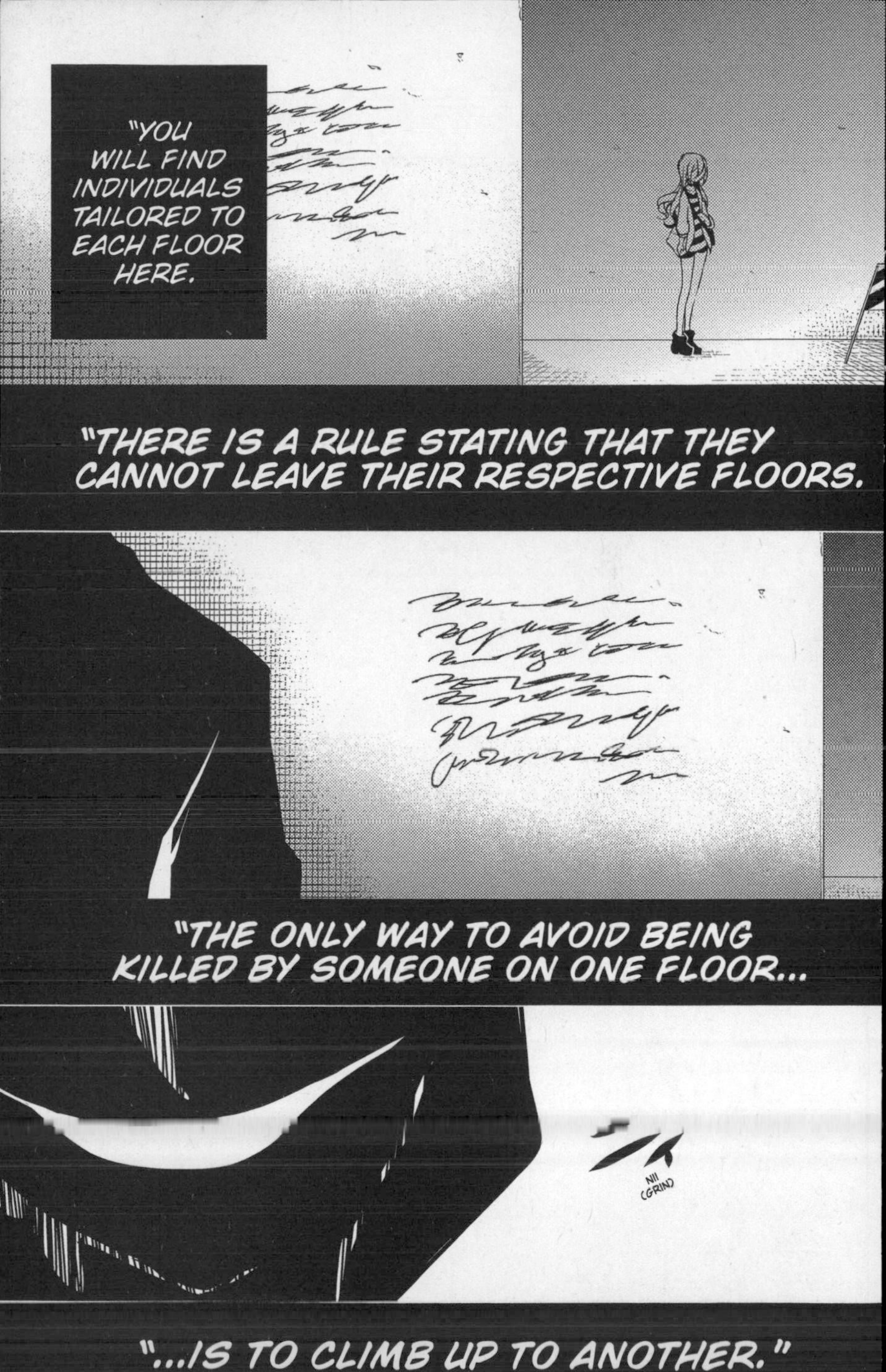
"YOU WILL FIND INDIVIDUALS TAILORED TO EACH FLOOR HERE.
"THERE IS A RULE STATING THAT THEY CANNOT LEAVE THEIR RESPECTIVE FLOORS.
"THE ONLY WAY TO AVOID BEING KILLED BY SOMEONE ON ONE FLOOR...
NII (GRIN)
"...IS TO CLIMB UP TO ANOTHER."

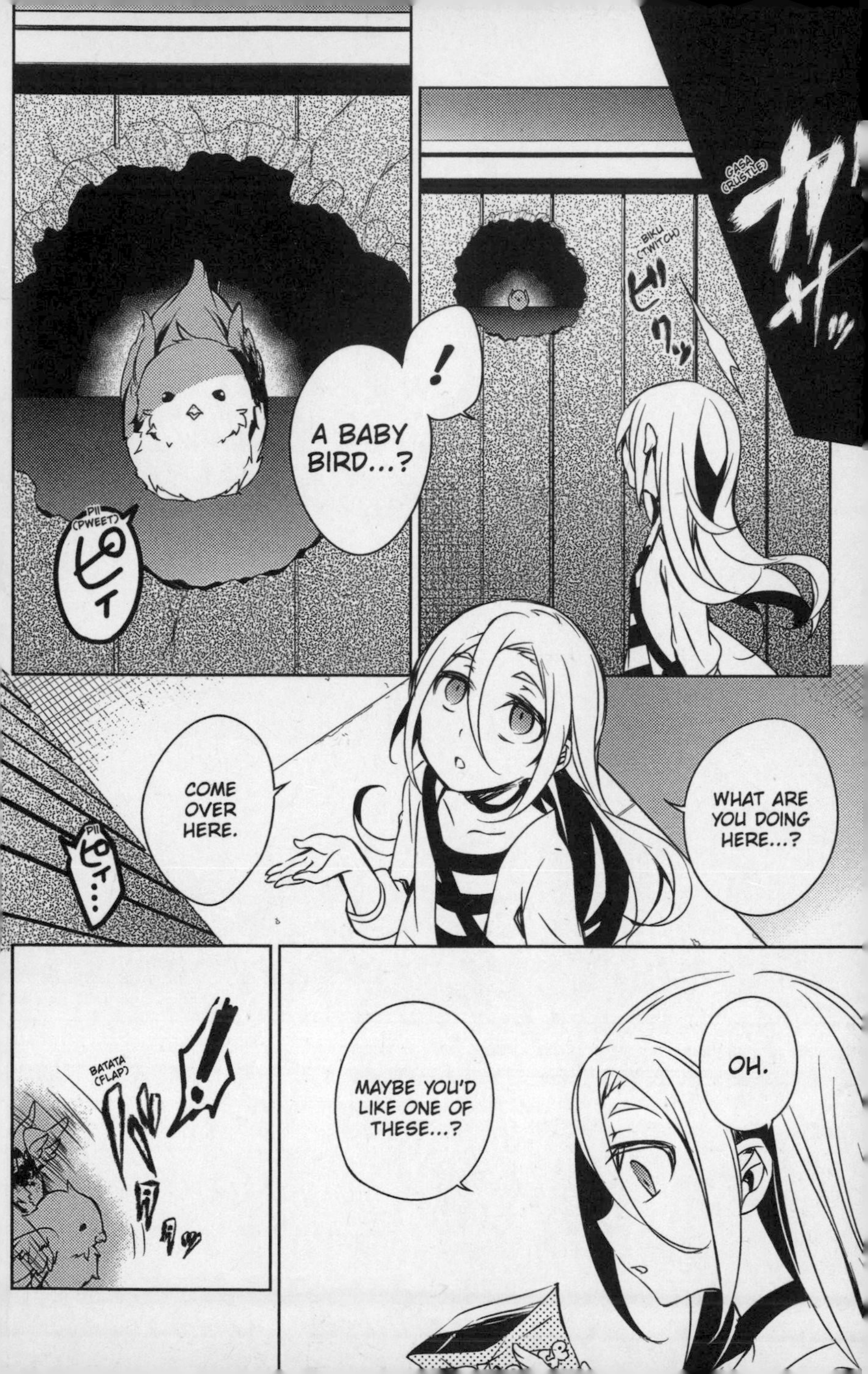
GASA (RUSTLE)
BIKU (TWITCH)
!
A BABY BIRD...?
PII (PWEET)
WHAT ARE YOU DOING HERE...?
COME OVER HERE.
PII...
OH.
MAYBE YOU'D LIKE ONE OF THESE...?
BATATA (FLAP)

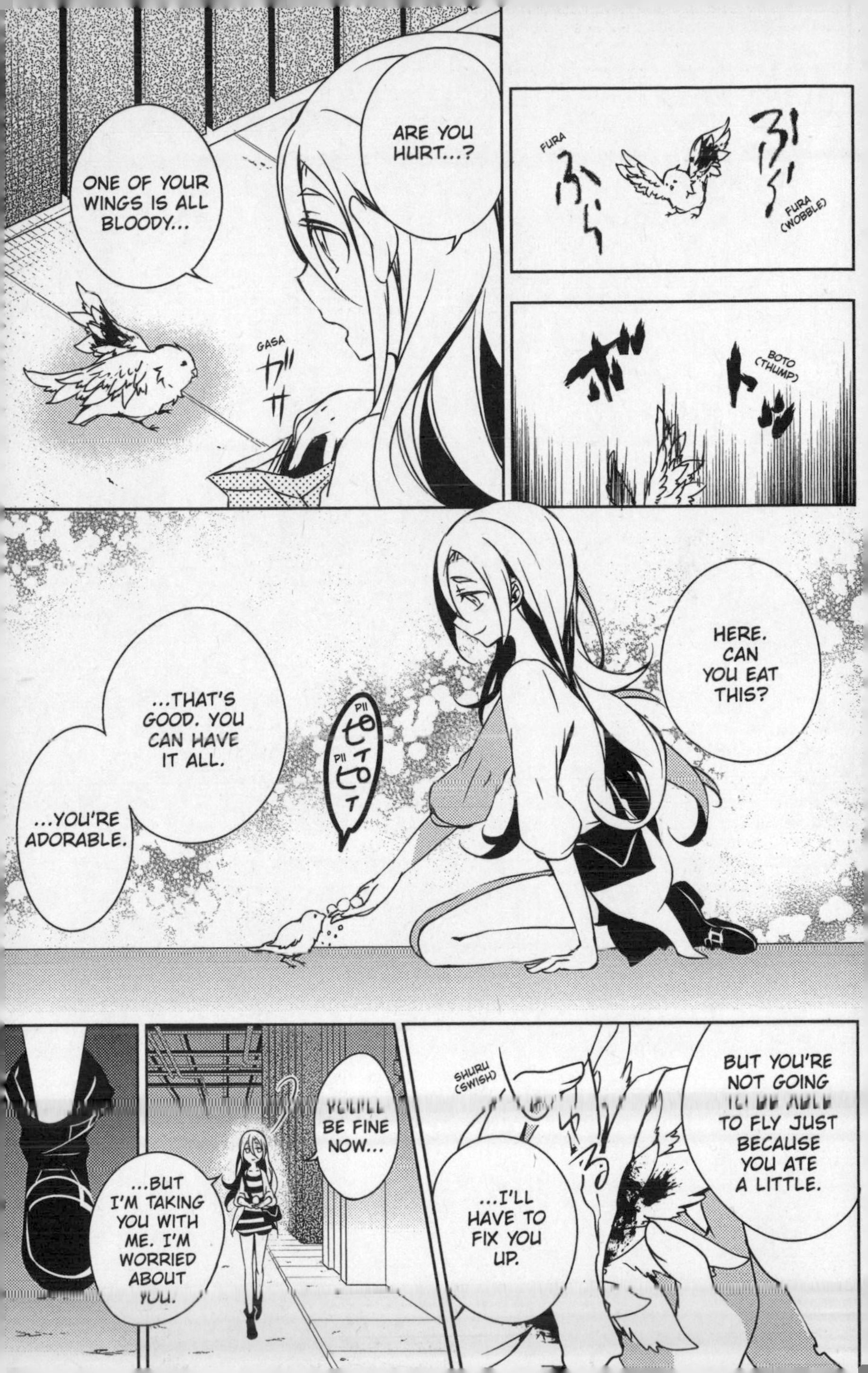
FURA
FURA (WOBBLE)
BOTO (THUMP)
ARE YOU HURT...?
ONE OF YOUR WINGS IS ALL BLOODY...
GASA
HERE. CAN YOU EAT THIS?
PII PII
...THAT'S GOOD. YOU CAN HAVE IT ALL.
...YOU'RE ADORABLE.
SHURU (SWISH)
BUT YOU'RE NOT GOING TO BE ABLE TO FLY JUST BECAUSE YOU ATE A LITTLE.
...I'LL HAVE TO FIX YOU UP.
YOU'LL BE FINE NOW...
...BUT I'M TAKING YOU WITH ME. I'M WORRIED ABOUT YOU.

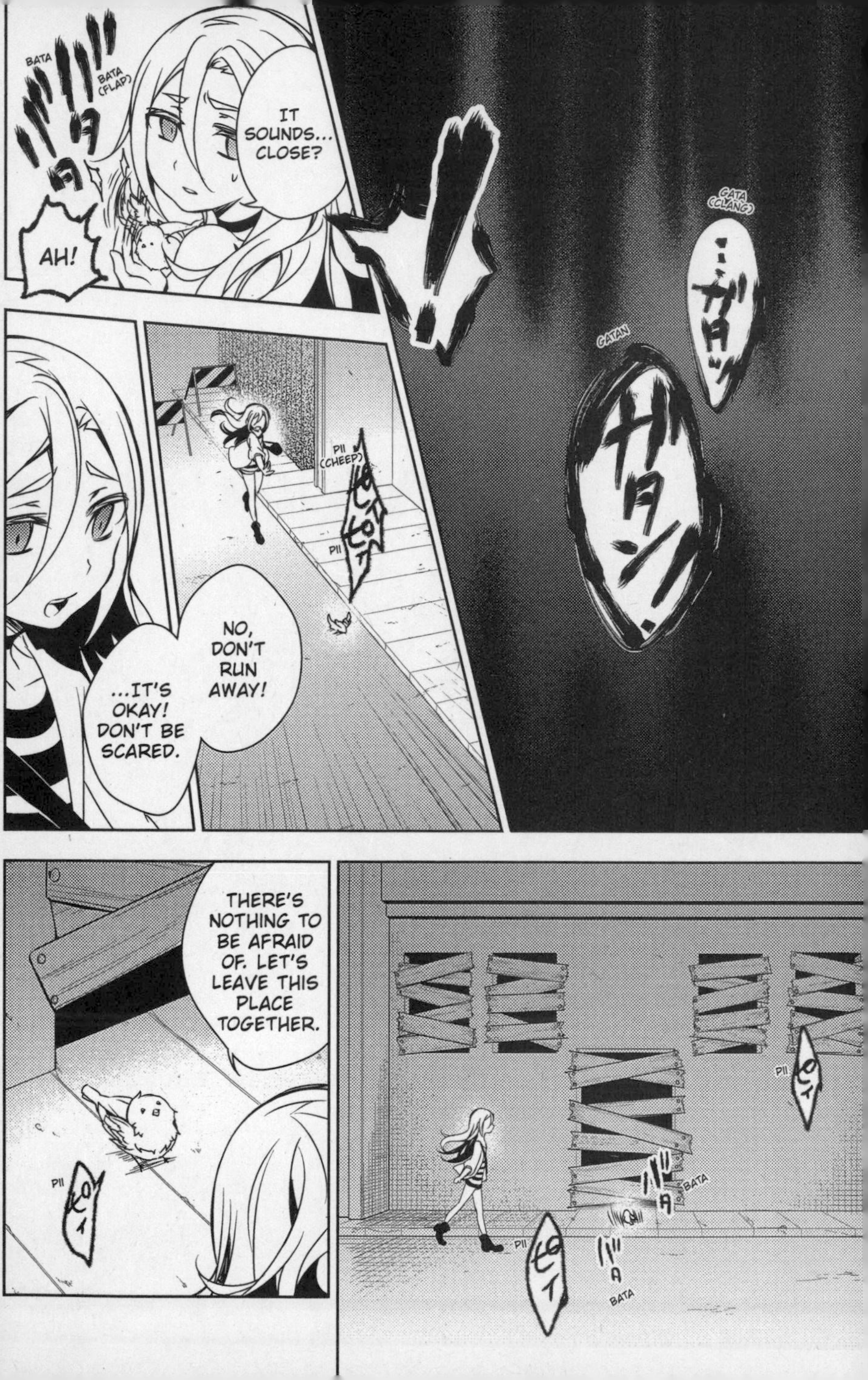
GATA (CLANG)
GATAN
IT SOUNDS... CLOSE?
BATA
BATA (FLAP)
AH!
PII (CHEEP)
PII
NO, DON'T RUN AWAY!
...IT'S OKAY! DON'T BE SCARED.
PII
BATA
PII
BATA
THERE'S NOTHING TO BE AFRAID OF. LET'S LEAVE THIS PLACE TOGETHER.
PII

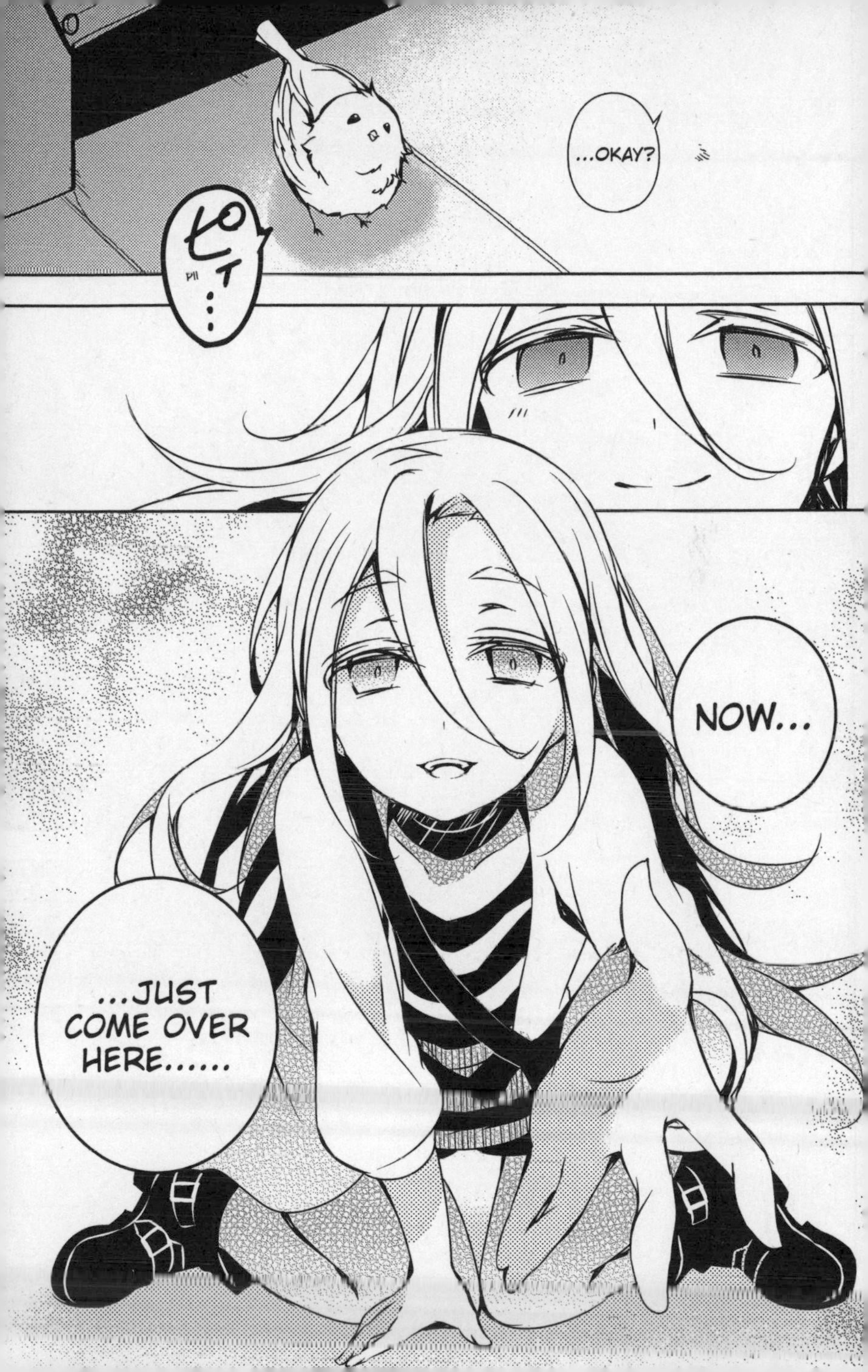
...OKAY?
ピッ...
PII
NOW...
...JUST COME OVER HERE......

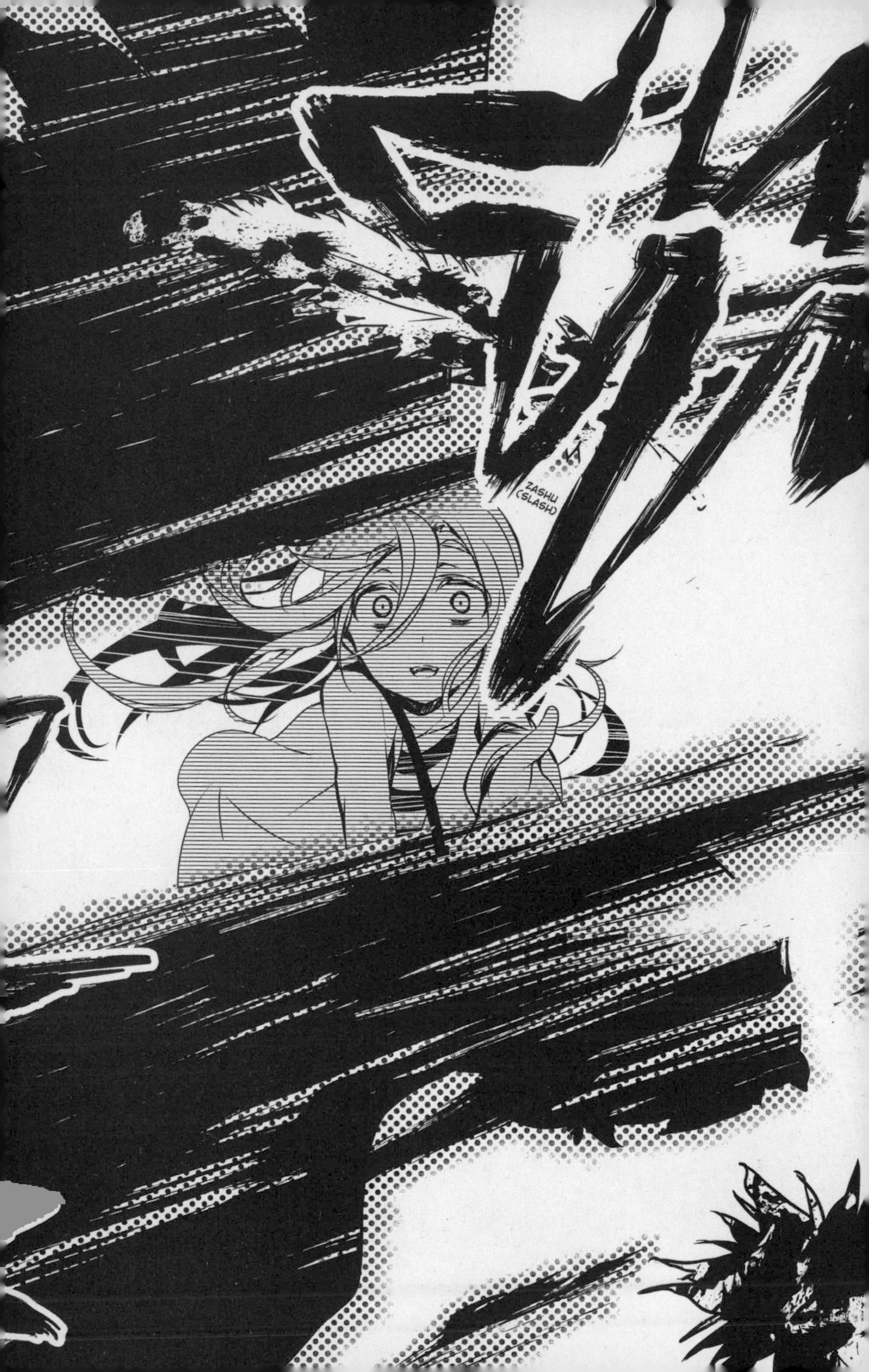
ZASHU
(SLASH)

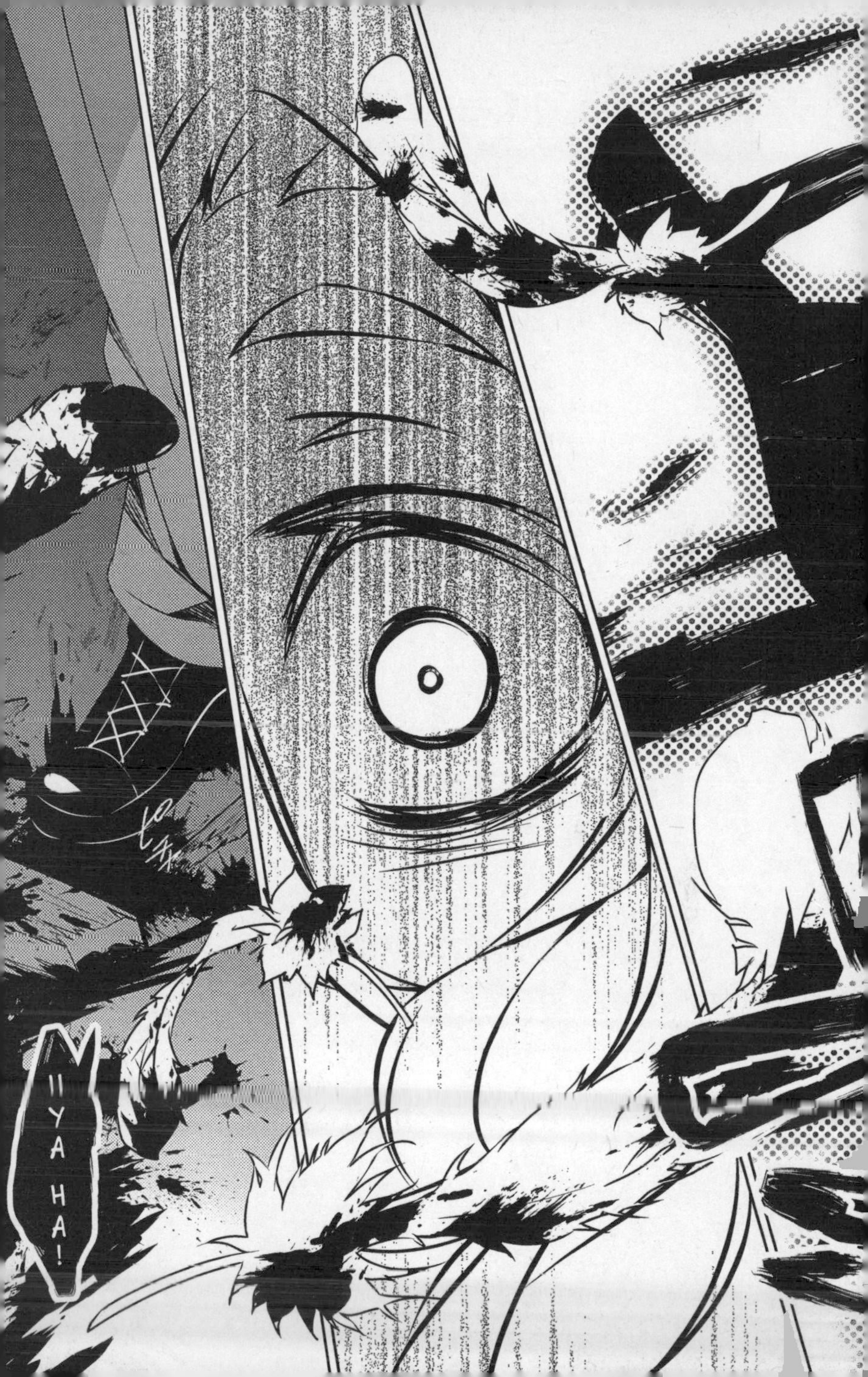
YA HA!

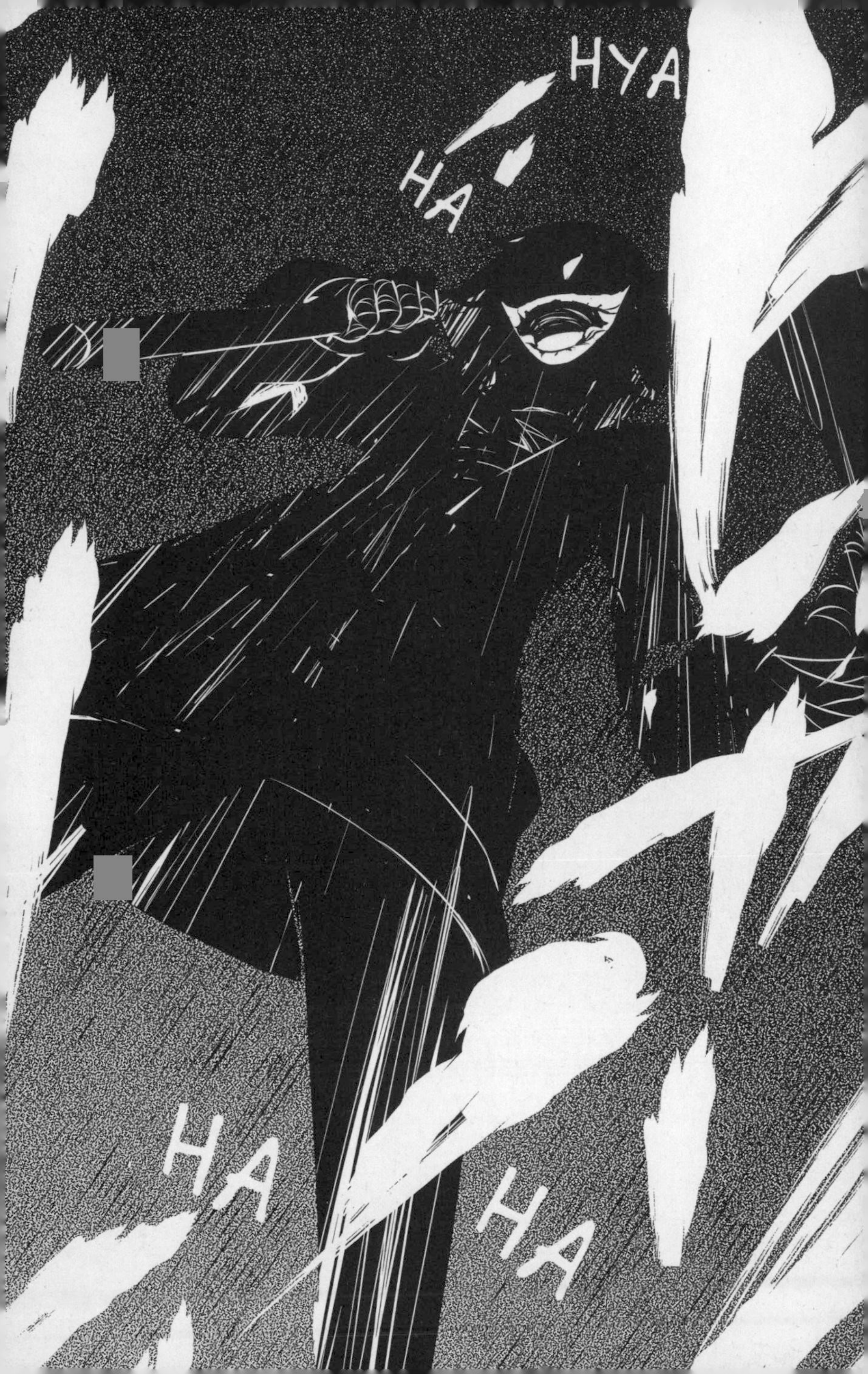
HYA
HA
HA
HA
HA

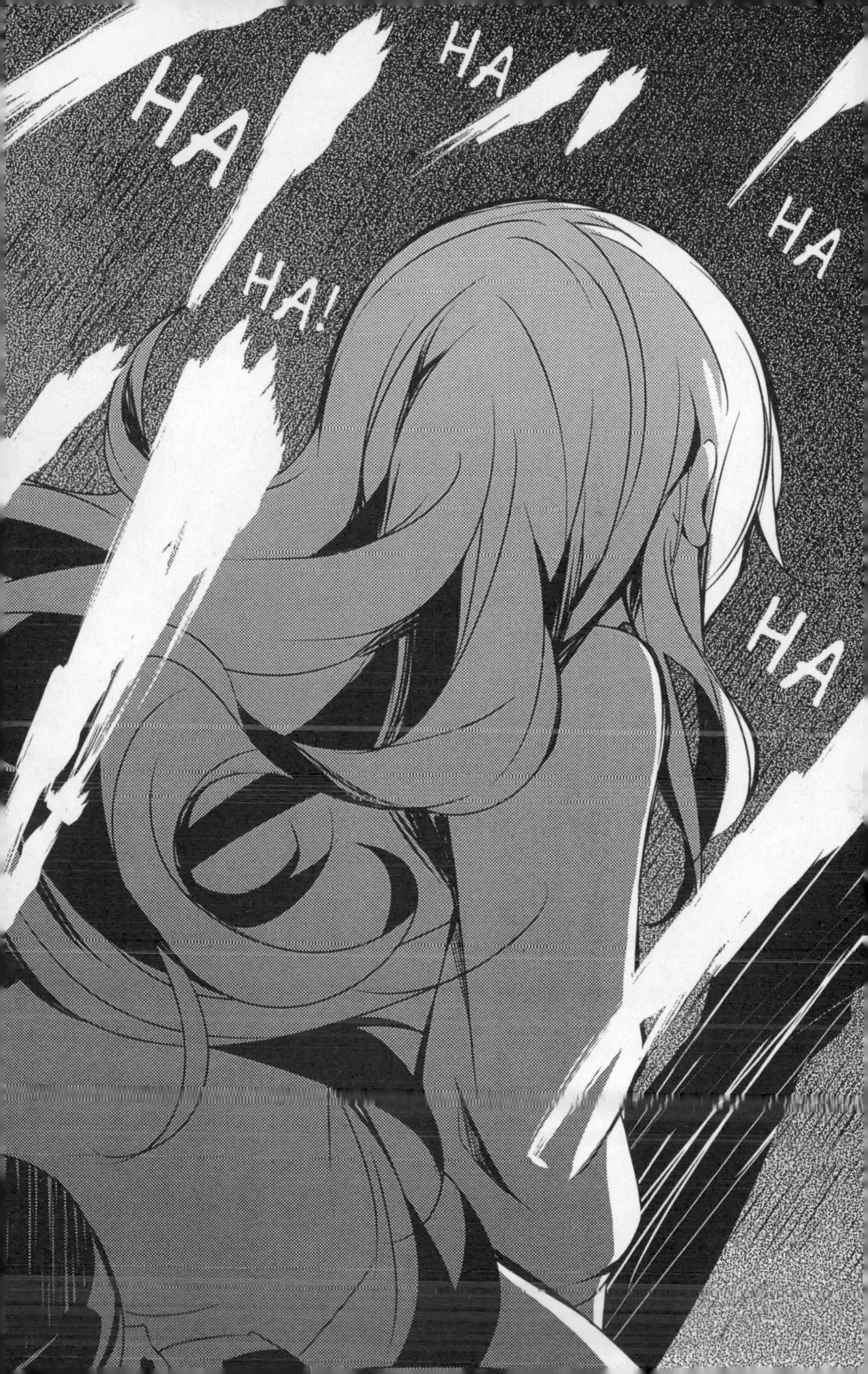
HA
HA
HA
HA!
HA

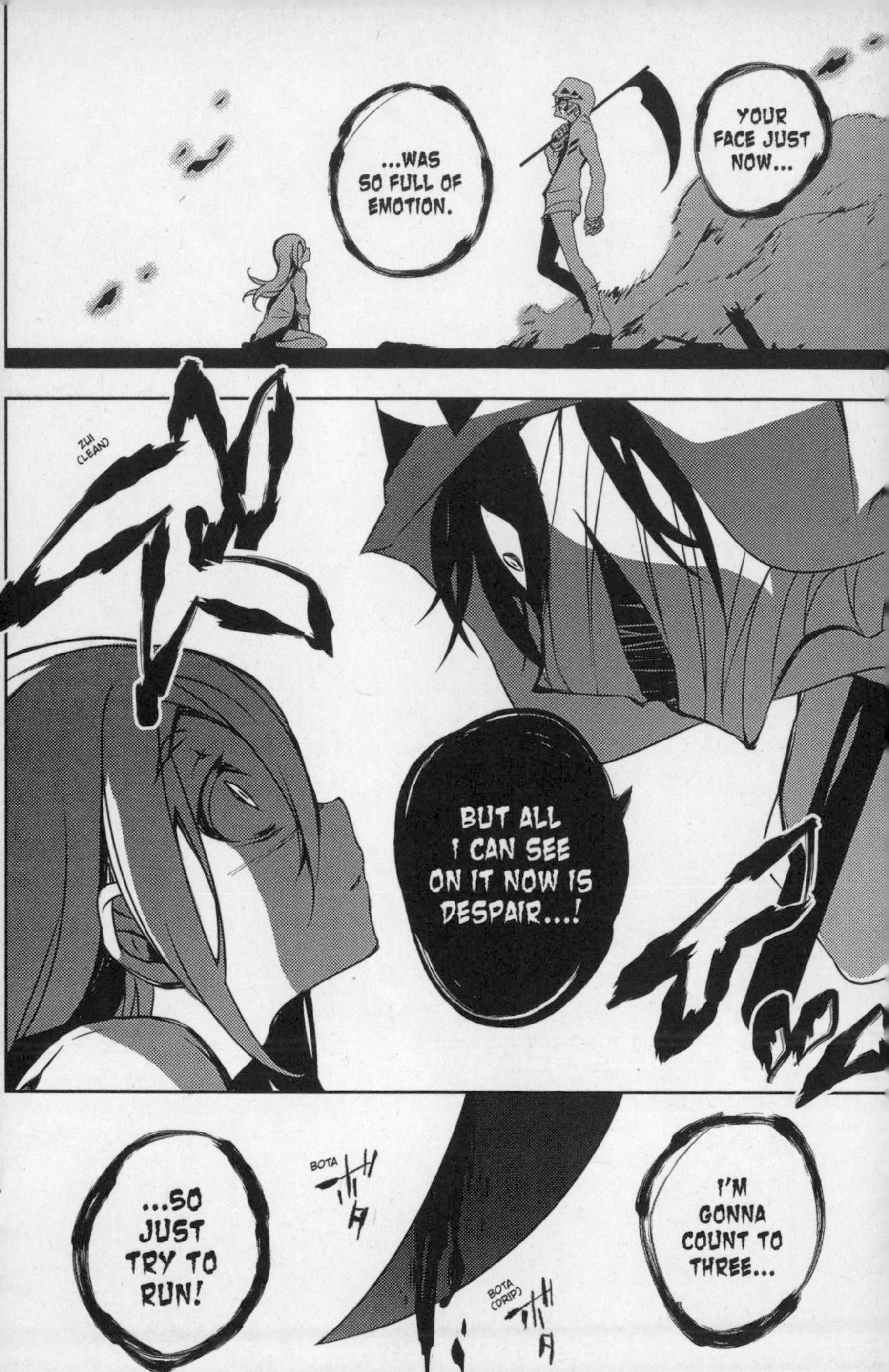
YOUR FACE JUST NOW...
...WAS SO FULL OF EMOTION.
BUT ALL I CAN SEE ON IT NOW IS DESPAIR...!
ZUI CLEAND
I'M GONNA COUNT TO THREE...
BOTA (DRIP)
BOTA
...SO JUST TRY TO RUN!

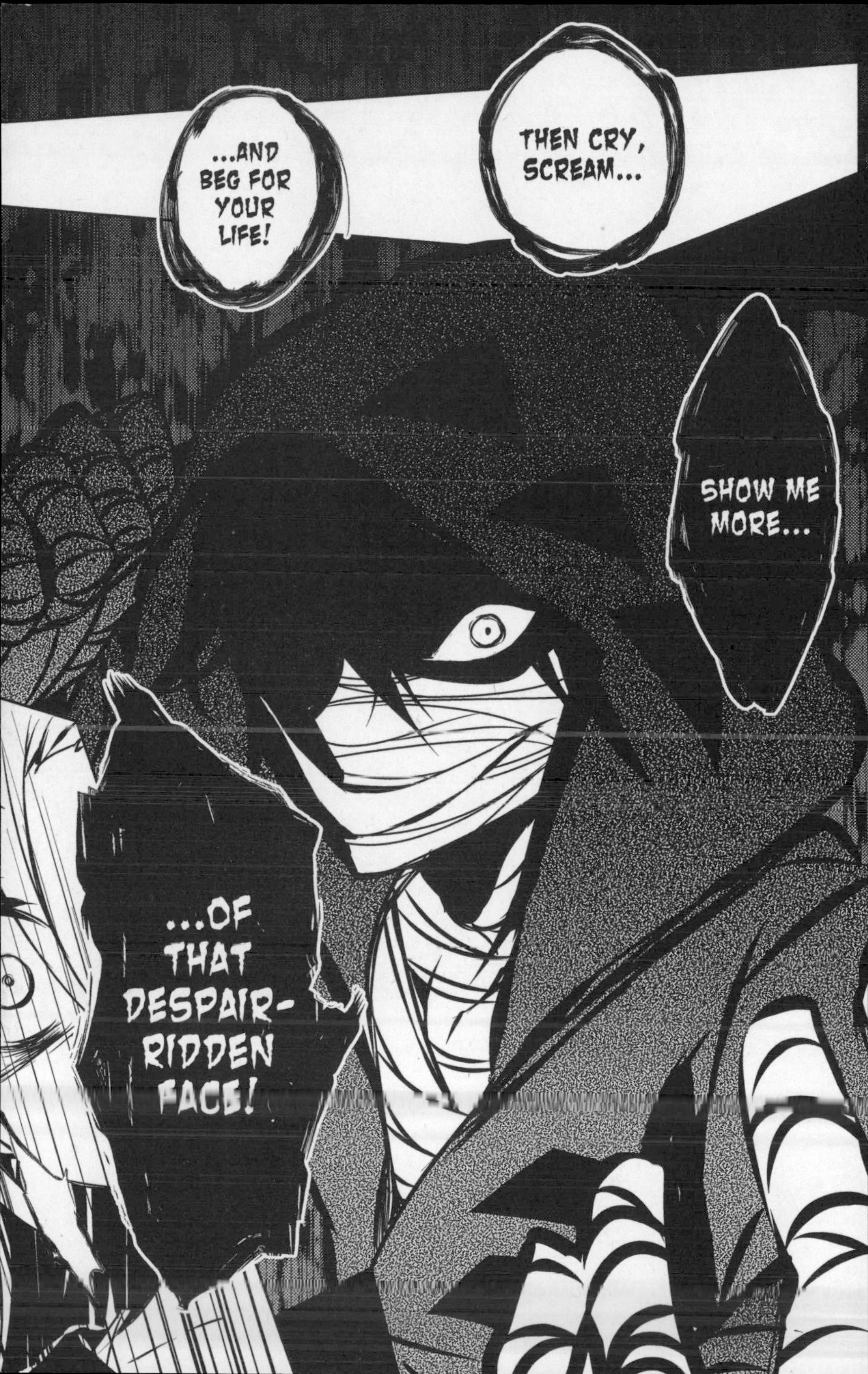
THEN CRY, SCREAM...
...AND BEG FOR YOUR LIFE!
SHOW ME MORE...
...OF THAT DESPAIR-RIDDEN FACE!

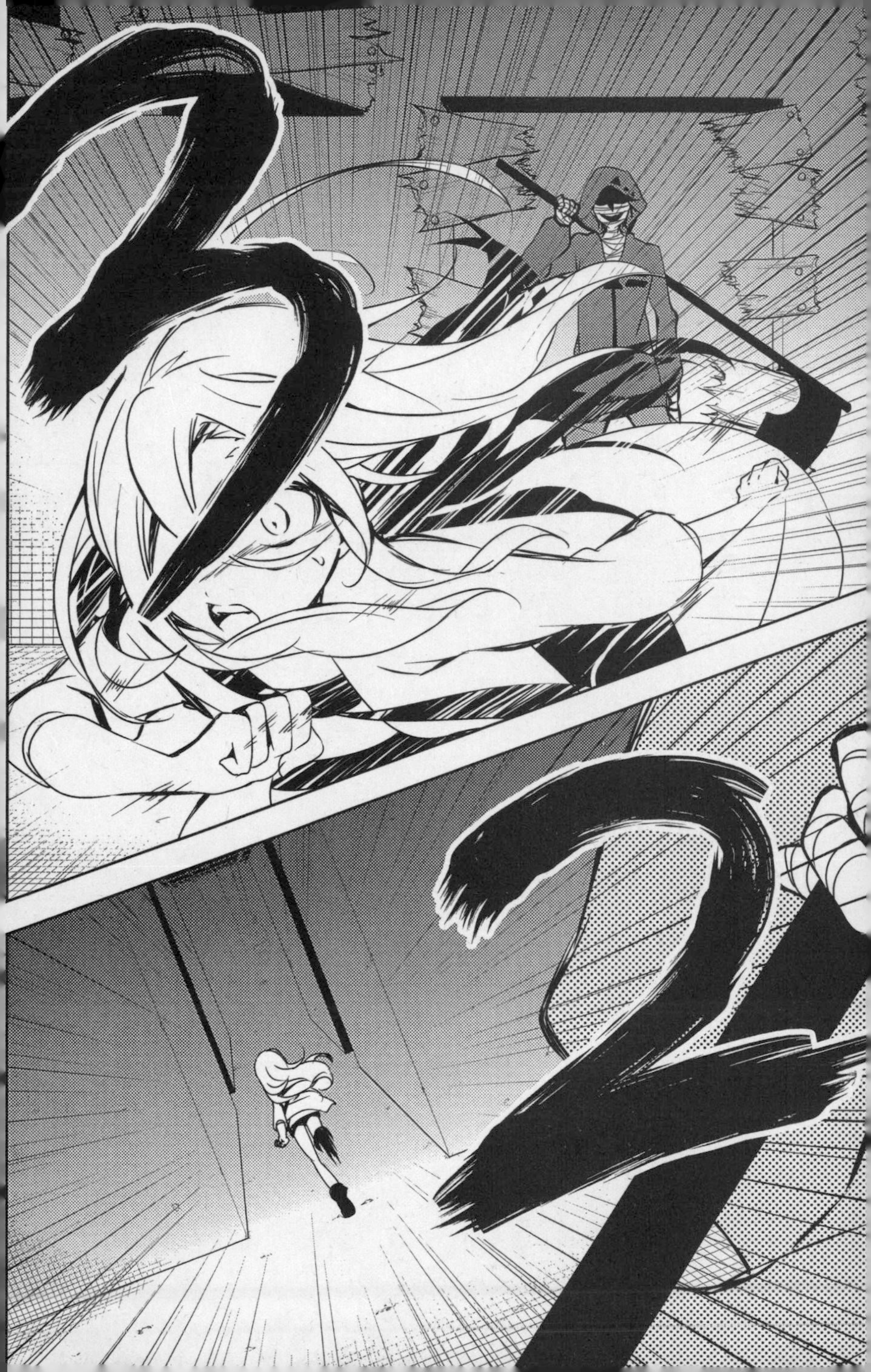

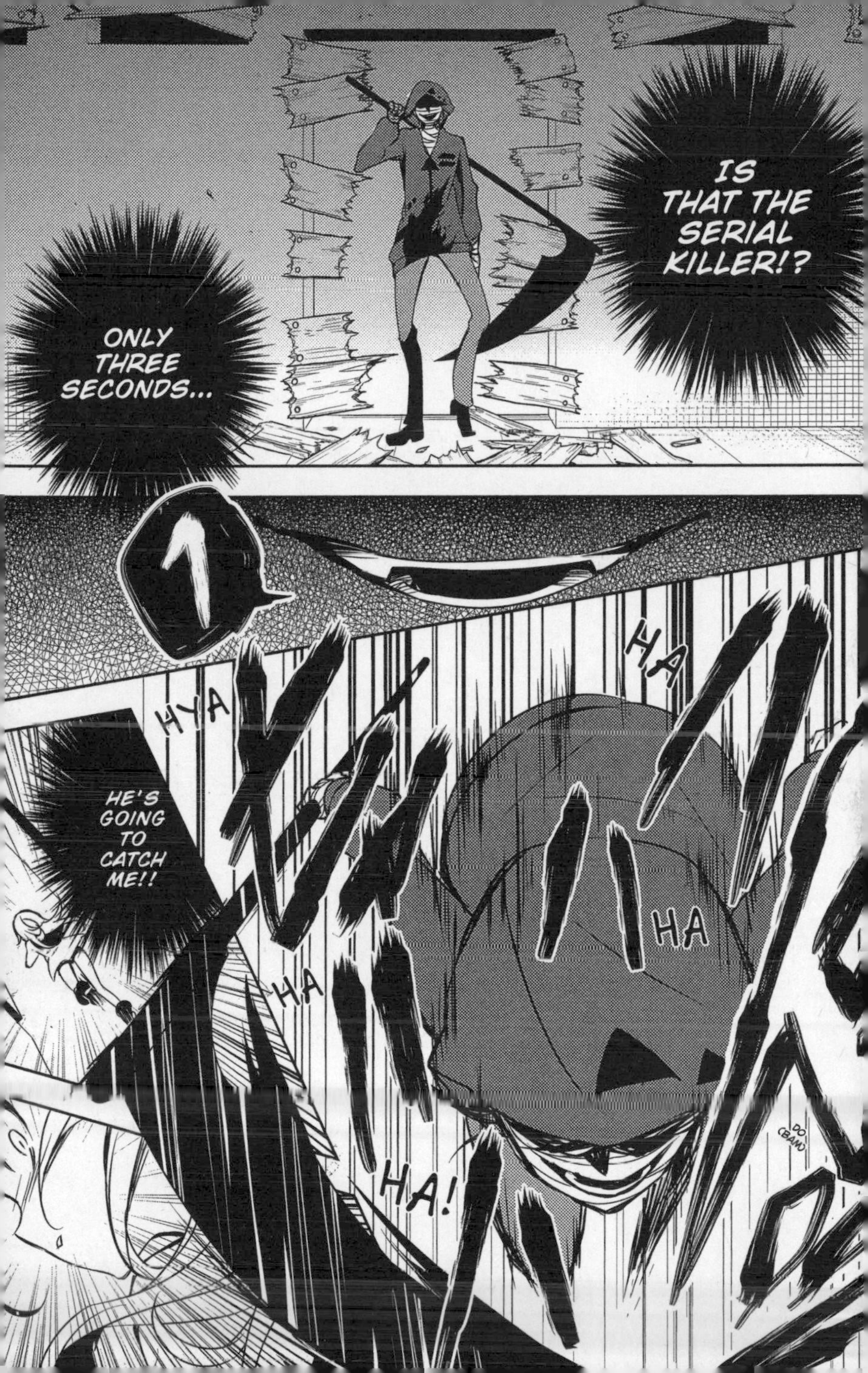
IS THAT THE SERIAL KILLER!?
ONLY THREE SECONDS...
1
HA
HYA
HE'S GOING TO CATCH ME!!
HA
HA
DO (BAM)
HA!

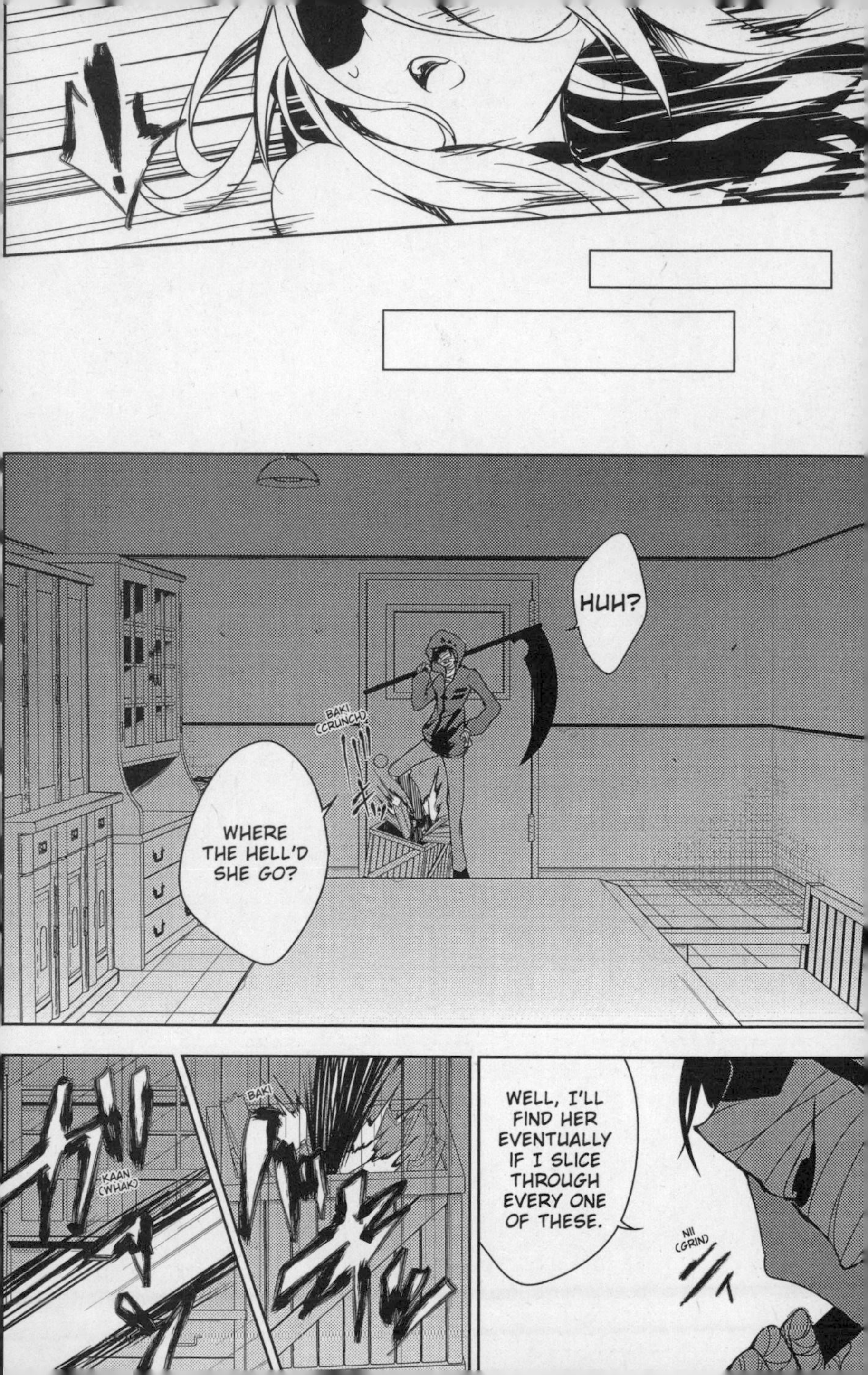
HUH?
BAKI (CRUNCH)
WHERE THE HELL'D SHE GO?
WELL, I'LL FIND HER EVENTUALLY IF I SLICE THROUGH EVERY ONE OF THESE.
NII (GRIND)
BAKI
KAAN (WHAK)

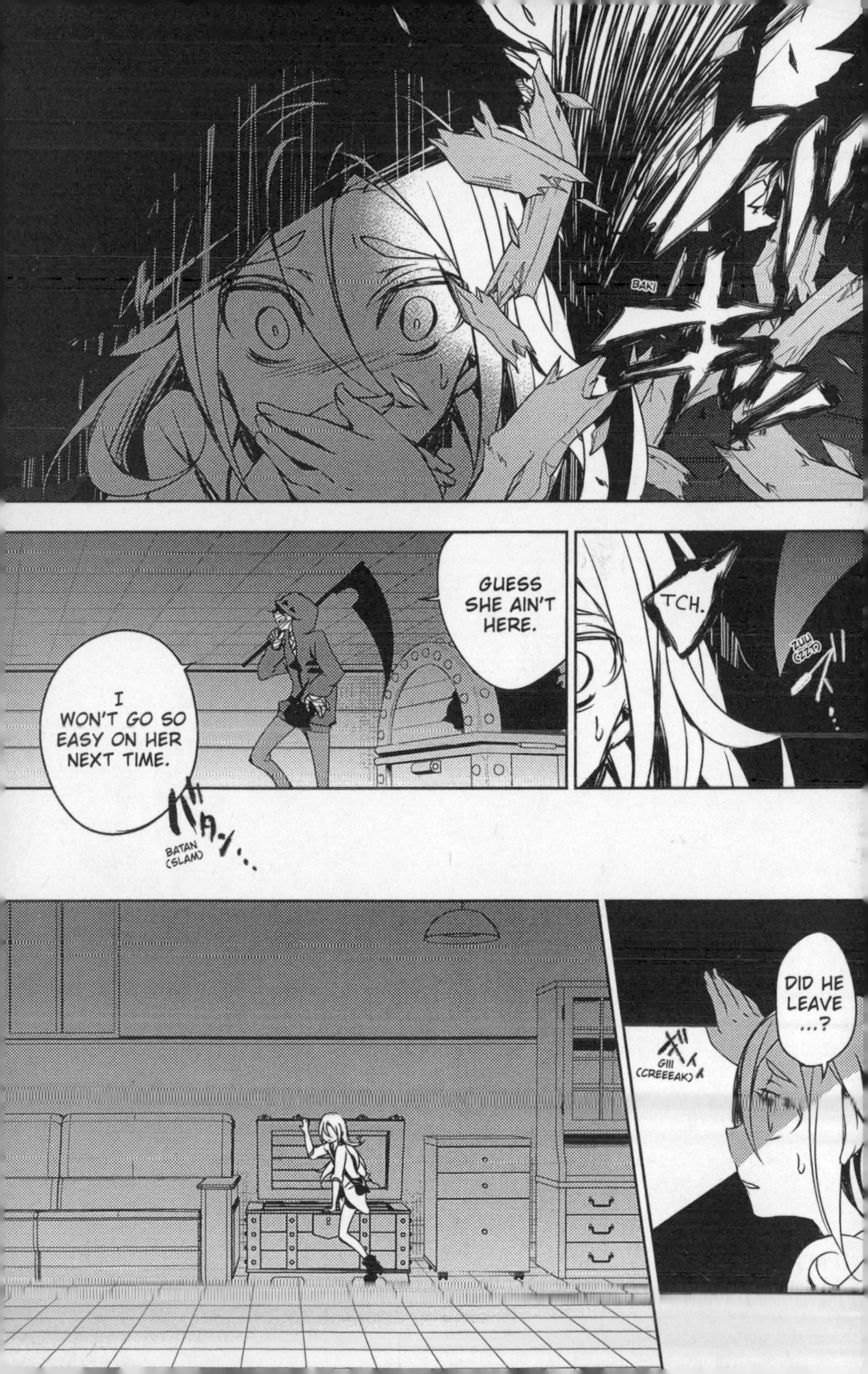
BAKI
TCH.
ZUU (ZZZT)
GUESS SHE AIN'T HERE.
I WON'T GO SO EASY ON HER NEXT TIME.
BATAN (SLAM)
DID HE LEAVE ...?
GIII (CREEEAK)

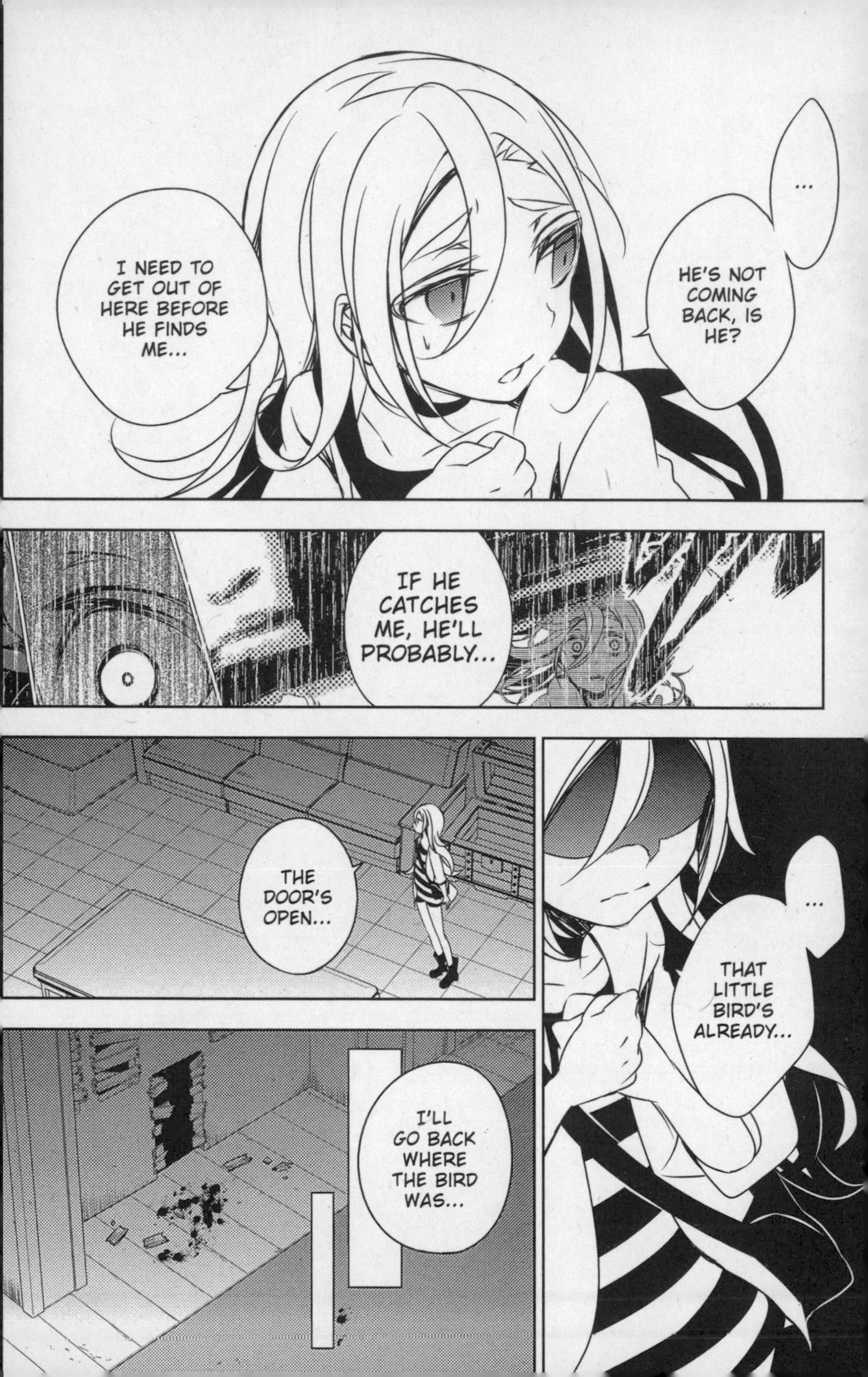
...
HE'S NOT COMING BACK, IS HE?
I NEED TO GET OUT OF HERE BEFORE HE FINDS ME...
IF HE CATCHES ME, HE'LL PROBABLY...
...
THAT LITTLE BIRD'S ALREADY...
THE DOOR'S OPEN...
I'LL GO BACK WHERE THE BIRD WAS...

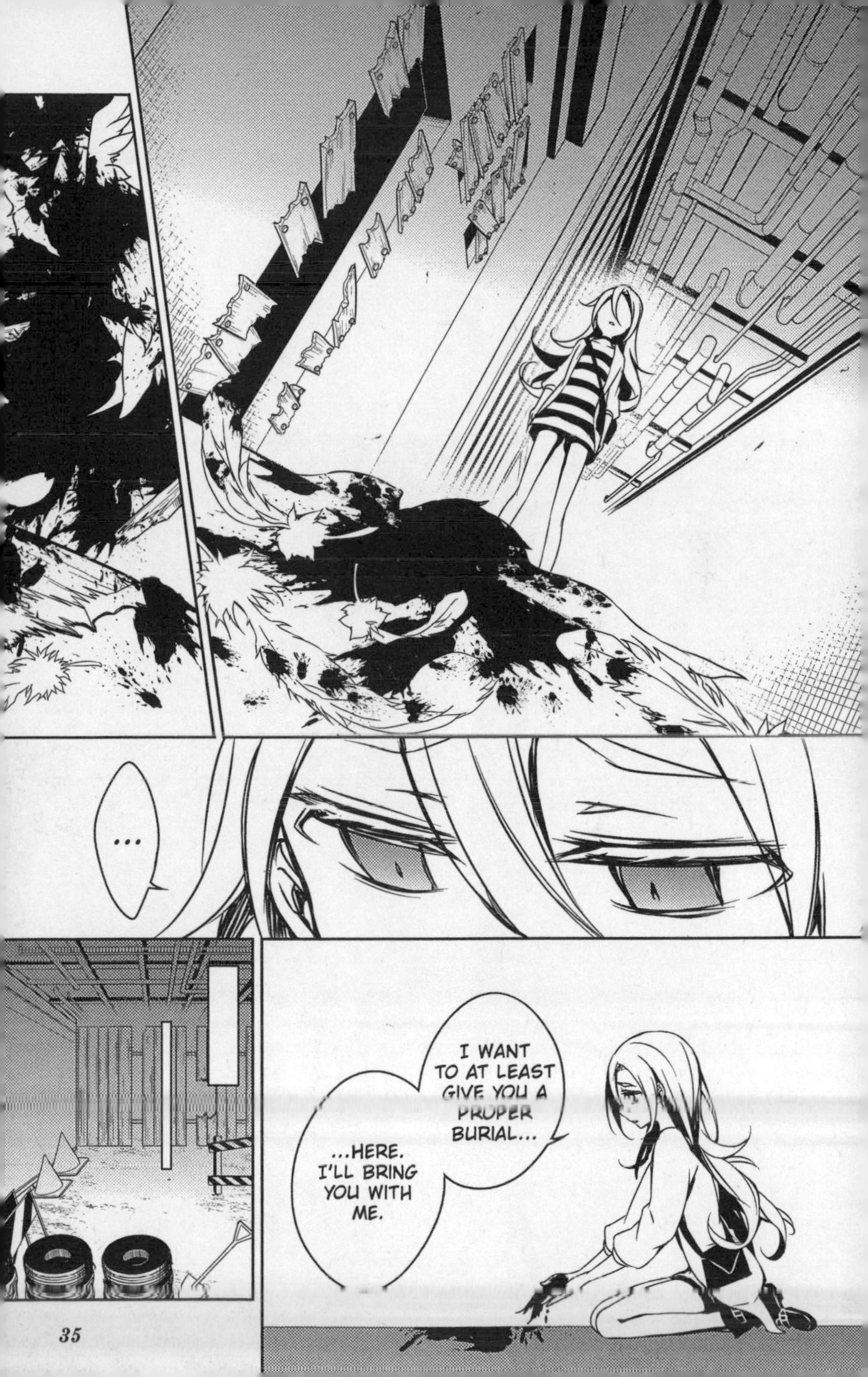
...
I WANT TO AT LEAST GIVE YOU A PROPER BURIAL...
...HERE. I'LL BRING YOU WITH ME.

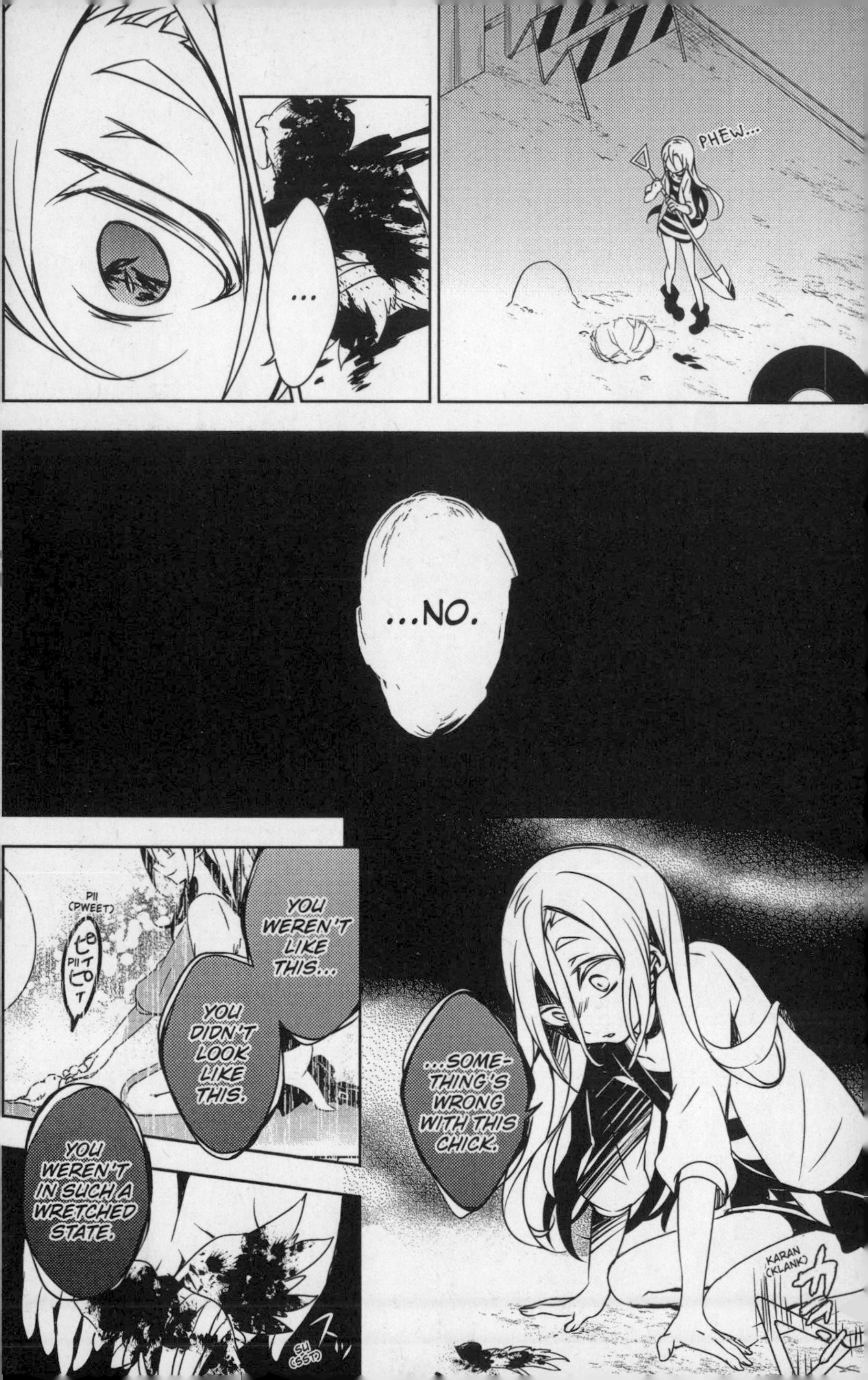
PHEW...
...
...NO.
...SOME-THING'S WRONG WITH THIS CHICK.
KARAN (KLANK)
YOU WEREN'T LIKE THIS...
YOU DIDN'T LOOK LIKE THIS.
PII (PWEET) PII
YOU WEREN'T IN SUCH A WRETCHED STATE.
SU (SSST)

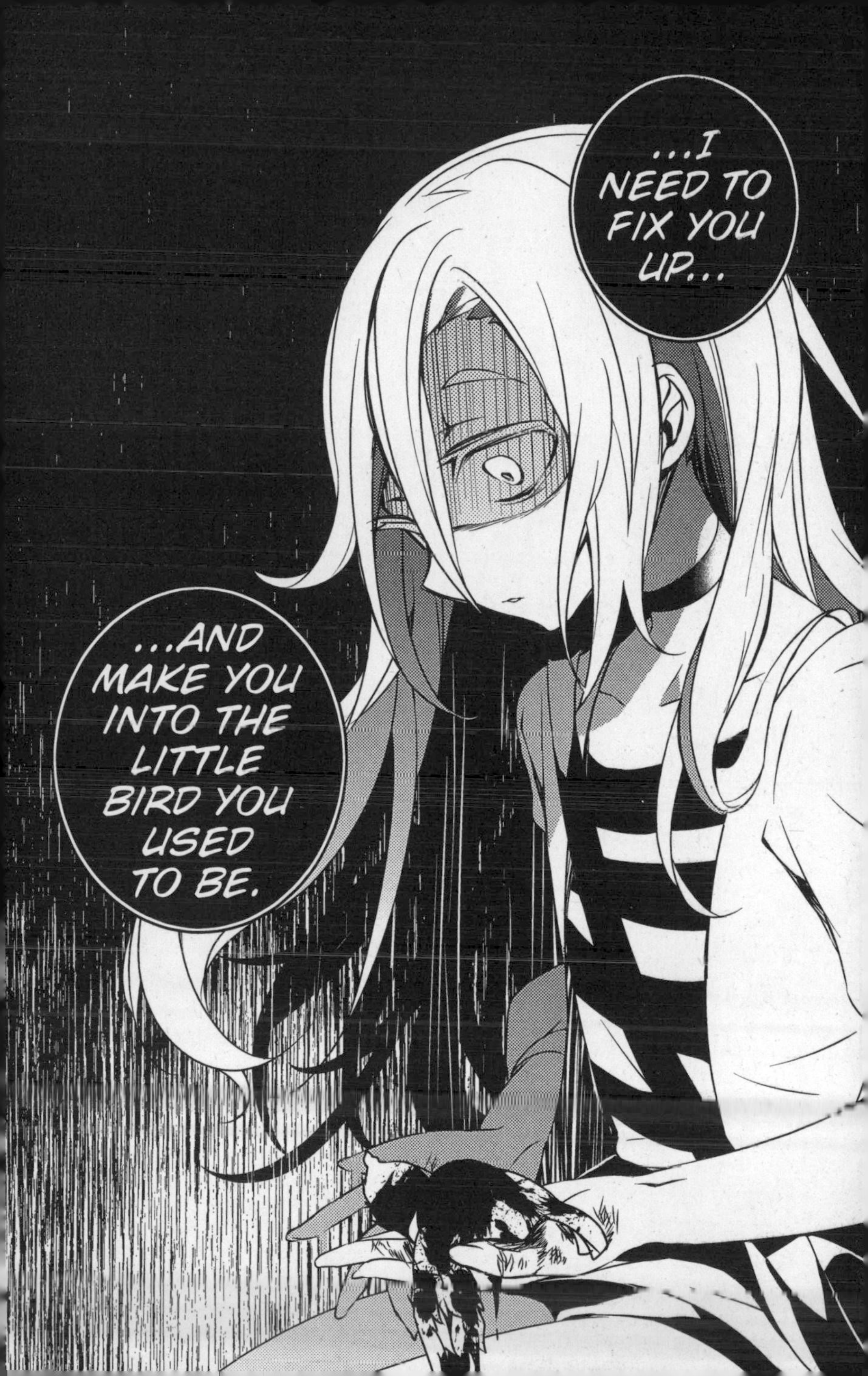
...I NEED TO FIX YOU UP...
...AND MAKE YOU INTO THE LITTLE BIRD YOU USED TO BE.

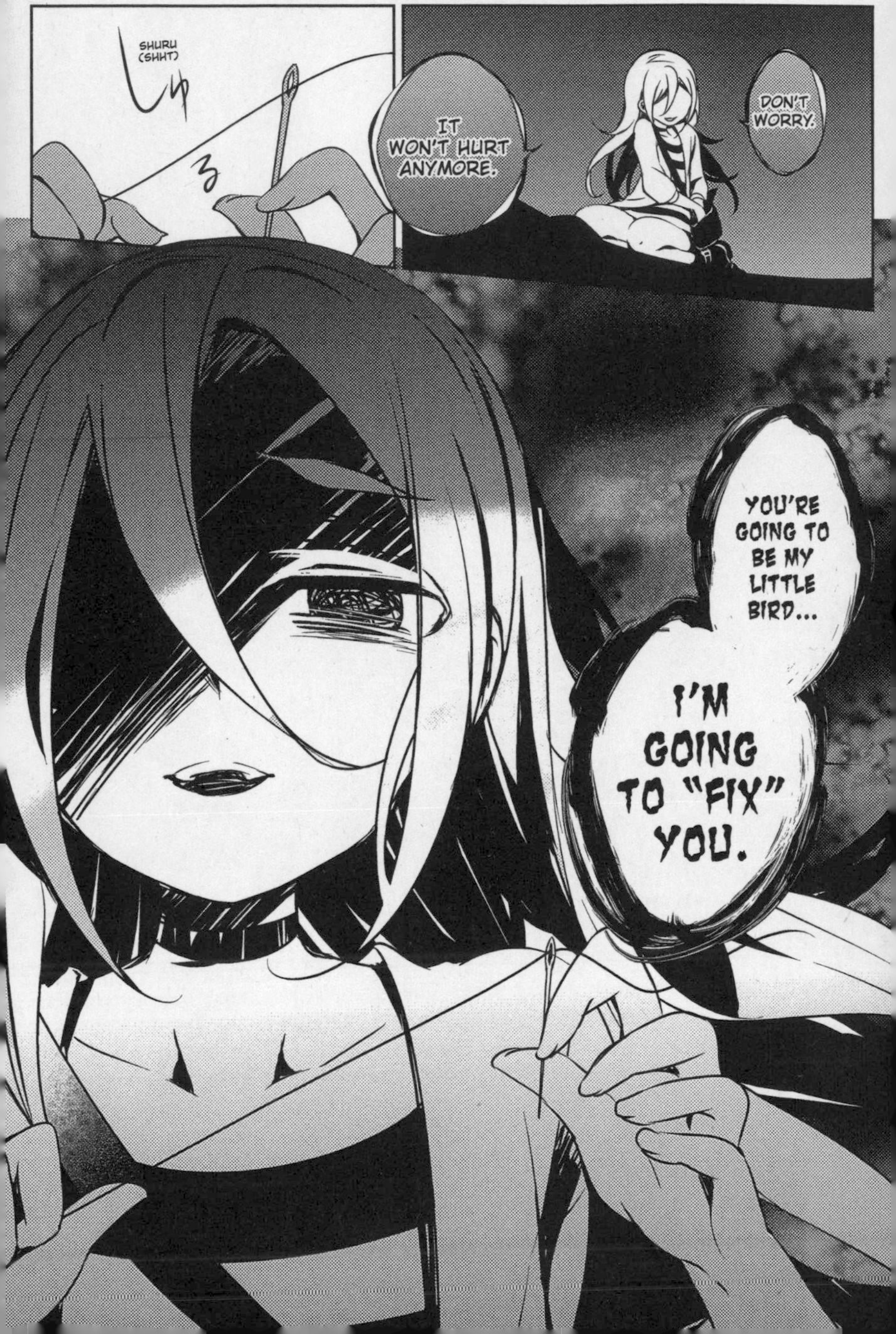
DON'T WORRY.
IT WON'T HURT ANYMORE.
SHURU (SHHT)
YOU'RE GOING TO BE MY LITTLE BIRD...
I'M GOING TO "FIX" YOU.

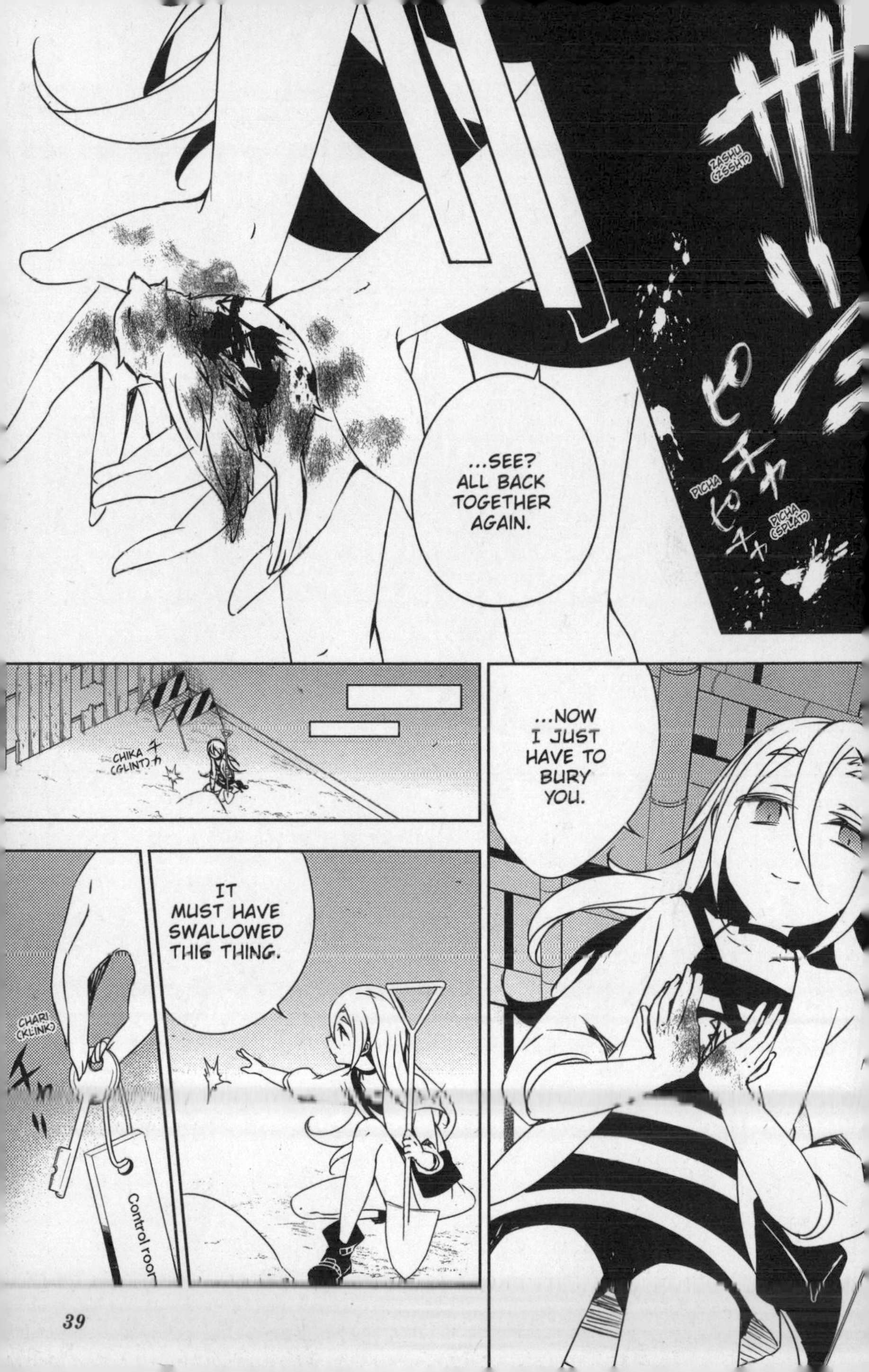
ZASHU (ZSSHT)
PICHA
PICHA (SPLAT)
...SEE? ALL BACK TOGETHER AGAIN.
...NOW I JUST HAVE TO BURY YOU.
CHIKA (GLINT)
IT MUST HAVE SWALLOWED THIS THING.
CHARI (KLINK)
Control roor

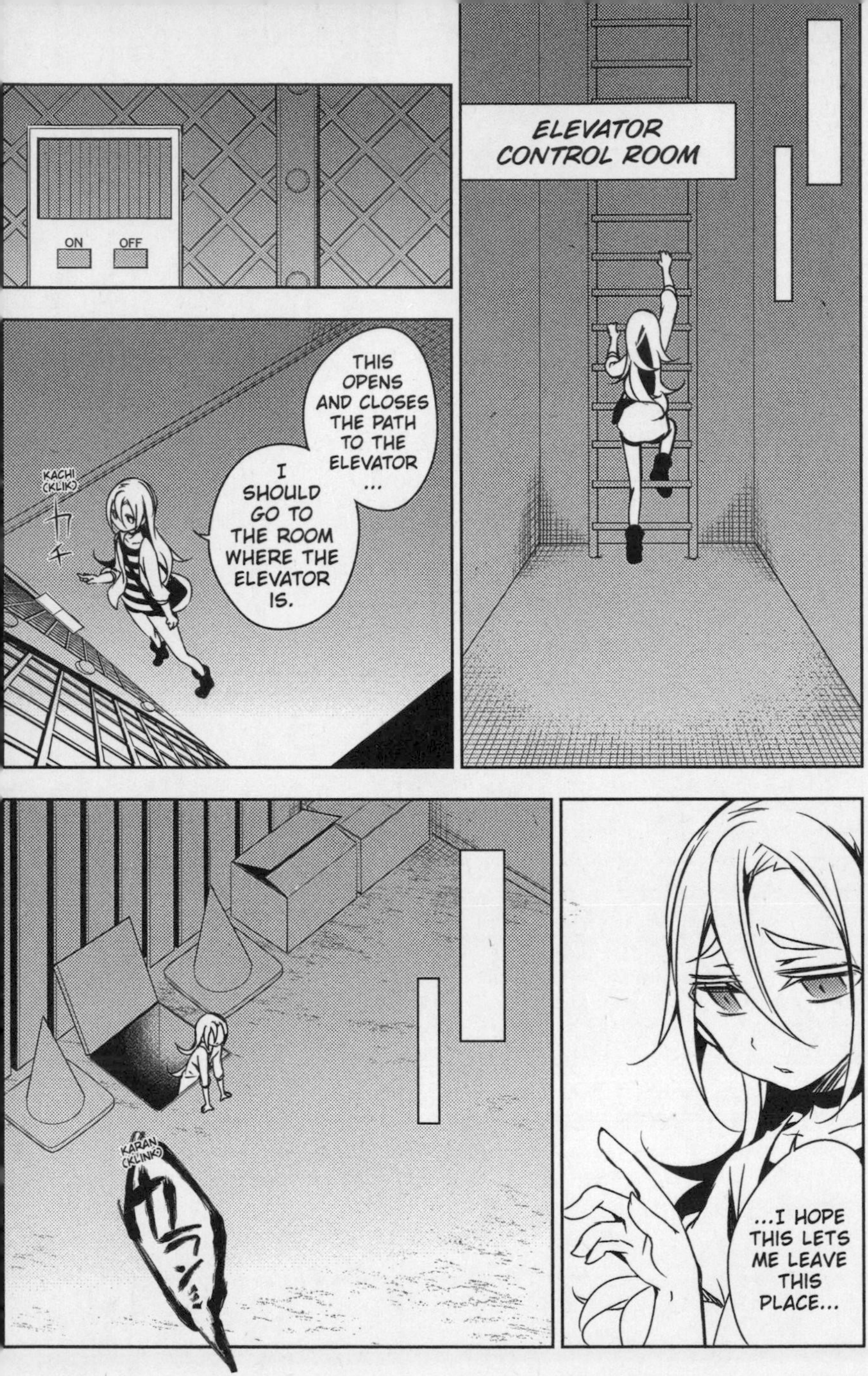
ELEVATOR CONTROL ROOM
ON
OFF
THIS OPENS AND CLOSES THE PATH TO THE ELEVATOR ...
I SHOULD GO TO THE ROOM WHERE THE ELEVATOR IS.
KACHI (KLIK)
...I HOPE THIS LETS ME LEAVE THIS PLACE...
KARAN (KLINK)

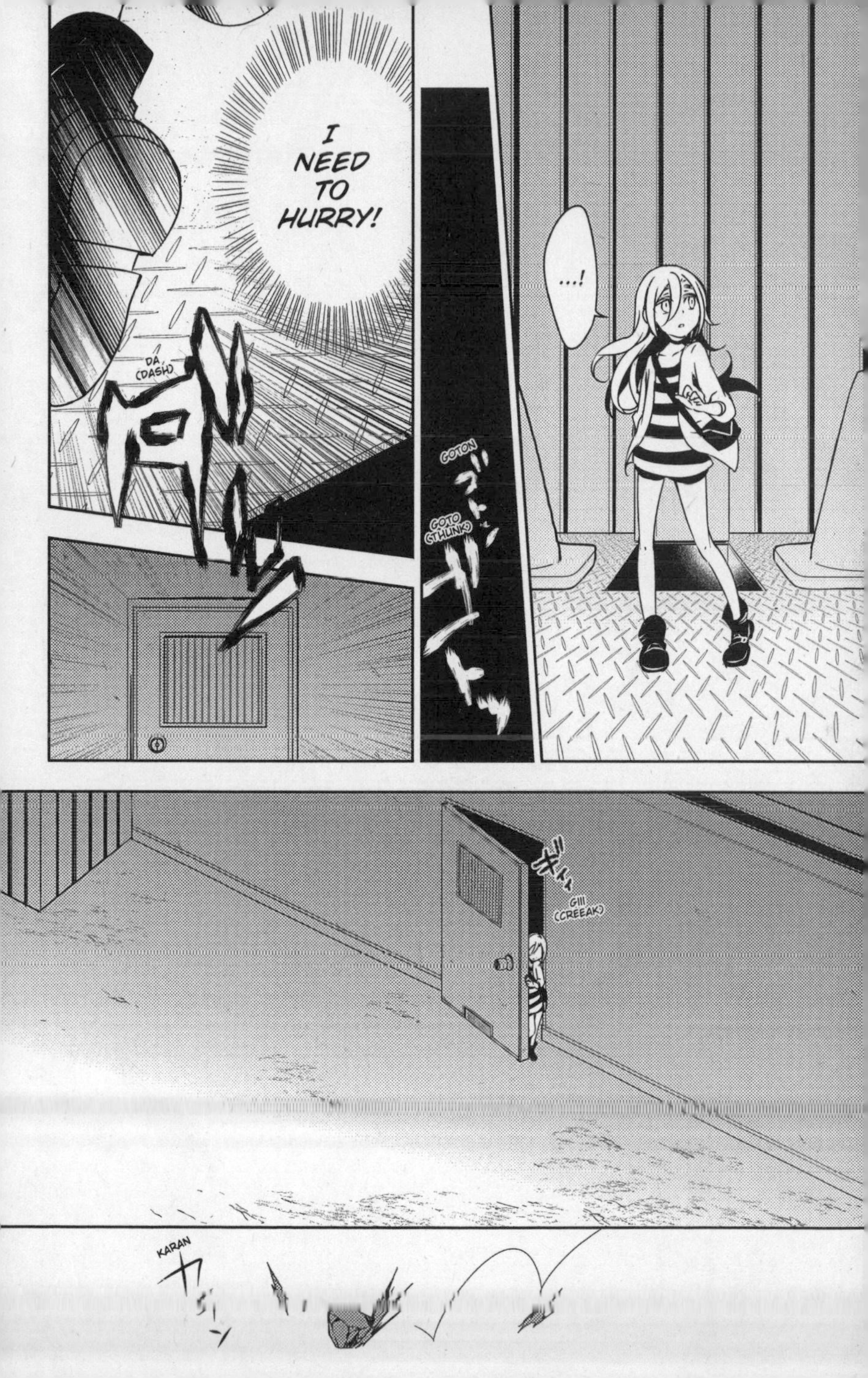

...!
GOTON
GOTO (THUNK)
I NEED TO HURRY!
DA (DASH)
GIII (CREEAK)
KARAN

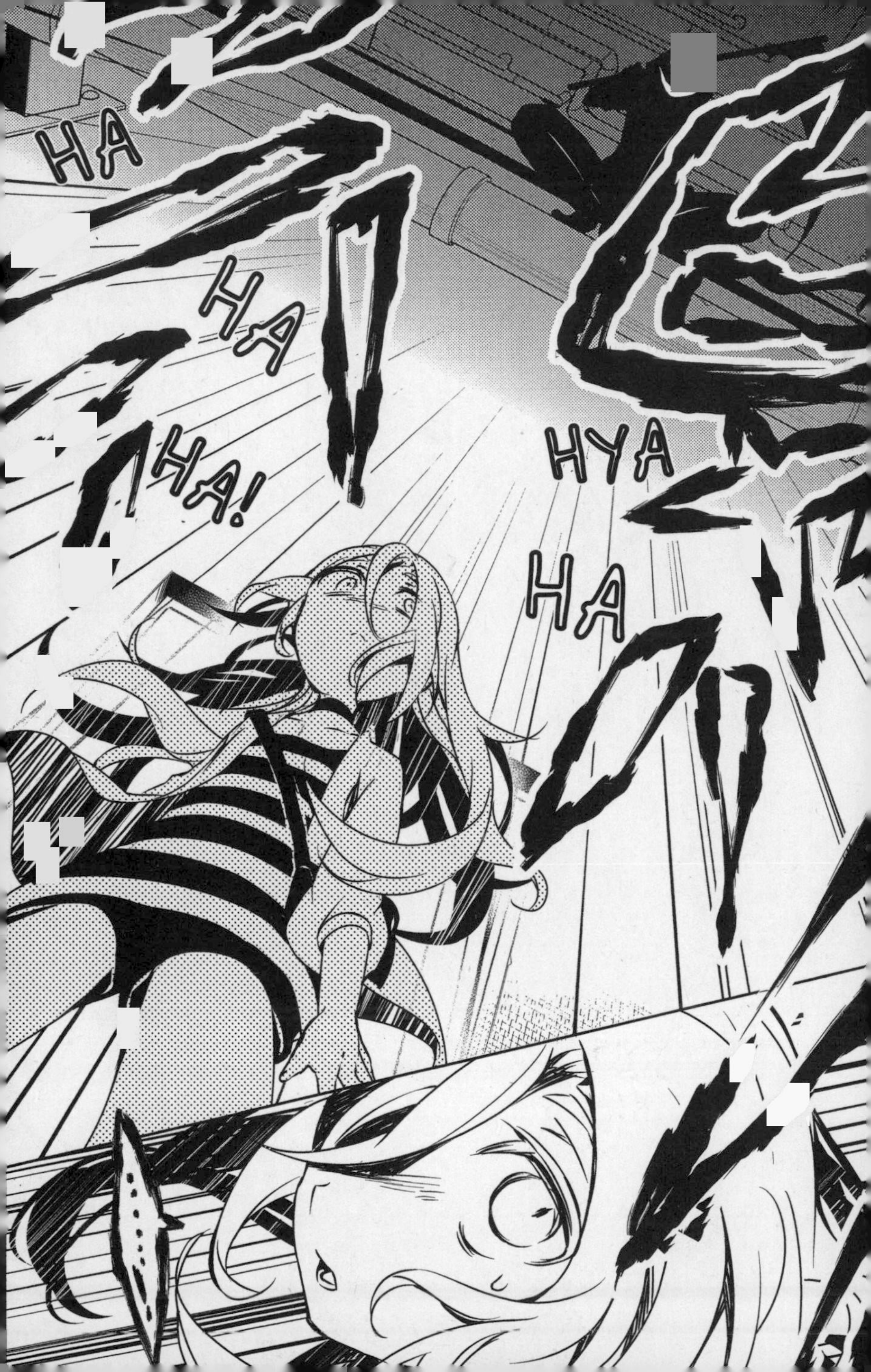
HA
HA
HA!
HYA
HA

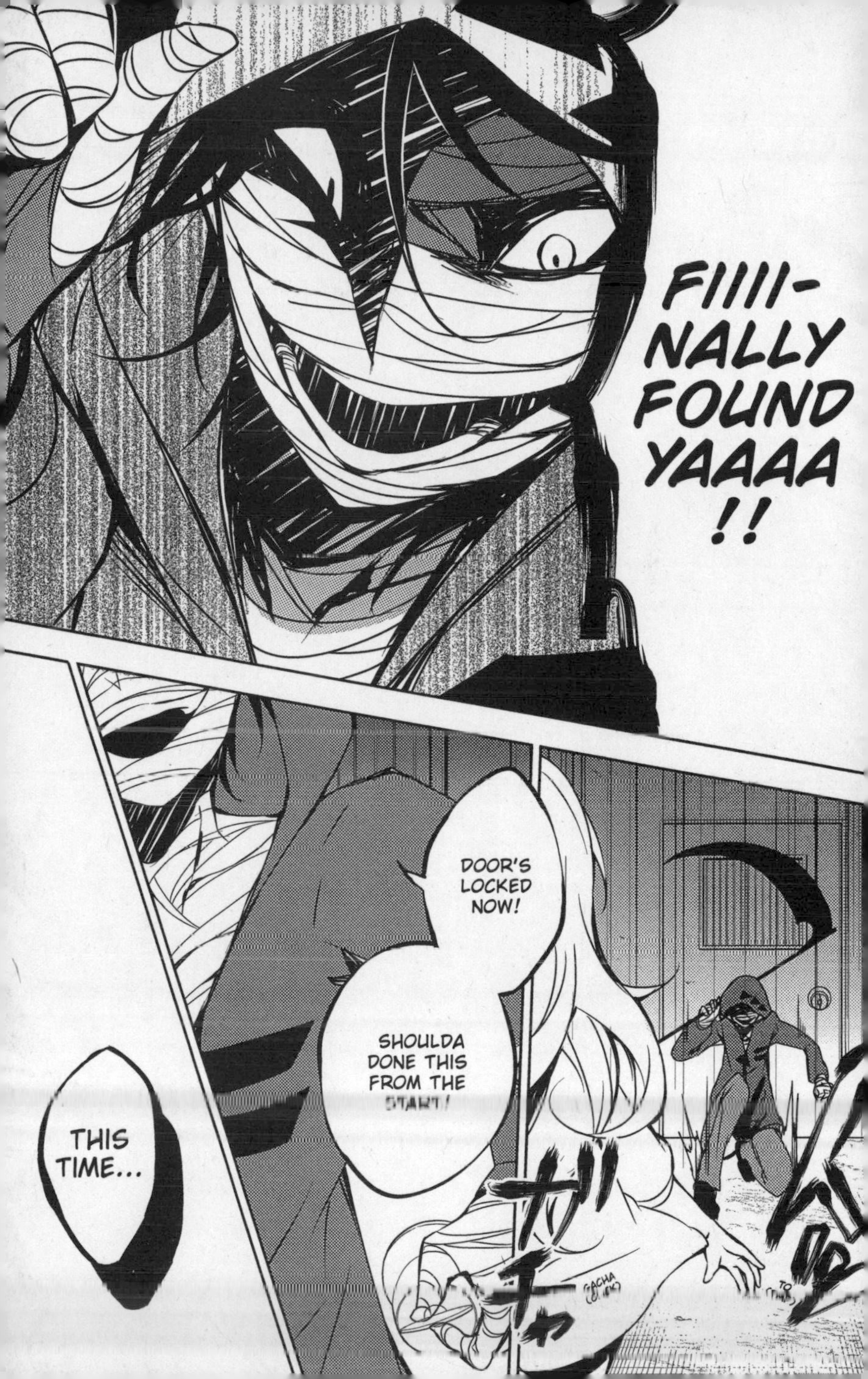
FIIII-NALLY FOUND YAAAA!!
DOOR'S LOCKED NOW!
SHOULDA DONE THIS FROM THE START!
THIS TIME...
GACHA

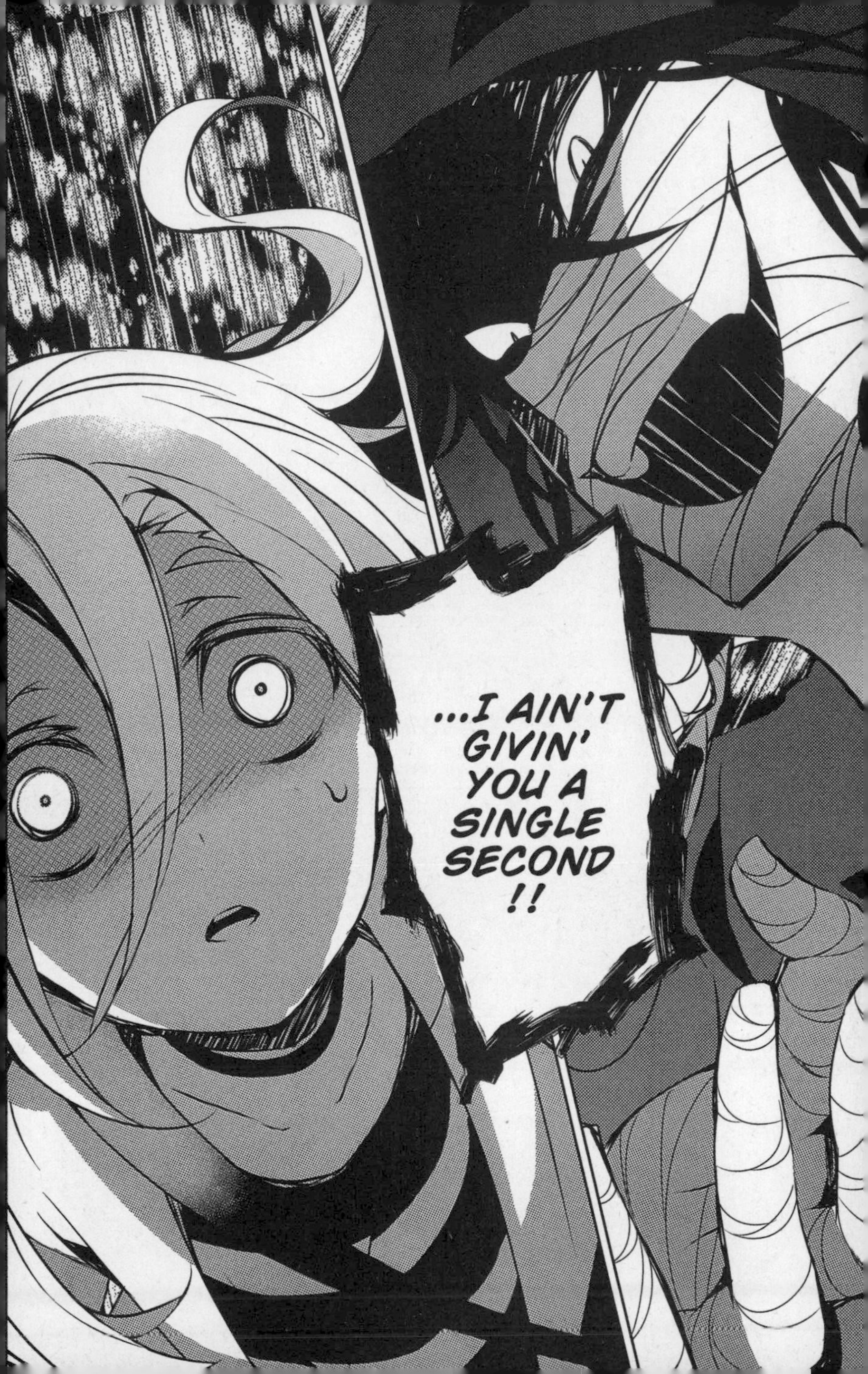
...I AIN'T GIVIN' YOU A SINGLE SECOND !!

Angels of DEATH

INSIDE STORY OF PRODUCTION VOL.1

BY MAKOTO SANADA

Before being given the opportunity by *Niconico Game Magazine* to serialize *Angels of Death* as a manga, I came up with its plot outline while working on my previous freeware game, *Kirisame ga Furu Mori* (*Forest of Drizzling Rain*).

As *Kirisame ga Furu Mori* is a game that deals with the fear of ancient customs and ghosts, for my next game, I wanted to make a horror title where people provoke that fear instead. I thought about what kind of story that would be, and this tale is the result.

However, the first draft was fairly rough, and the characters were only vaguely fleshed out. Looking at my sketchbook from back then, Rachel and Zack were still unnamed, described only as "hapless" and "killer with no self-restraint."

It's also interesting to see how different the story's setting was. Zack didn't have his bandages, both he and Rachel were older, and their personalities were a bit different as well. It's surprising now, but Rachel was a regular girl, while Zack was a little nihilistic and not quite as noisy as he ended up being. The story was also untitled at the time.

Compared to then, the current *Angels of Death* is quite complex, and each of its characters has more to them that makes them unique. Once serialization talks had commenced, I began giving a lot of thought to the character designs to further develop them for this adaptation.

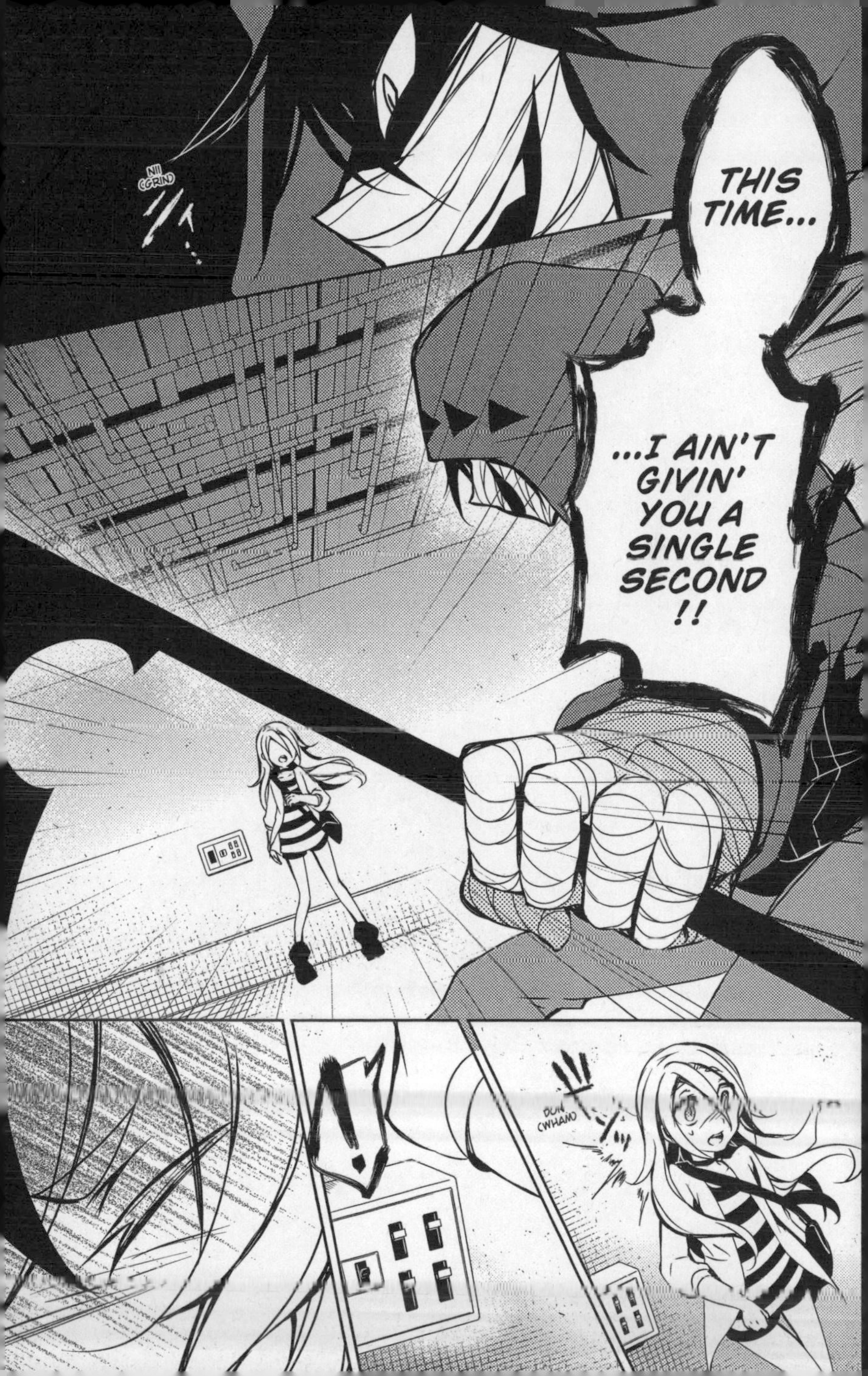
NII (GRIN)
THIS TIME...
...I AIN'T GIVIN' YOU A SINGLE SECOND!!
DON (WHAM)

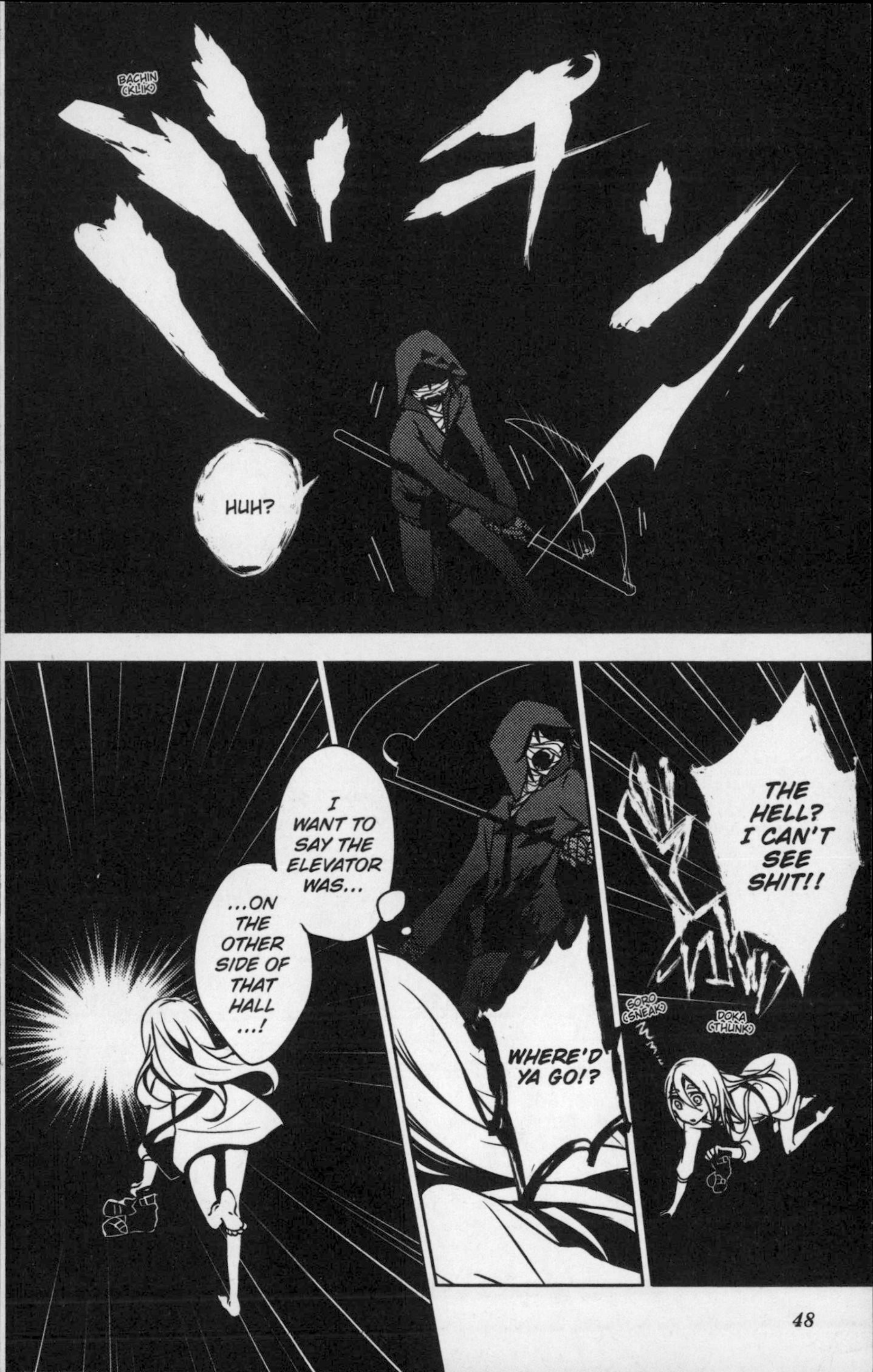
BACHIN (KLIK)
HUH?
THE HELL? I CAN'T SEE SHIT!!
SORO (SNEAK)
DOKA (THUNK)
WHERE'D YA GO!?
I WANT TO SAY THE ELEVATOR WAS...
...ON THE OTHER SIDE OF THAT HALL...!

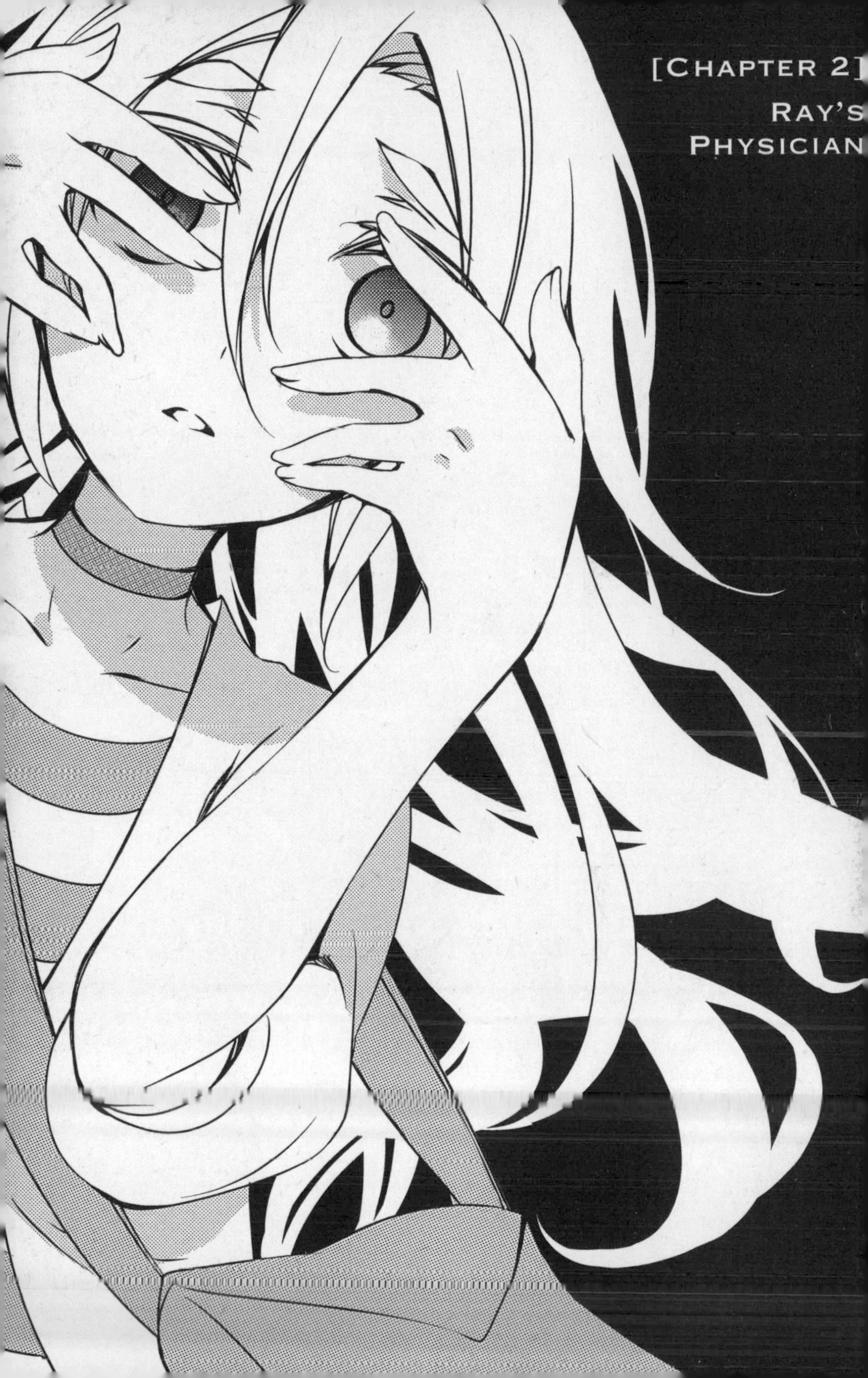

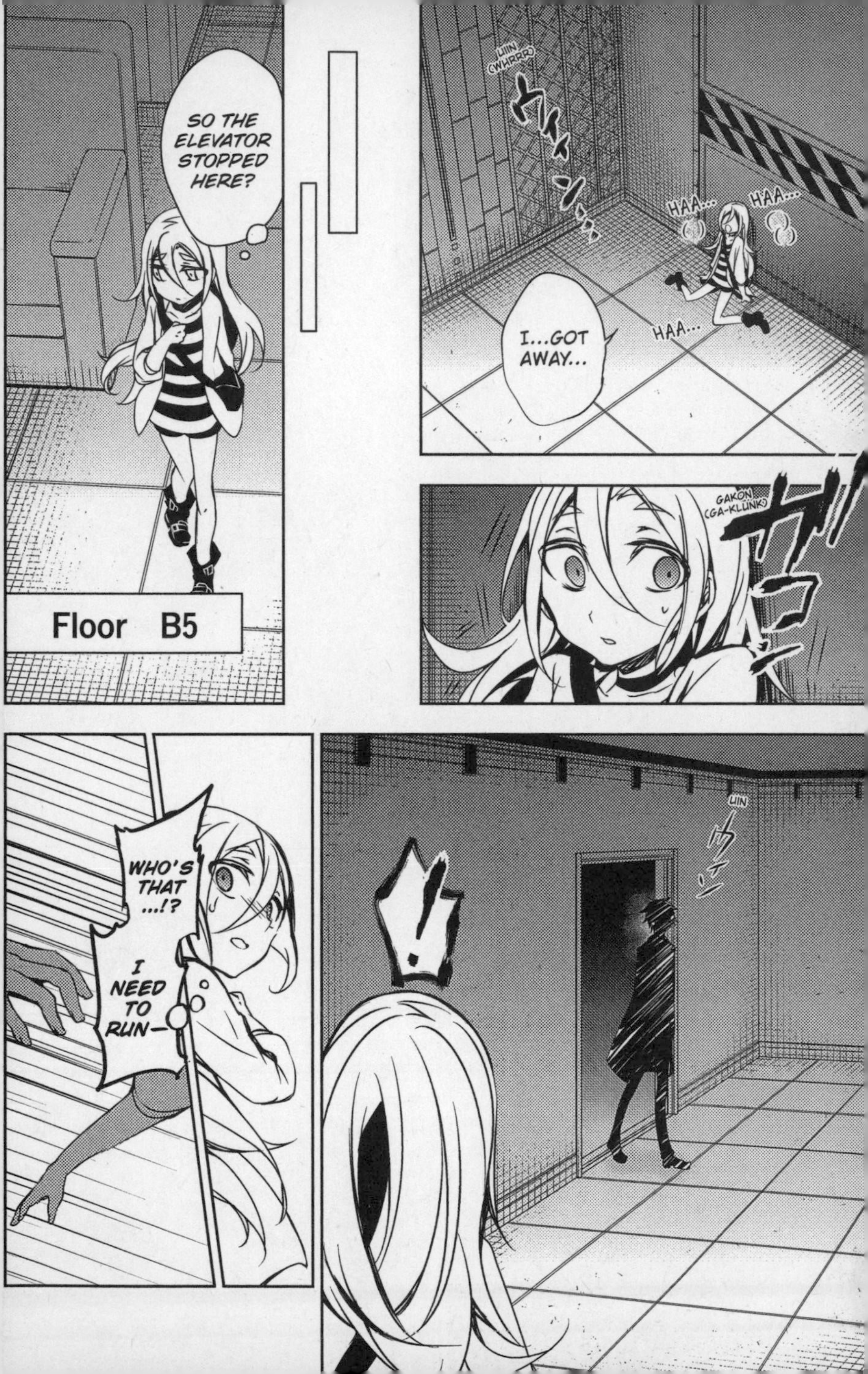
LIIN (WHRRR)
HAA...
HAA...
HAA...
I...GOT AWAY...
GAKON (GA-KLUNK)
SO THE ELEVATOR STOPPED HERE?
Floor B5
LIIN
!
WHO'S THAT ...!?
I NEED TO RUN—

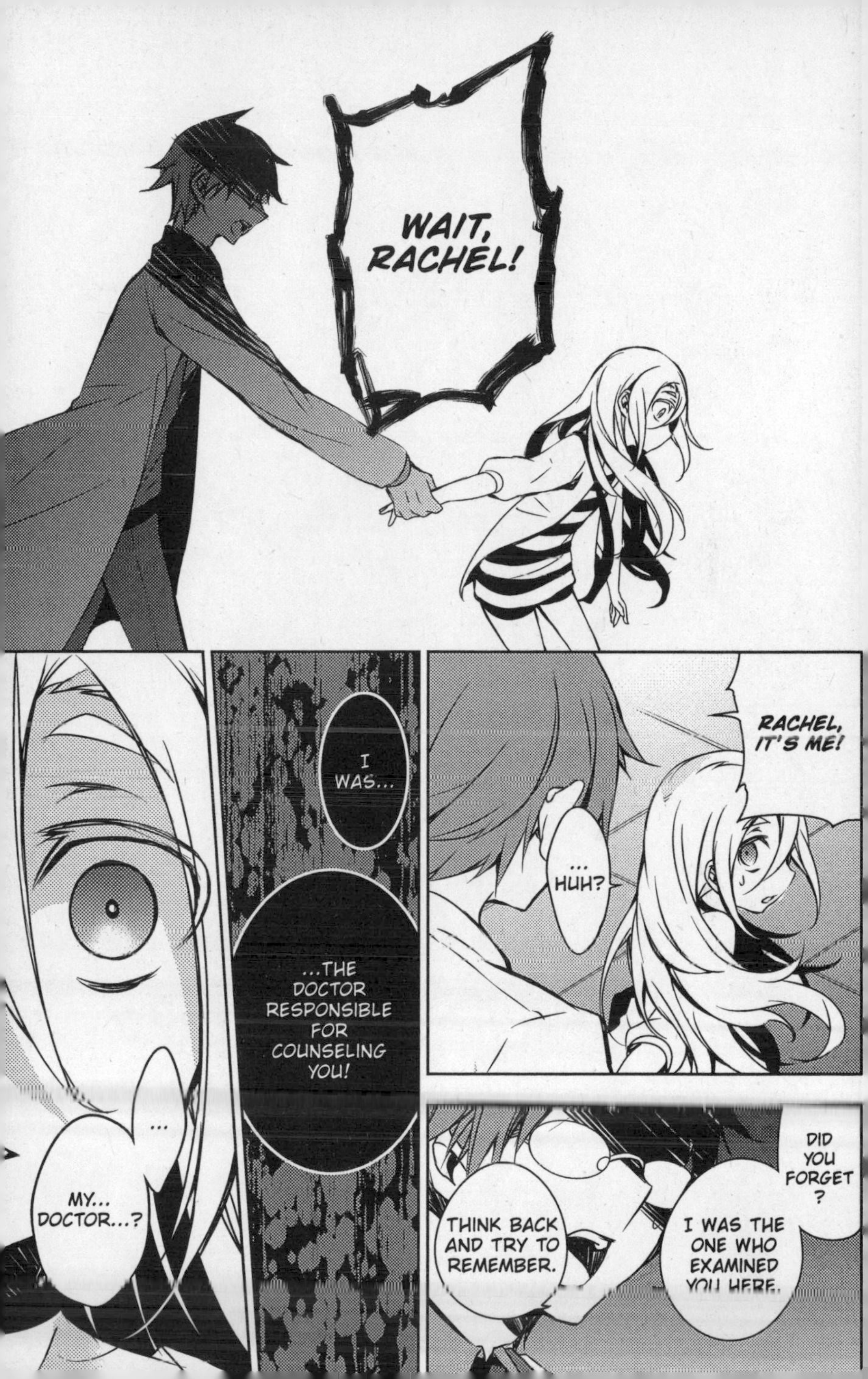
WAIT, RACHEL!
RACHEL, IT'S ME!
... HUH?
DID YOU FORGET?
I WAS THE ONE WHO EXAMINED YOU HERE.
THINK BACK AND TRY TO REMEMBER.
I WAS...
...THE DOCTOR RESPONSIBLE FOR COUNSELING YOU!
...
MY... DOCTOR...?

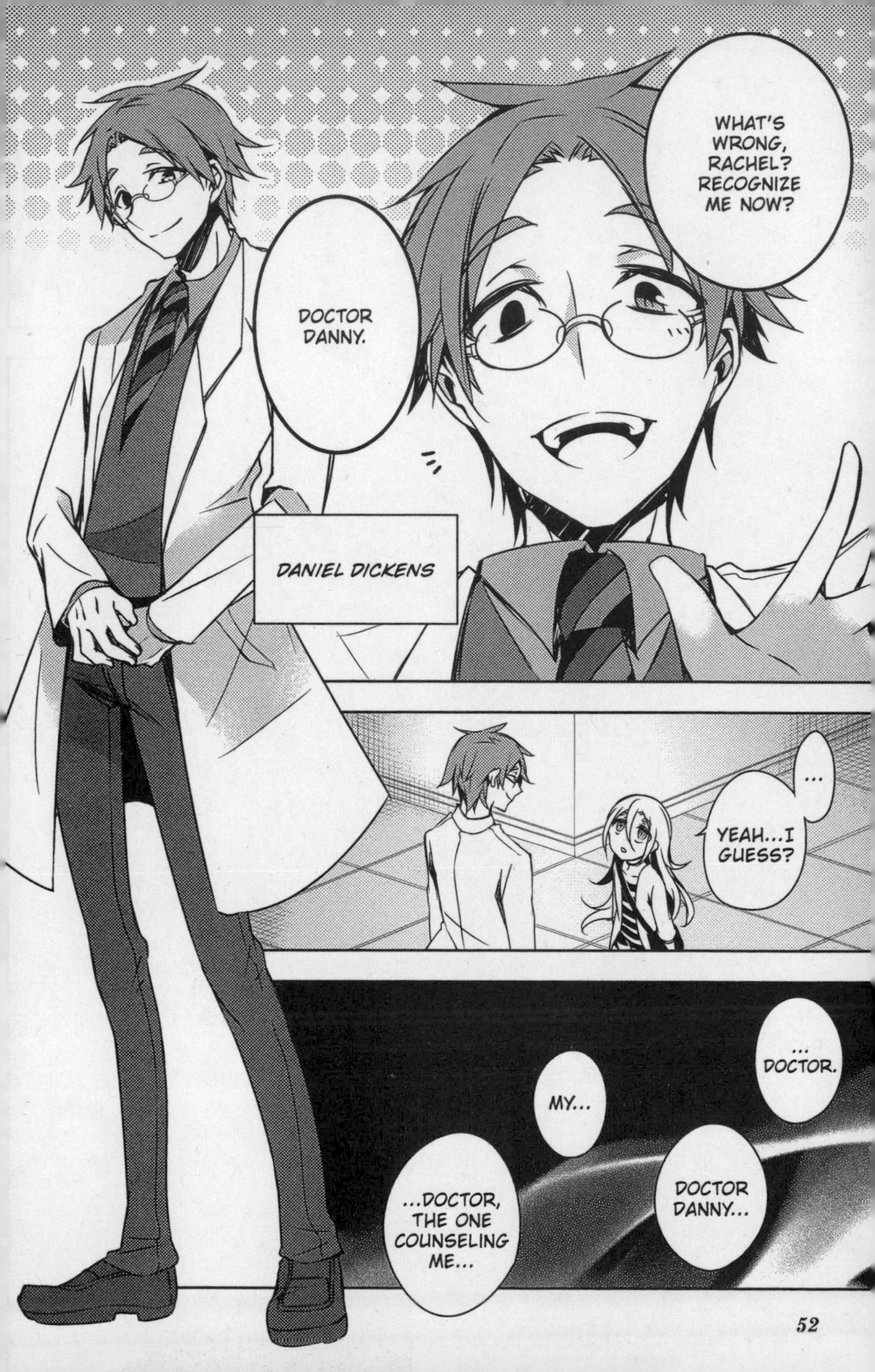
WHAT'S WRONG, RACHEL? RECOGNIZE ME NOW?
DOCTOR DANNY.
DANIEL DICKENS
...
YEAH...I GUESS?
...DOCTOR.
MY...
DOCTOR DANNY...
...DOCTOR, THE ONE COUNSELING ME...

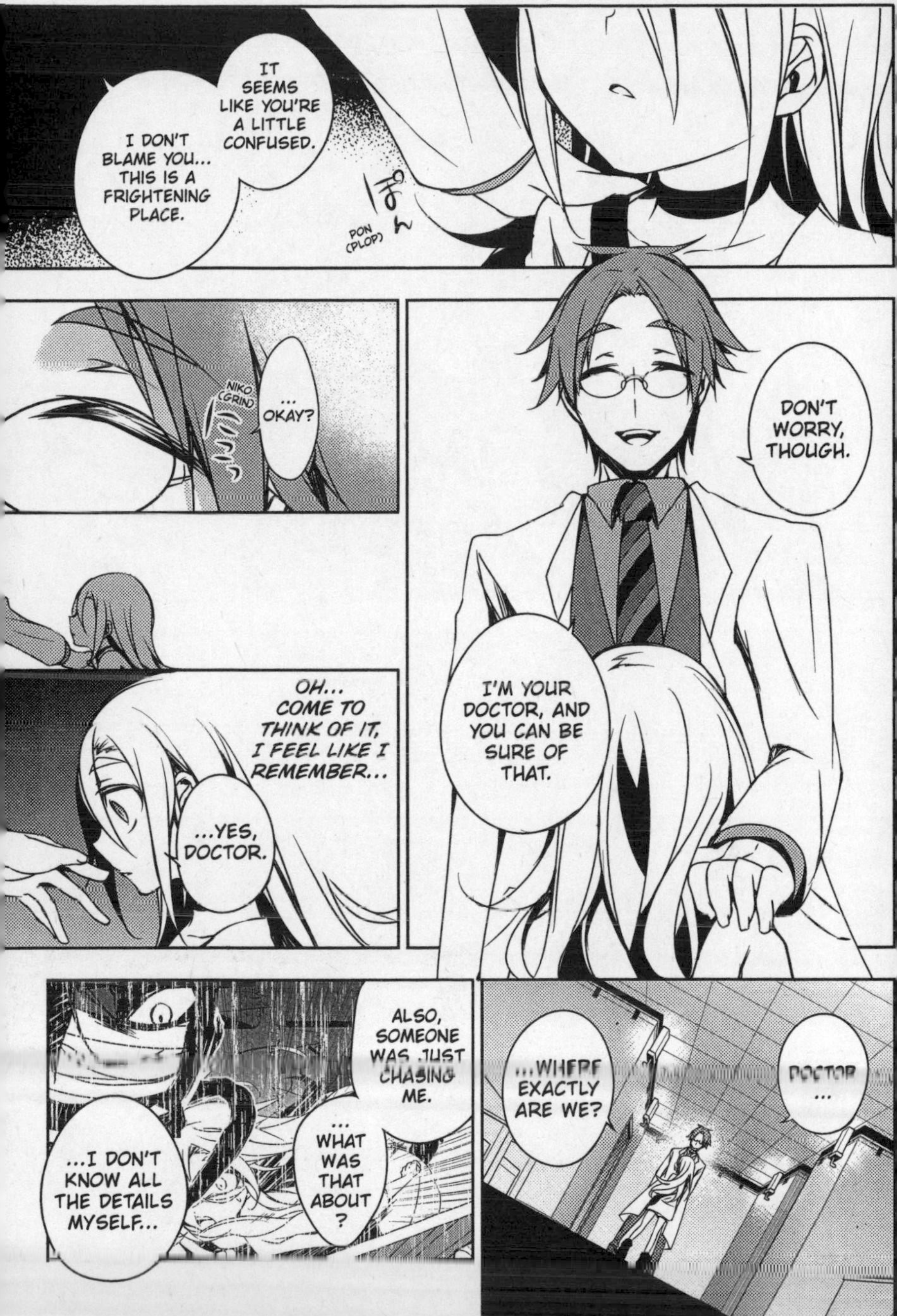
IT SEEMS LIKE YOU'RE A LITTLE CONFUSED.
I DON'T BLAME YOU... THIS IS A FRIGHTENING PLACE.
ぽん
PON (PLOP)
DON'T WORRY, THOUGH.
I'M YOUR DOCTOR, AND YOU CAN BE SURE OF THAT.
...OKAY?
NIKO (GRIN)
OH... COME TO THINK OF IT, I FEEL LIKE I REMEMBER...
...YES, DOCTOR.
DOCTOR...
...WHERE EXACTLY ARE WE?
ALSO, SOMEONE WAS JUST CHASING ME.
...WHAT WAS THAT ABOUT?
...I DON'T KNOW ALL THE DETAILS MYSELF...

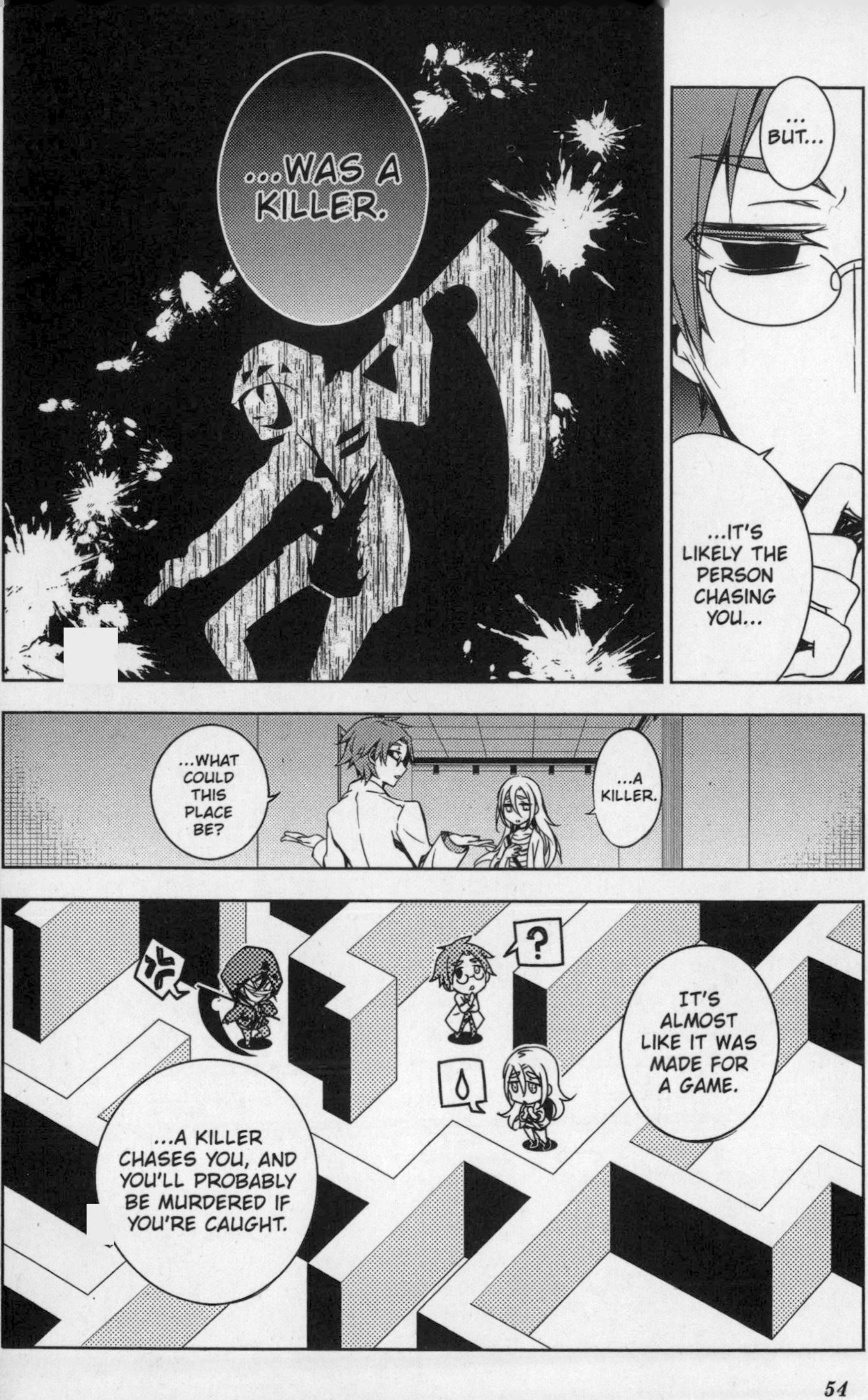
... BUT...
...IT'S LIKELY THE PERSON CHASING YOU...
...WAS A KILLER.
...A KILLER.
...WHAT COULD THIS PLACE BE?
?
IT'S ALMOST LIKE IT WAS MADE FOR A GAME.
...A KILLER CHASES YOU, AND YOU'LL PROBABLY BE MURDERED IF YOU'RE CAUGHT.

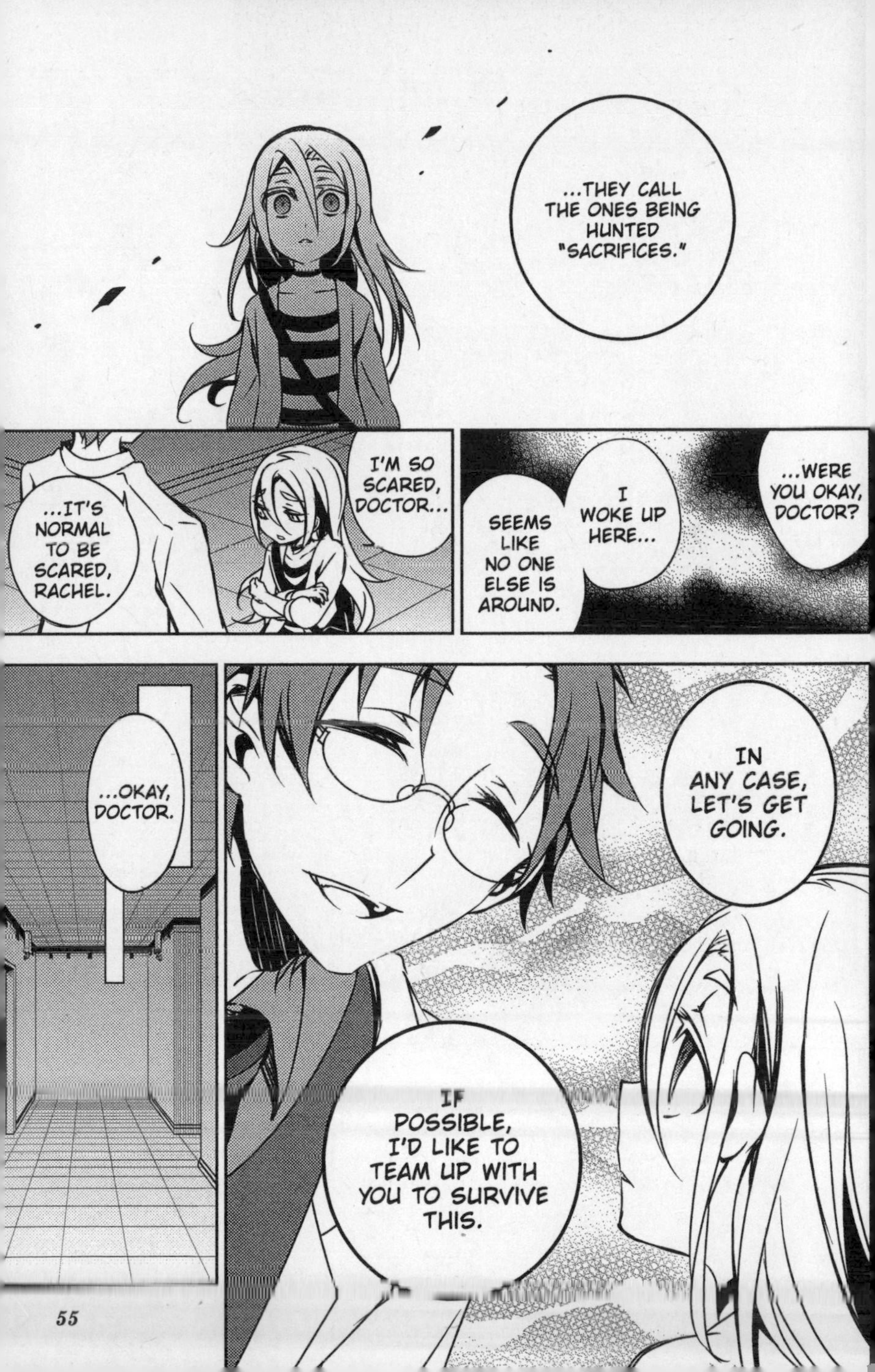
...THEY CALL THE ONES BEING HUNTED "SACRIFICES."
...WERE YOU OKAY, DOCTOR?
I WOKE UP HERE...
SEEMS LIKE NO ONE ELSE IS AROUND.
I'M SO SCARED, DOCTOR...
...IT'S NORMAL TO BE SCARED, RACHEL.
IN ANY CASE, LET'S GET GOING.
IF POSSIBLE, I'D LIKE TO TEAM UP WITH YOU TO SURVIVE THIS.
...OKAY, DOCTOR.

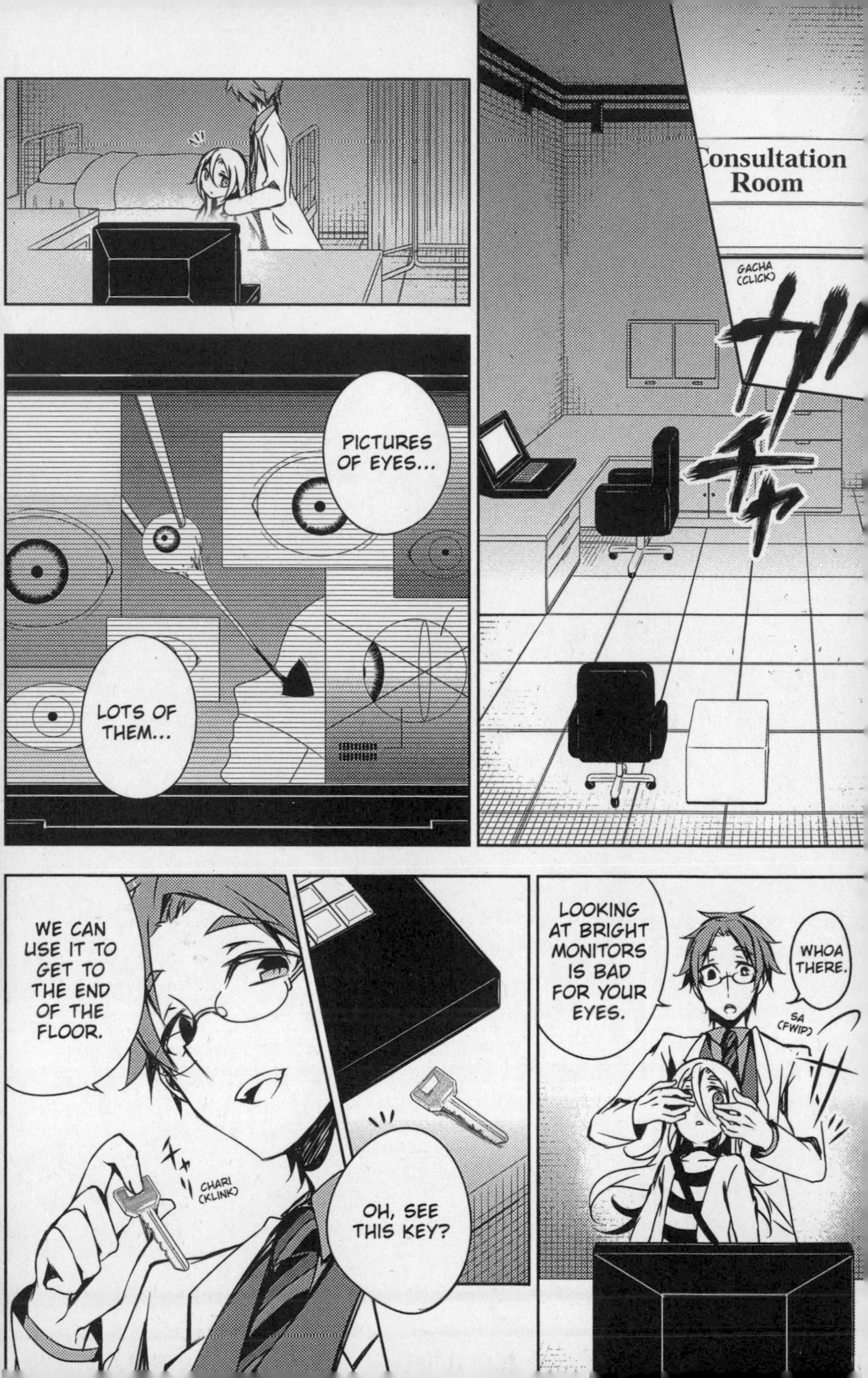
Consultation Room
GACHA (CLICK)
PICTURES OF EYES...
LOTS OF THEM...
WHOA THERE.
LOOKING AT BRIGHT MONITORS IS BAD FOR YOUR EYES.
SA (FWIP)
OH, SEE THIS KEY?
CHARI (KLINK)
WE CAN USE IT TO GET TO THE END OF THE FLOOR.

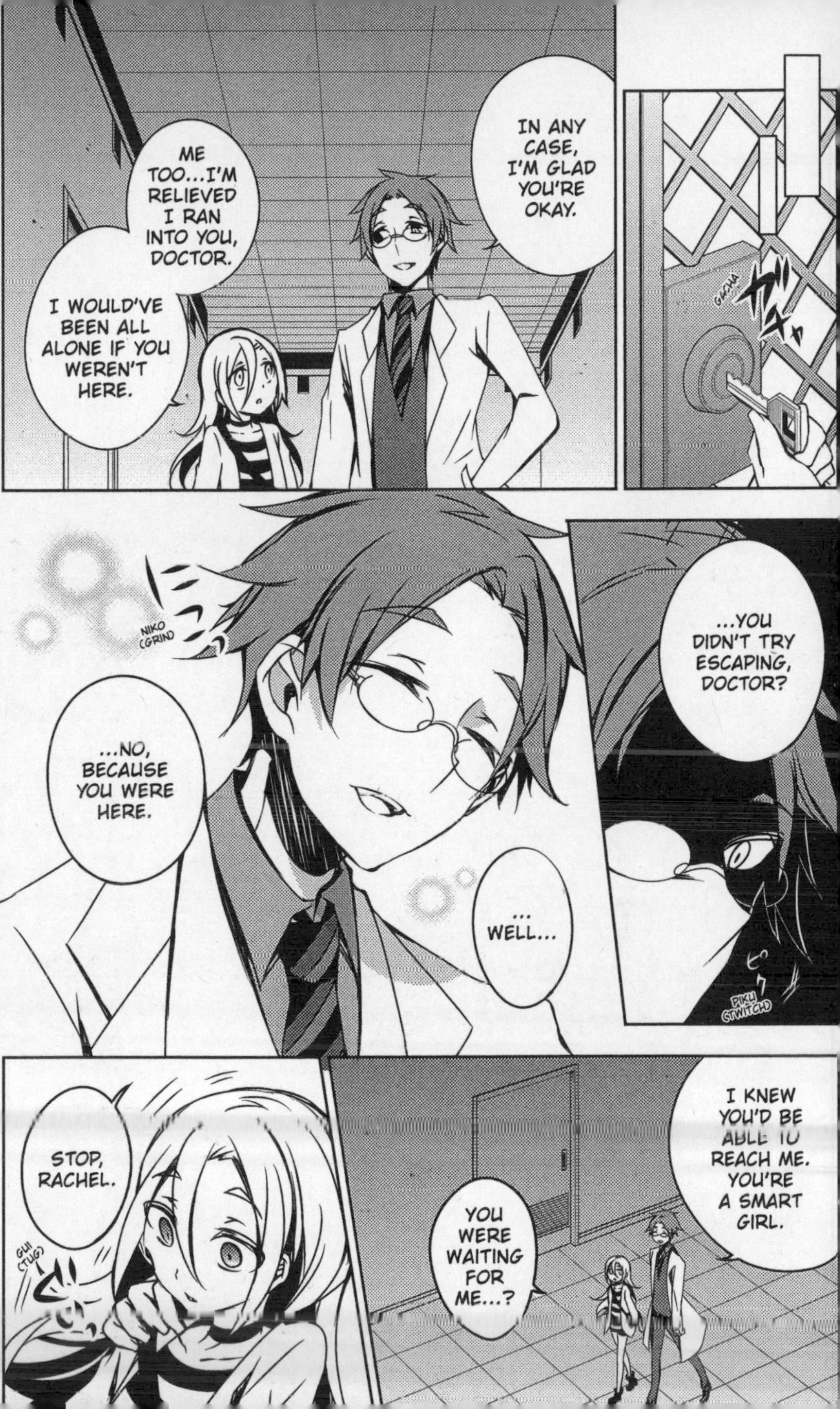
GACHA
IN ANY CASE, I'M GLAD YOU'RE OKAY.
ME TOO...I'M RELIEVED I RAN INTO YOU, DOCTOR.
I WOULD'VE BEEN ALL ALONE IF YOU WEREN'T HERE.
...YOU DIDN'T TRY ESCAPING, DOCTOR?
PIKU (TWITCH)
... WELL...
...NO, BECAUSE YOU WERE HERE.
NIKO (GRIND)
I KNEW YOU'D BE ABLE TO REACH ME. YOU'RE A SMART GIRL.
YOU WERE WAITING FOR ME...?
STOP, RACHEL.
GUI (TUG)

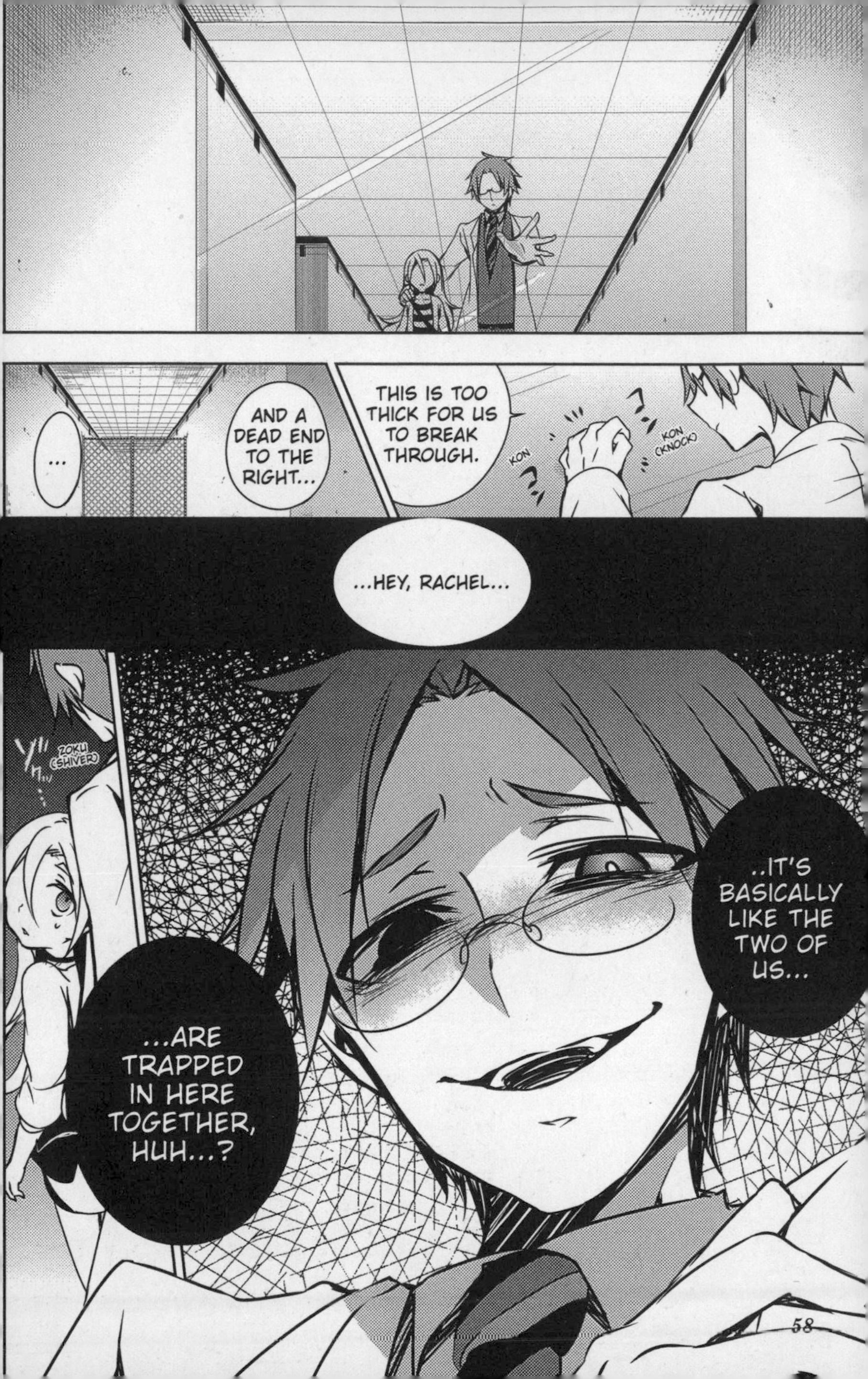
KON
KON (KNOCK)
THIS IS TOO THICK FOR US TO BREAK THROUGH.
AND A DEAD END TO THE RIGHT...
...
...HEY, RACHEL...
..IT'S BASICALLY LIKE THE TWO OF US...
ZOKU (SHIVER)
...ARE TRAPPED IN HERE TOGETHER, HUH...?

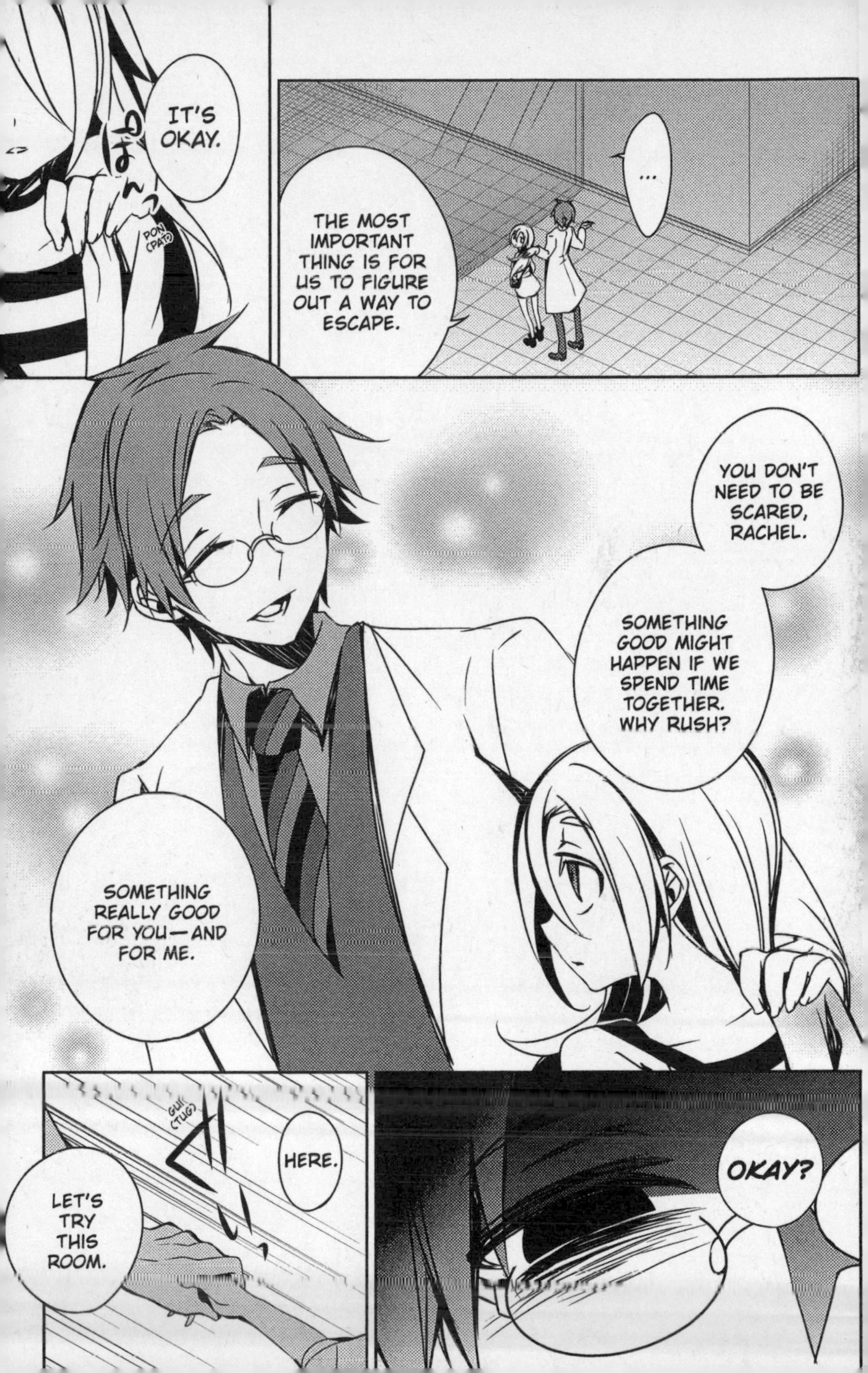
...
THE MOST IMPORTANT THING IS FOR US TO FIGURE OUT A WAY TO ESCAPE.
IT'S OKAY.
PON (PAT)
YOU DON'T NEED TO BE SCARED, RACHEL.
SOMETHING GOOD MIGHT HAPPEN IF WE SPEND TIME TOGETHER. WHY RUSH?
SOMETHING REALLY GOOD FOR YOU—AND FOR ME.
OKAY?
GUI (TUG)
HERE.
LET'S TRY THIS ROOM.

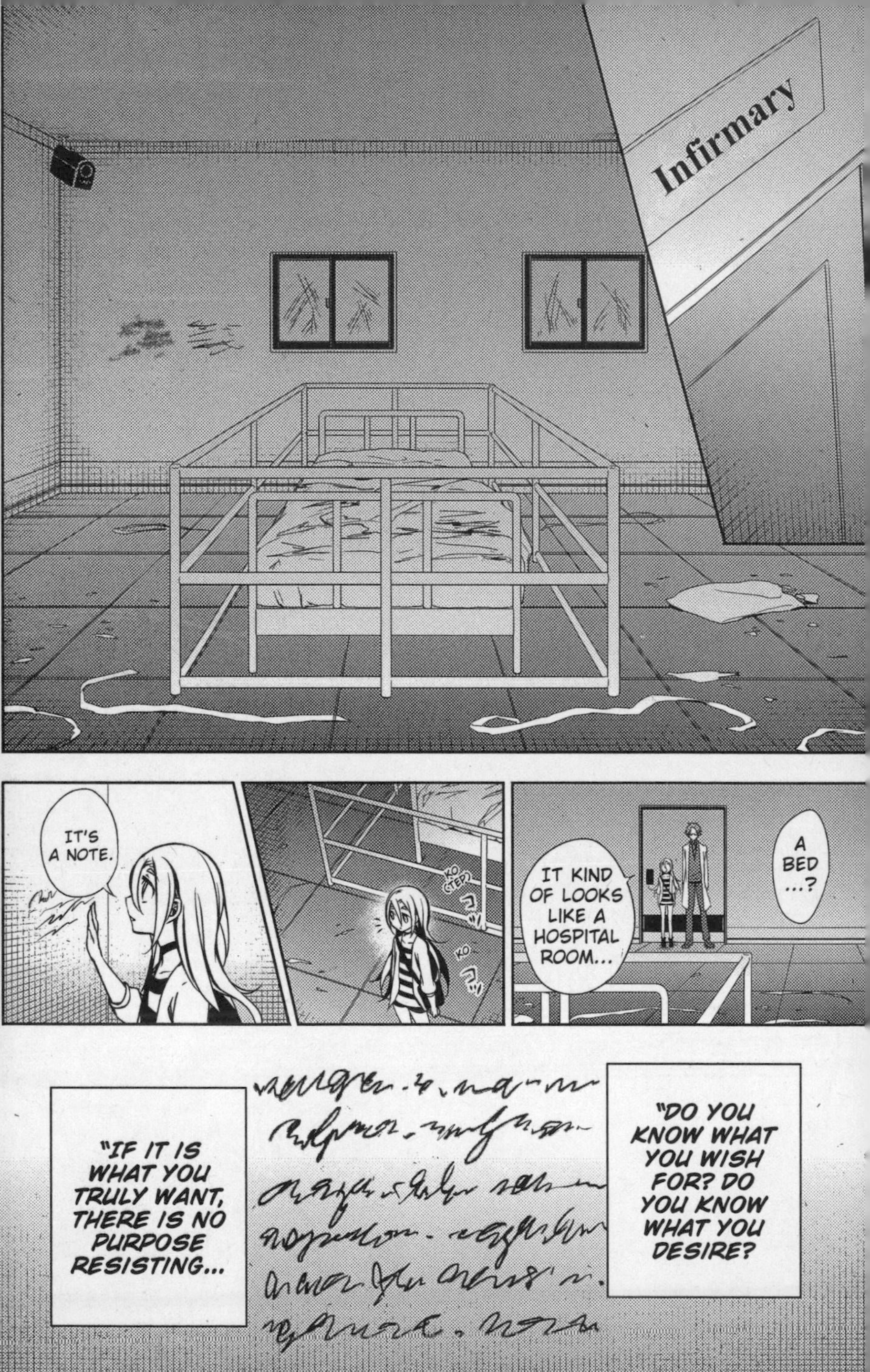
Infirmary
A BED ...?
IT KIND OF LOOKS LIKE A HOSPITAL ROOM...
KO (TEP)
KO
IT'S A NOTE.
"DO YOU KNOW WHAT YOU WISH FOR? DO YOU KNOW WHAT YOU DESIRE?
"IF IT IS WHAT YOU TRULY WANT, THERE IS NO PURPOSE RESISTING...

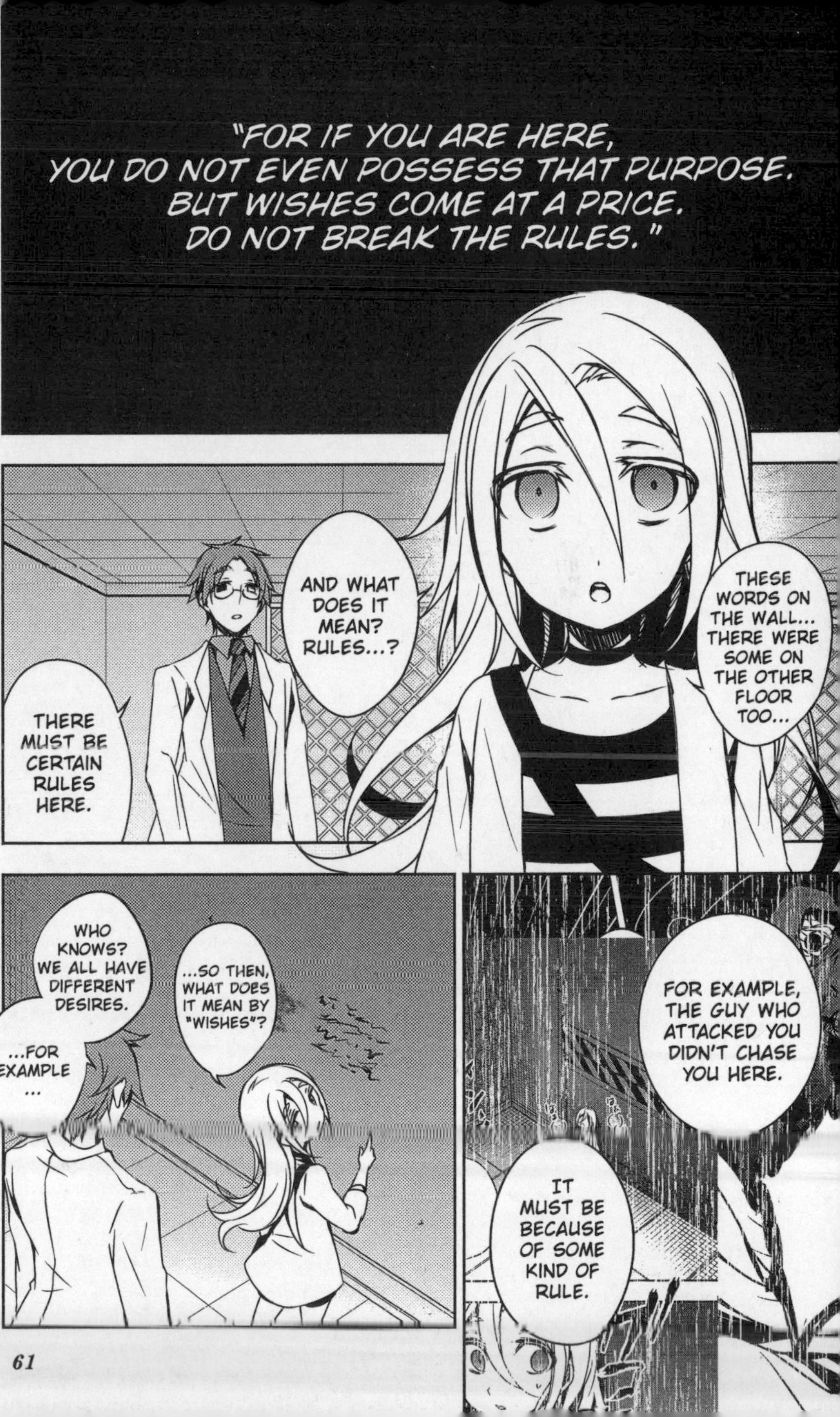
"FOR IF YOU ARE HERE, YOU DO NOT EVEN POSSESS THAT PURPOSE. BUT WISHES COME AT A PRICE. DO NOT BREAK THE RULES."
THESE WORDS ON THE WALL... THERE WERE SOME ON THE OTHER FLOOR TOO...
AND WHAT DOES IT MEAN? RULES...?
THERE MUST BE CERTAIN RULES HERE.
FOR EXAMPLE, THE GUY WHO ATTACKED YOU DIDN'T CHASE YOU HERE.
IT MUST BE BECAUSE OF SOME KIND OF RULE.
...SO THEN, WHAT DOES IT MEAN BY "WISHES"?
WHO KNOWS? WE ALL HAVE DIFFERENT DESIRES.
...FOR EXAMPLE ...

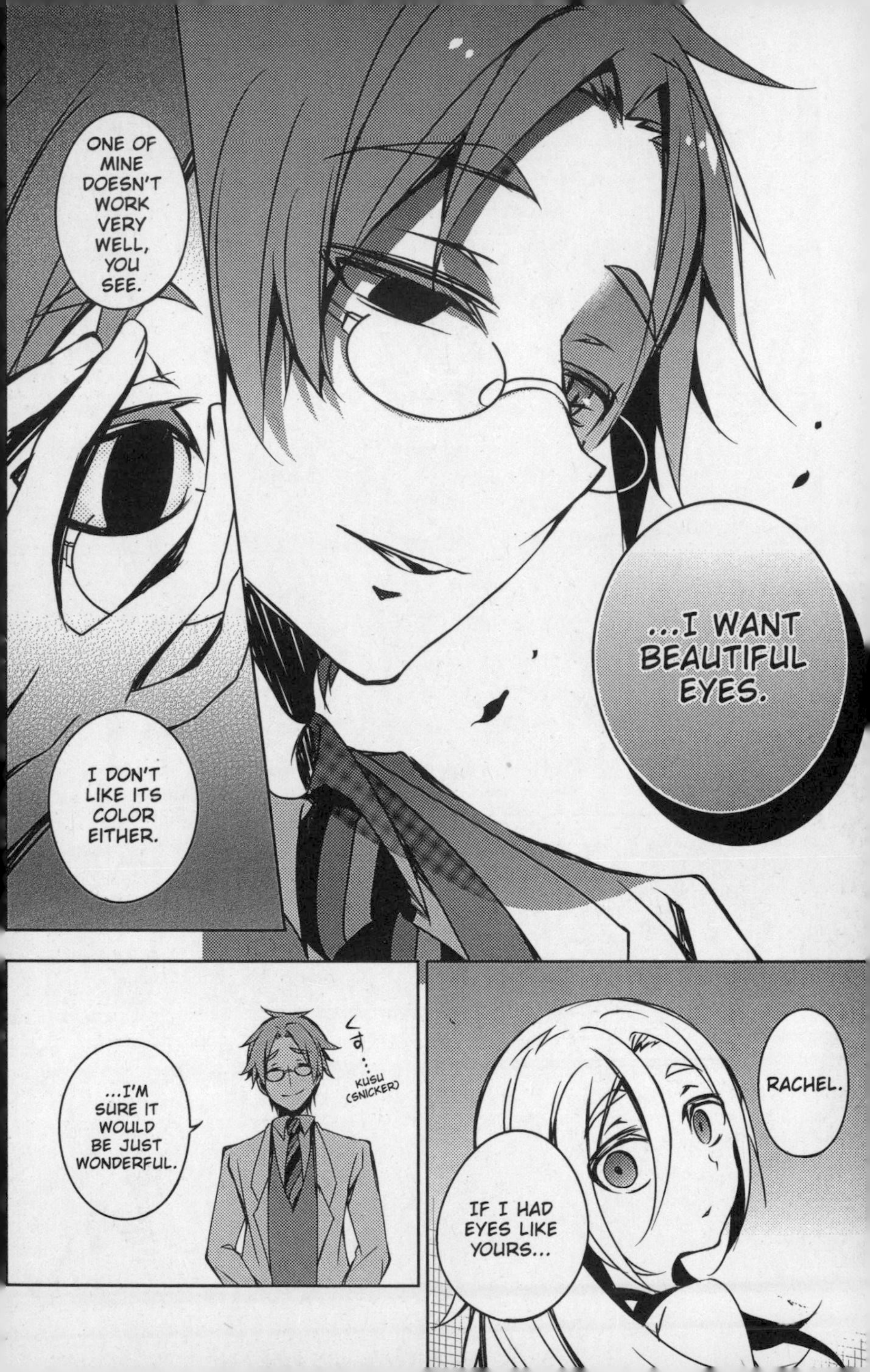
ONE OF MINE DOESN'T WORK VERY WELL, YOU SEE.
I DON'T LIKE ITS COLOR EITHER.
...I WANT BEAUTIFUL EYES.
RACHEL.
IF I HAD EYES LIKE YOURS...
くす…
KUSU (SNICKER)
...I'M SURE IT WOULD BE JUST WONDERFUL.

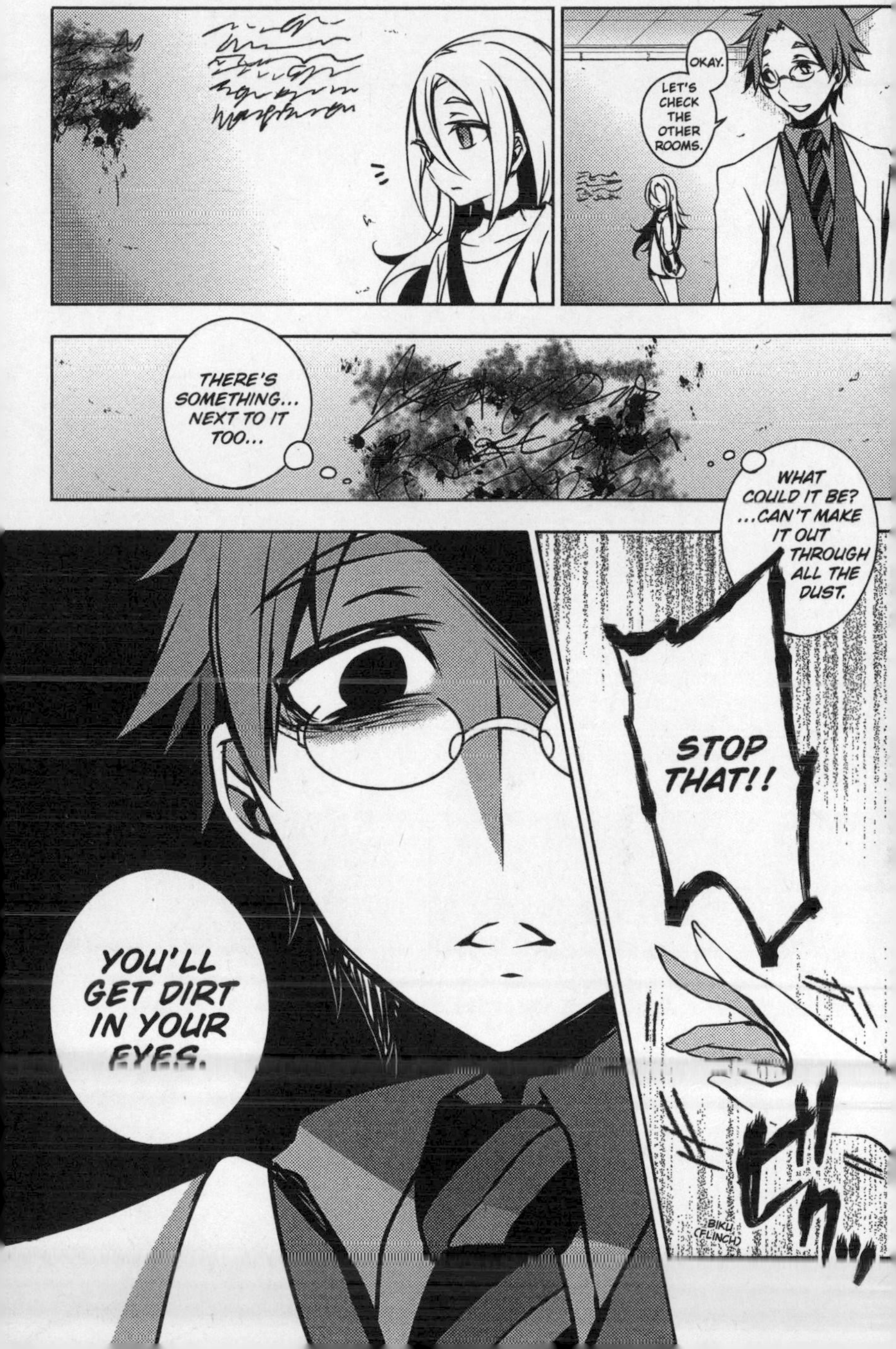
OKAY.
LET'S CHECK THE OTHER ROOMS.
THERE'S SOMETHING... NEXT TO IT TOO...
WHAT COULD IT BE? ...CAN'T MAKE IT OUT THROUGH ALL THE DUST.
STOP THAT!!
BIKU (FLINCH)
YOU'LL GET DIRT IN YOUR EYES.

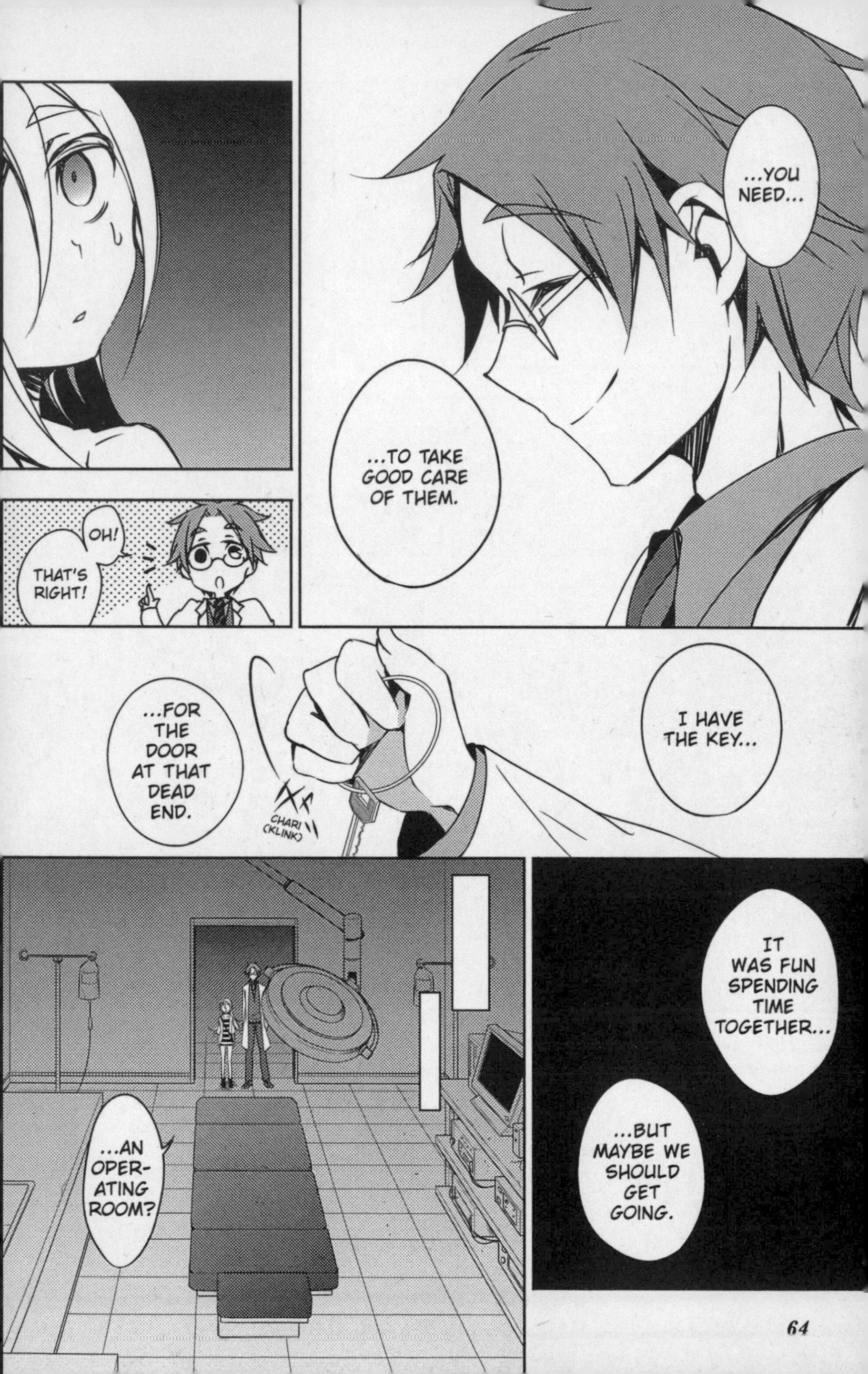
...YOU NEED...
...TO TAKE GOOD CARE OF THEM.
OH!
THAT'S RIGHT!
I HAVE THE KEY...
...FOR THE DOOR AT THAT DEAD END.
CHARI (KLINK)
IT WAS FUN SPENDING TIME TOGETHER...
...BUT MAYBE WE SHOULD GET GOING.
...AN OPER-ATING ROOM?

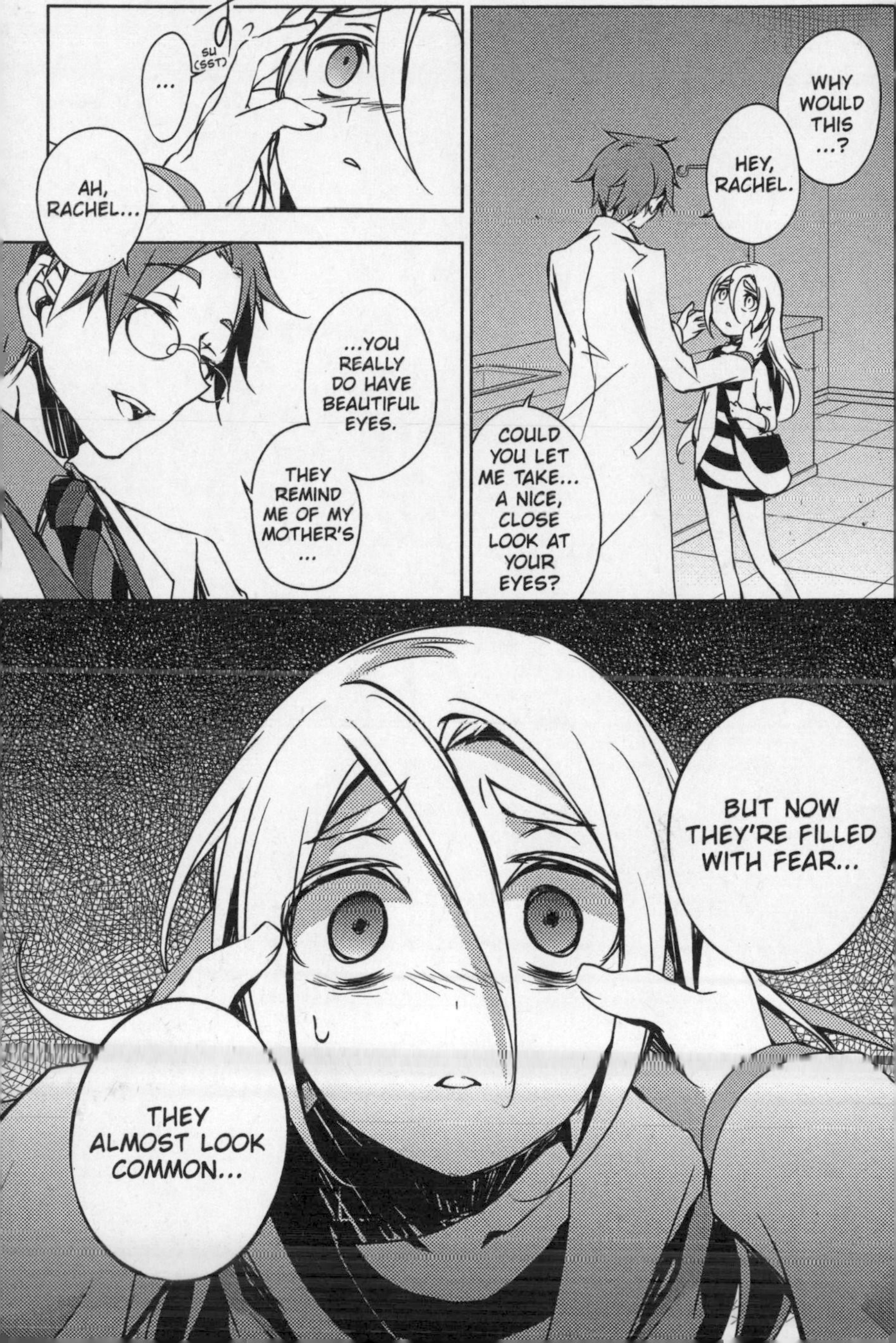
WHY WOULD THIS ...?
HEY, RACHEL.
COULD YOU LET ME TAKE... A NICE, CLOSE LOOK AT YOUR EYES?
SU (SST)
...
AH, RACHEL...
...YOU REALLY DO HAVE BEAUTIFUL EYES.
THEY REMIND ME OF MY MOTHER'S ...
BUT NOW THEY'RE FILLED WITH FEAR...
THEY ALMOST LOOK COMMON...

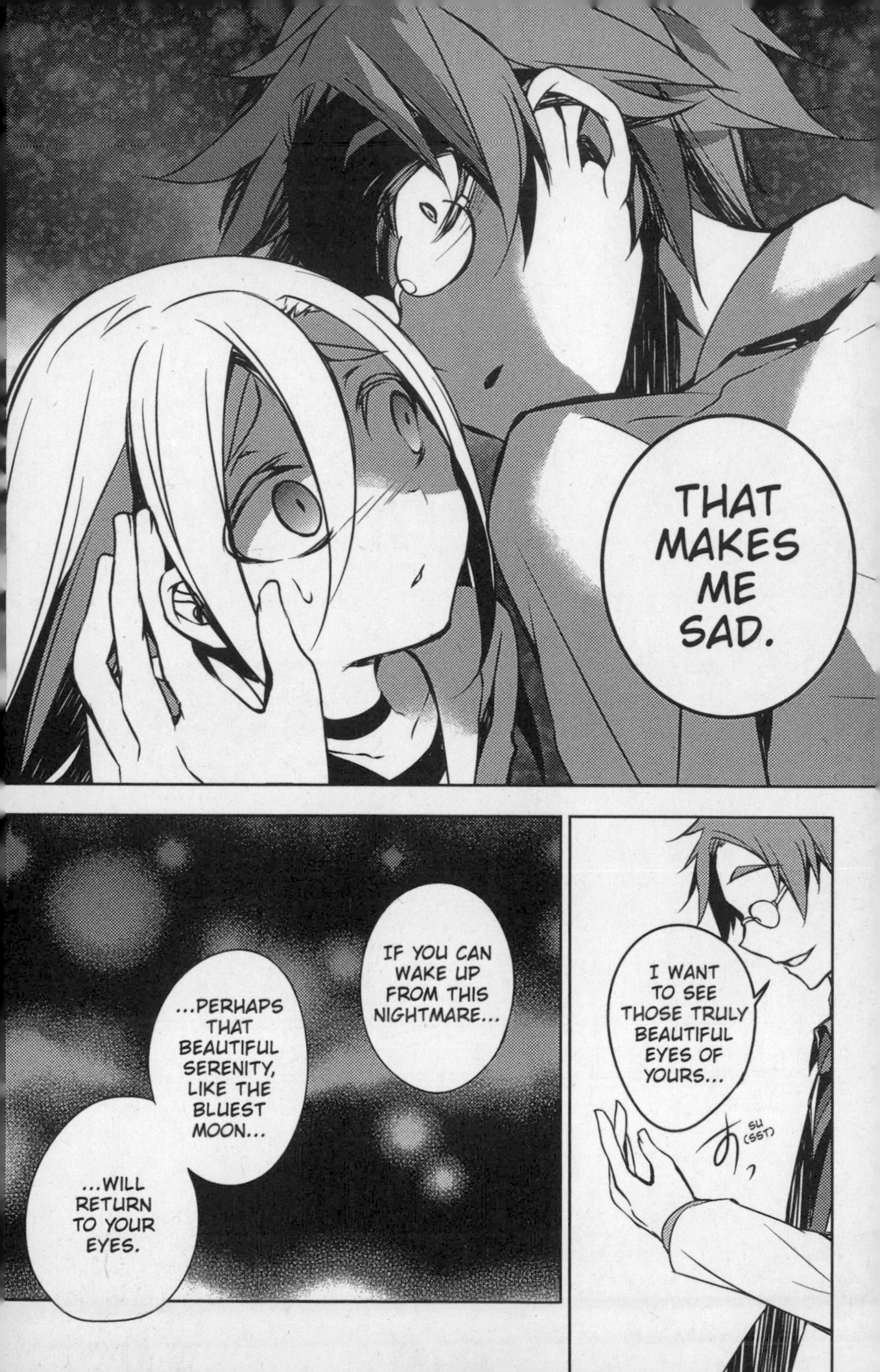
THAT MAKES ME SAD.
I WANT TO SEE THOSE TRULY BEAUTIFUL EYES OF YOURS...
SU (SST)
IF YOU CAN WAKE UP FROM THIS NIGHTMARE...
...PERHAPS THAT BEAUTIFUL SERENITY, LIKE THE BLUEST MOON...
...WILL RETURN TO YOUR EYES.

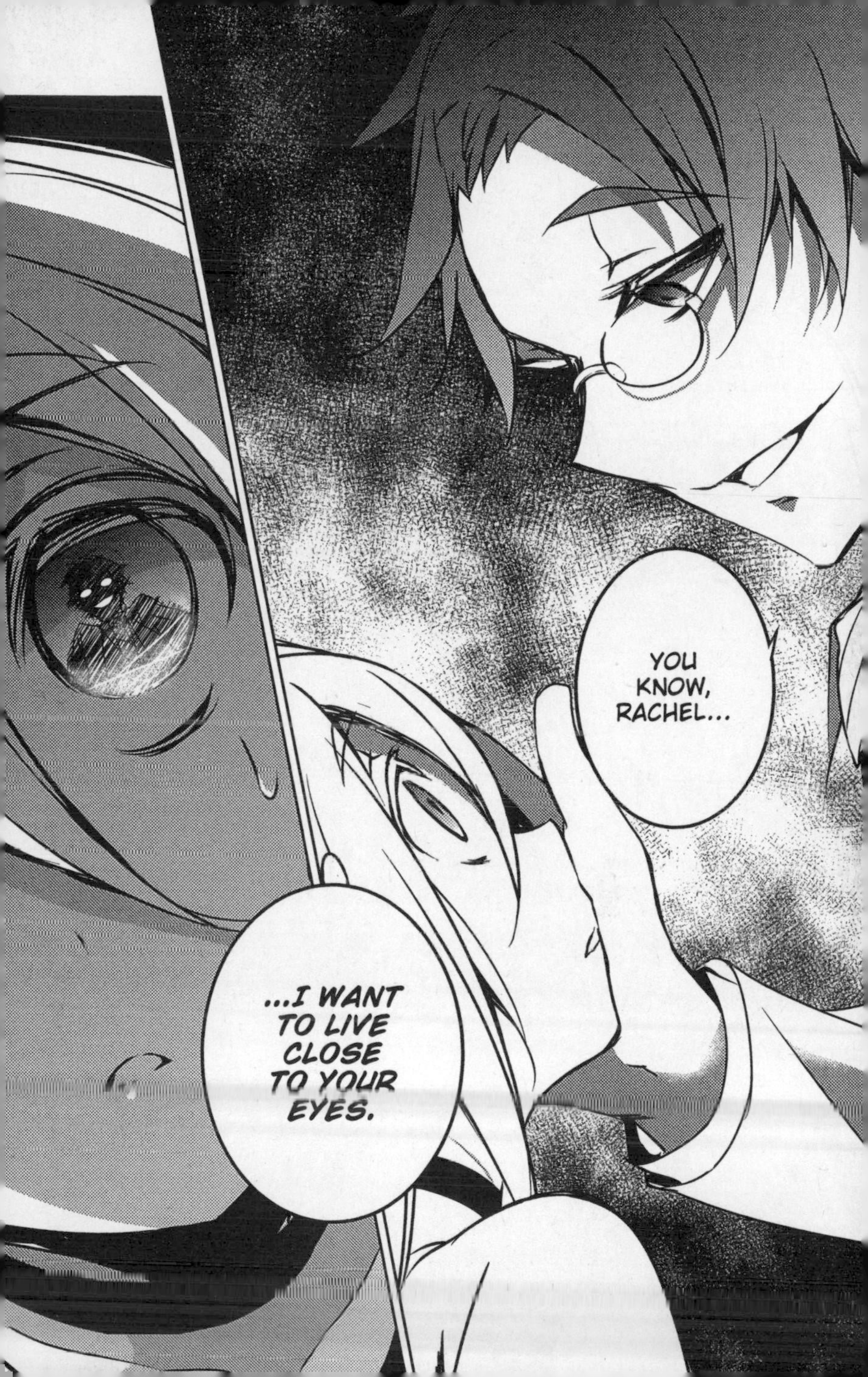
YOU KNOW, RACHEL...
...I WANT TO LIVE CLOSE TO YOUR EYES.

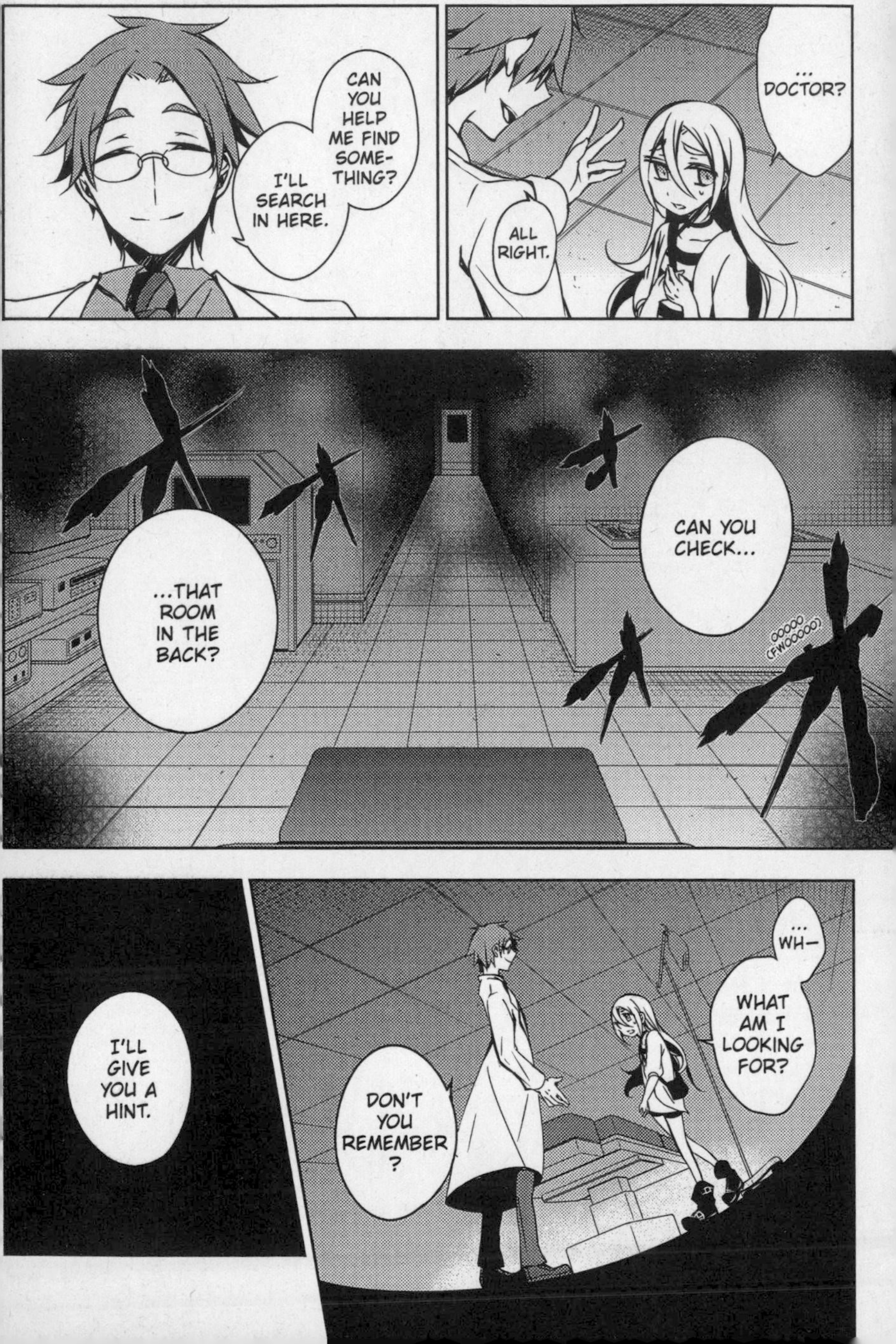
...DOCTOR?
ALL RIGHT.
CAN YOU HELP ME FIND SOME-THING?
I'LL SEARCH IN HERE.
CAN YOU CHECK...
OOOOO (FWOOOOO)
...THAT ROOM IN THE BACK?
...WH—
WHAT AM I LOOKING FOR?
DON'T YOU REMEMBER?
I'LL GIVE YOU A HINT.

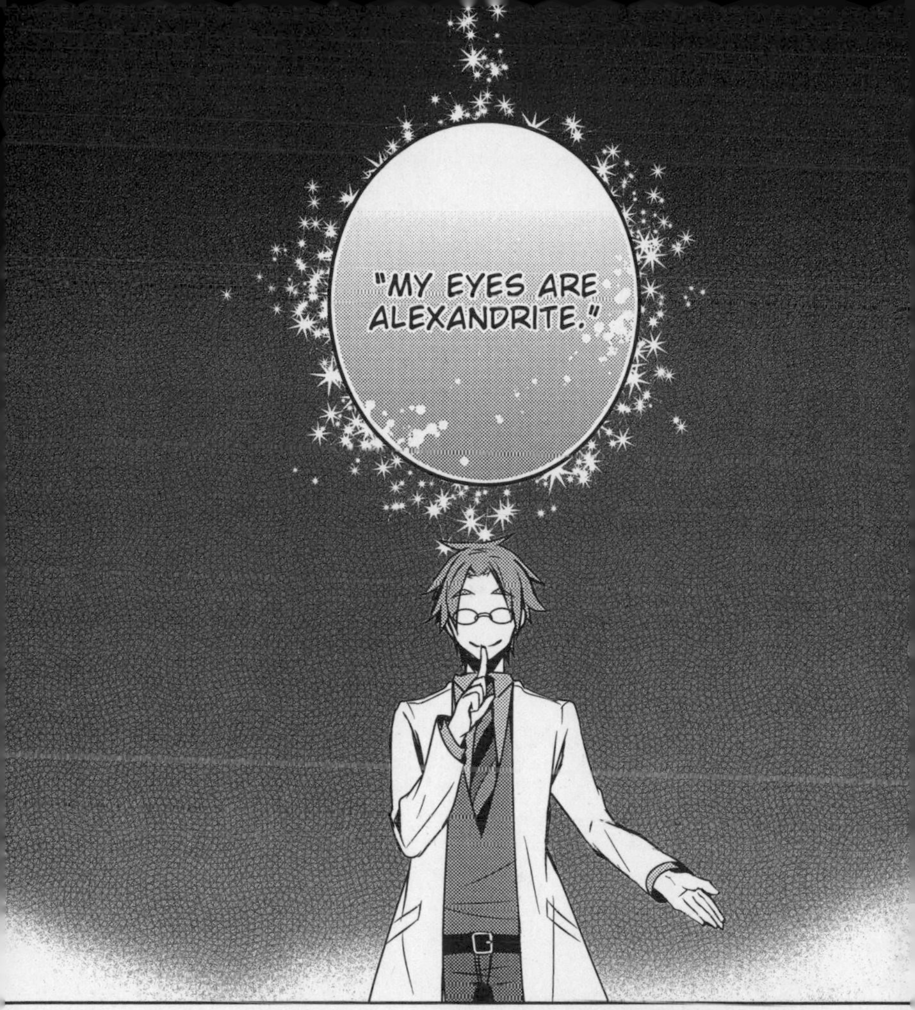
"MY EYES ARE ALEXANDRITE."
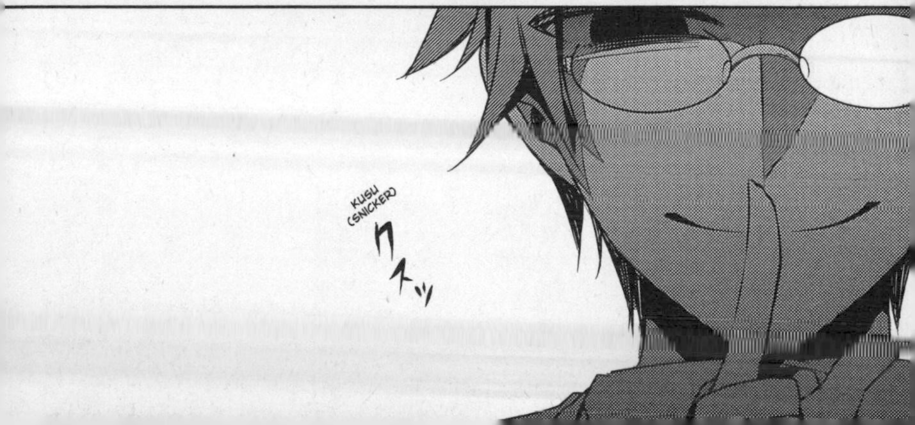
KUSU (SNICKER)
クスッ

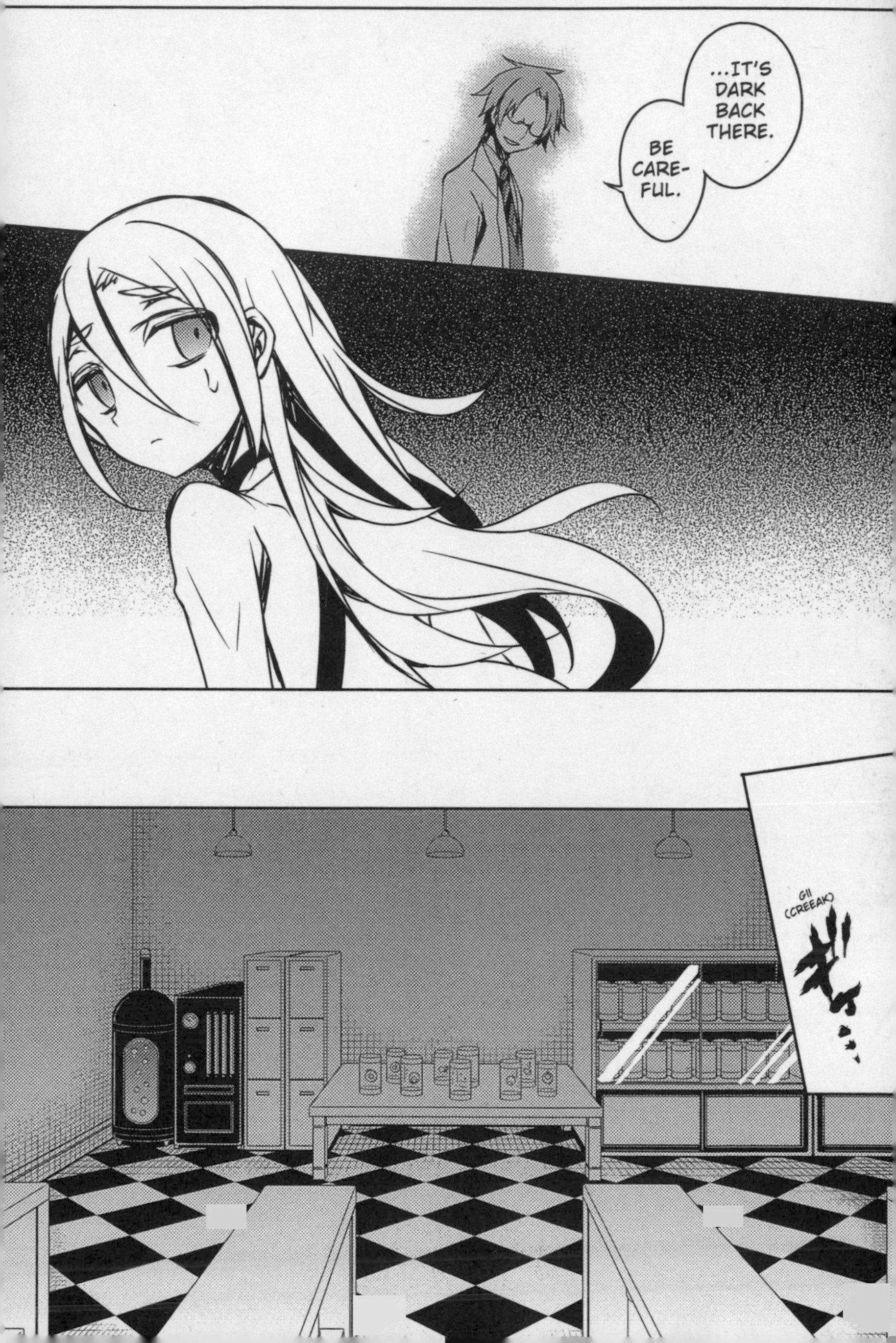
...IT'S DARK BACK THERE.
BE CARE-FUL.
GII (CREEAK)

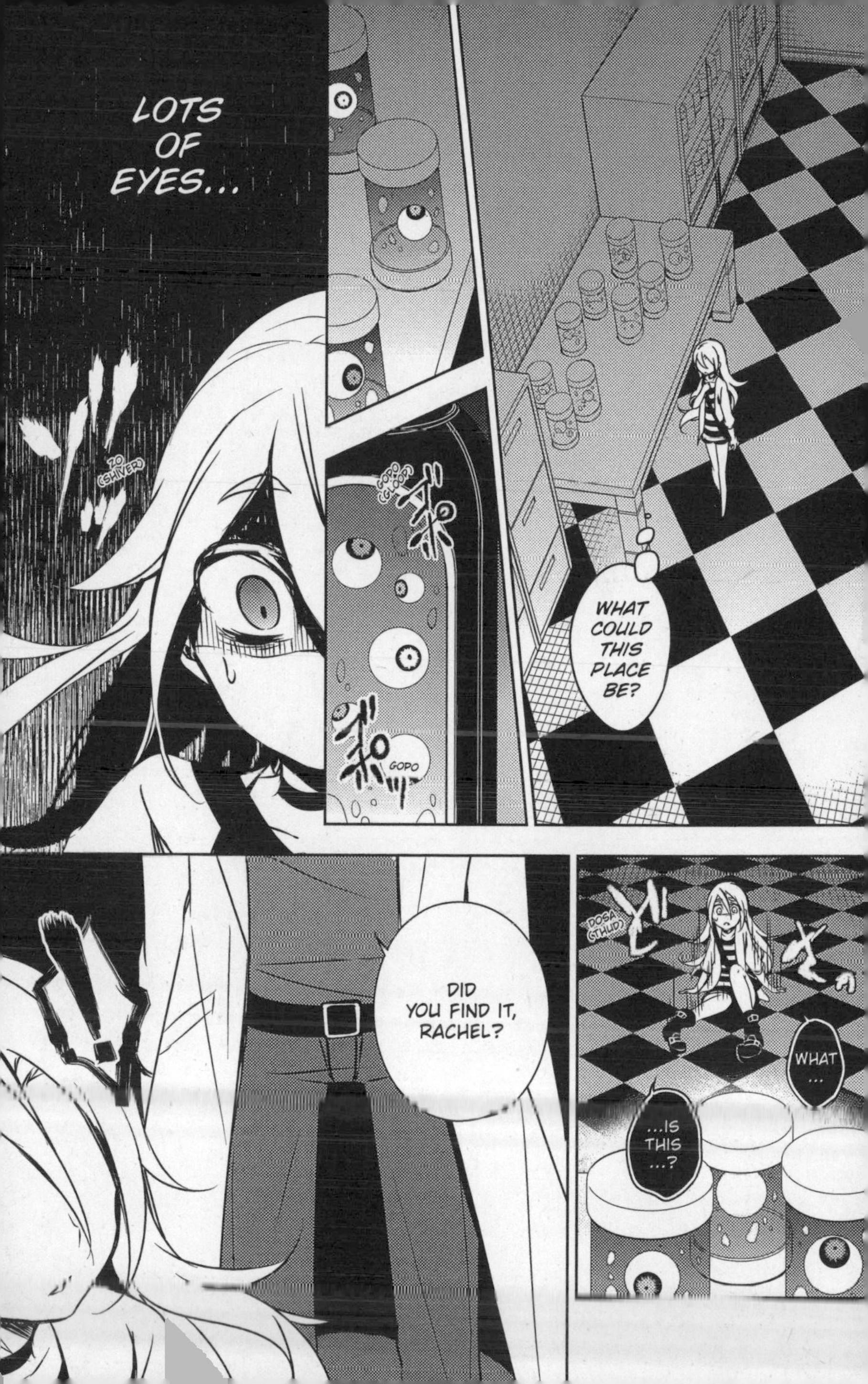
WHAT COULD THIS PLACE BE?
GOPO (GLOOP)
GOPO
LOTS OF EYES...
ZO (SHIVER)
DOSA (THUD)
WHAT...
...IS THIS...?
DID YOU FIND IT, RACHEL?

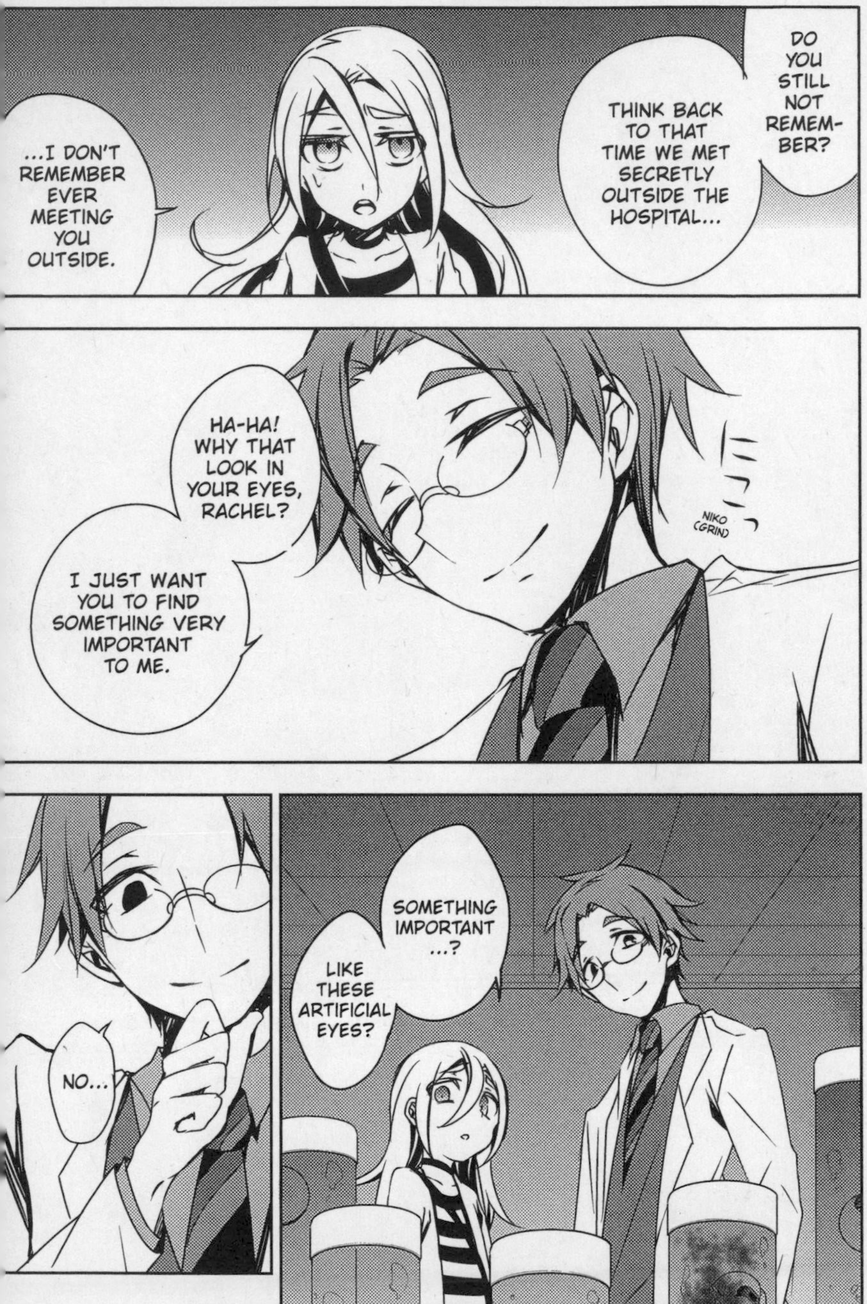
DO YOU STILL NOT REMEMBER?
THINK BACK TO THAT TIME WE MET SECRETLY OUTSIDE THE HOSPITAL...
...I DON'T REMEMBER EVER MEETING YOU OUTSIDE.
NIKO (GRIN)
HA-HA! WHY THAT LOOK IN YOUR EYES, RACHEL?
I JUST WANT YOU TO FIND SOMETHING VERY IMPORTANT TO ME.
SOMETHING IMPORTANT ...?
LIKE THESE ARTIFICIAL EYES?
NO...

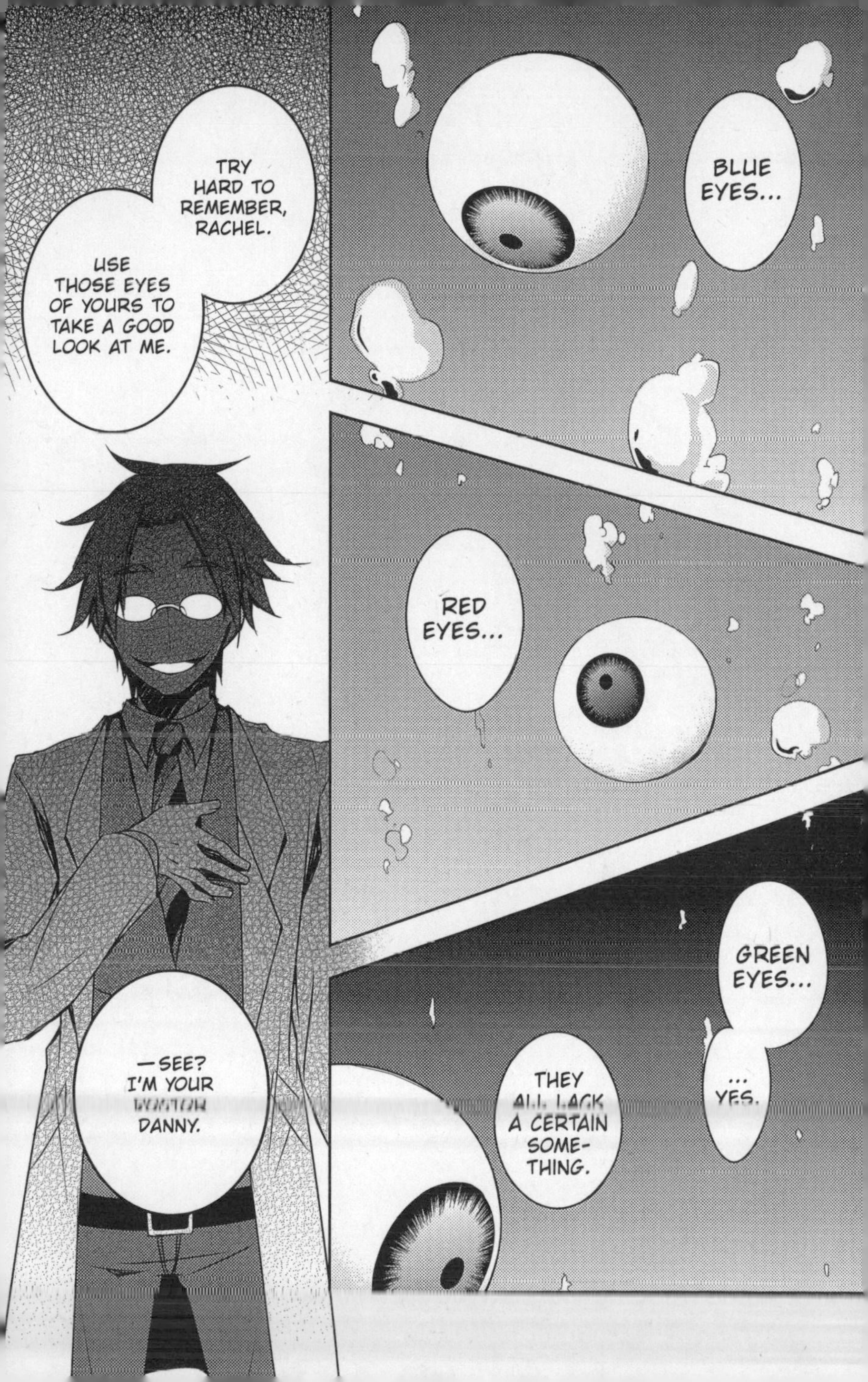
BLUE EYES...
RED EYES...
GREEN EYES...
...YES.
THEY ALL LACK A CERTAIN SOME-THING.
TRY HARD TO REMEMBER, RACHEL.
USE THOSE EYES OF YOURS TO TAKE A GOOD LOOK AT ME.
—SEE? I'M YOUR
DANNY.

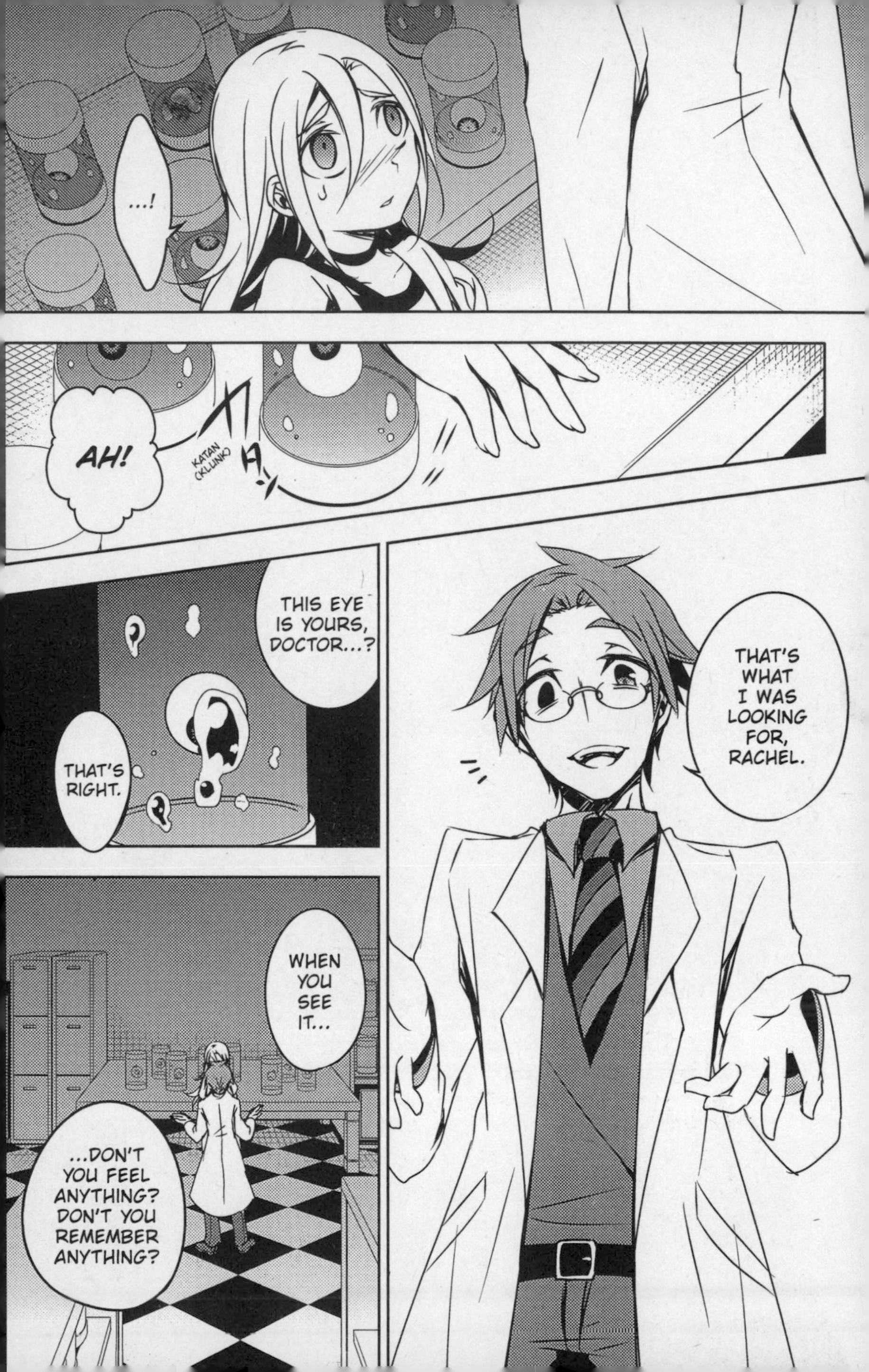
...!
AH!
KATAN (KLUNK)
THAT'S WHAT I WAS LOOKING FOR, RACHEL.
THIS EYE IS YOURS, DOCTOR...?
THAT'S RIGHT.
WHEN YOU SEE IT...
...DON'T YOU FEEL ANYTHING? DON'T YOU REMEMBER ANYTHING?

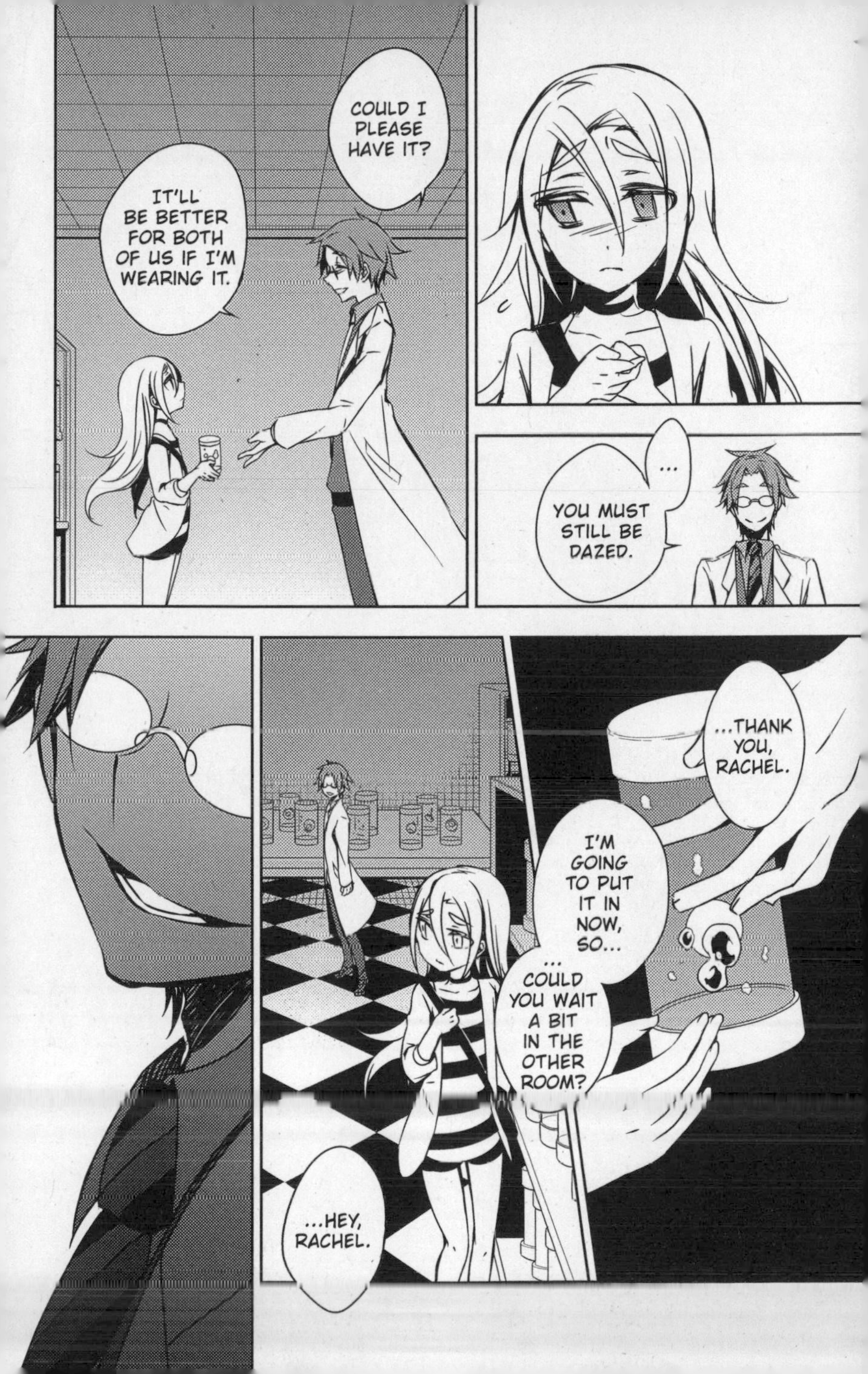
...
YOU MUST STILL BE DAZED.
COULD I PLEASE HAVE IT?
IT'LL BE BETTER FOR BOTH OF US IF I'M WEARING IT.
...THANK YOU, RACHEL.
I'M GOING TO PUT IT IN NOW, SO...
... COULD YOU WAIT A BIT IN THE OTHER ROOM?
...HEY, RACHEL.

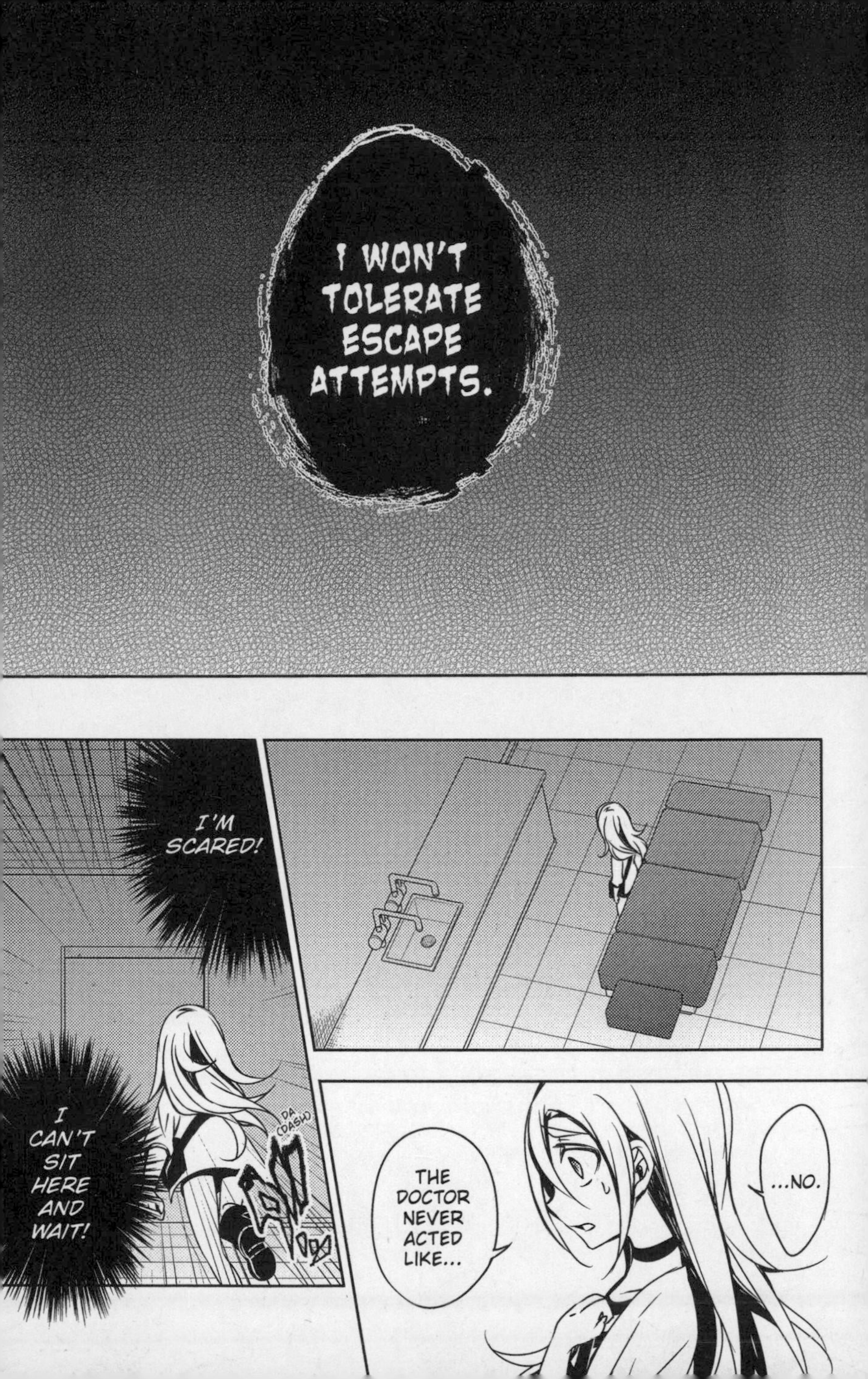
I WON'T TOLERATE ESCAPE ATTEMPTS.
...NO.
THE DOCTOR NEVER ACTED LIKE...
I'M SCARED!
I CAN'T SIT HERE AND WAIT!
DA (DASH)

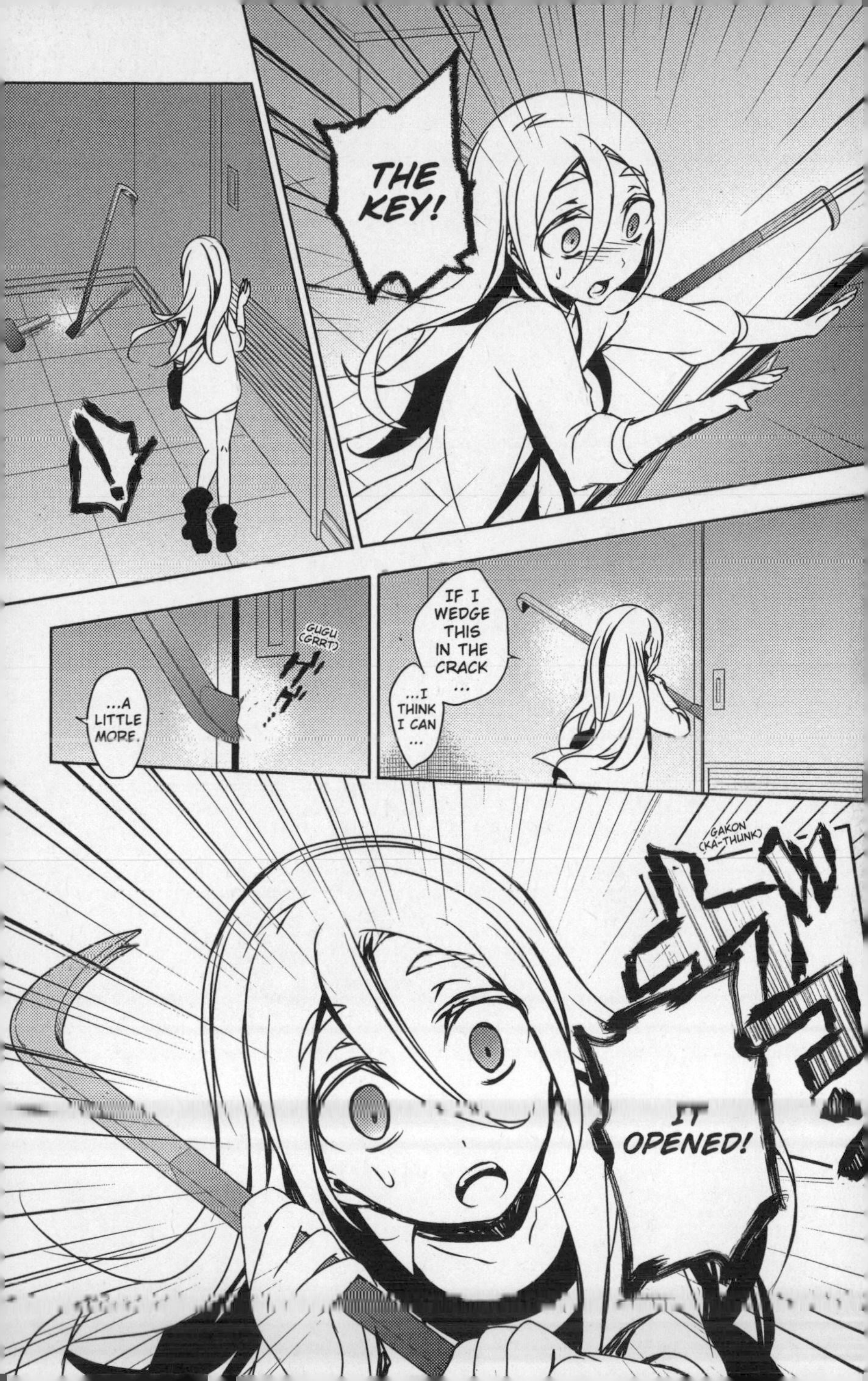
THE KEY!
IF I WEDGE THIS IN THE CRACK ...
...I THINK I CAN ...
GUGU (GRRT)
...A LITTLE MORE.
GAKON (KA-THUNK)
IT OPENED!

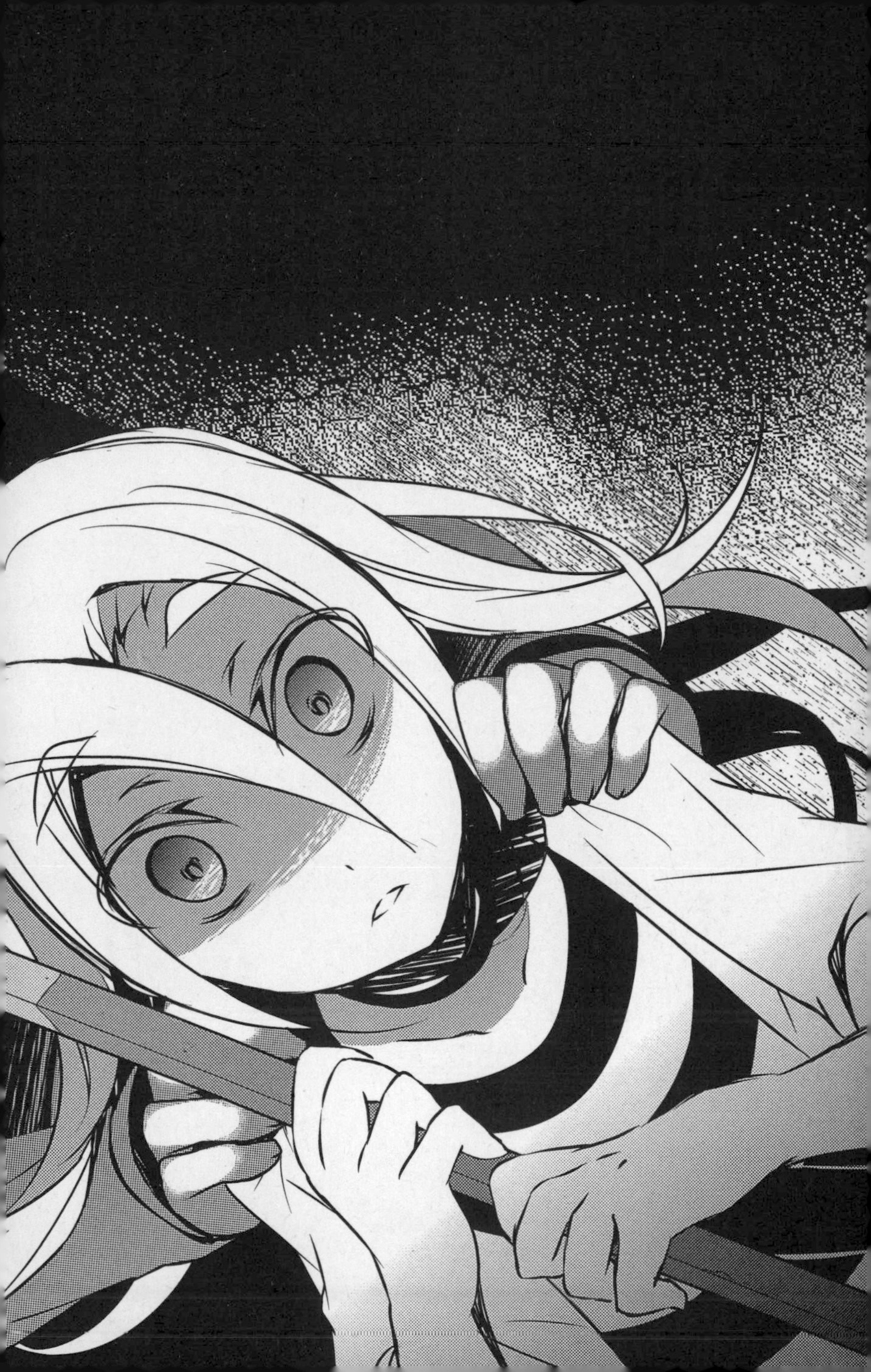

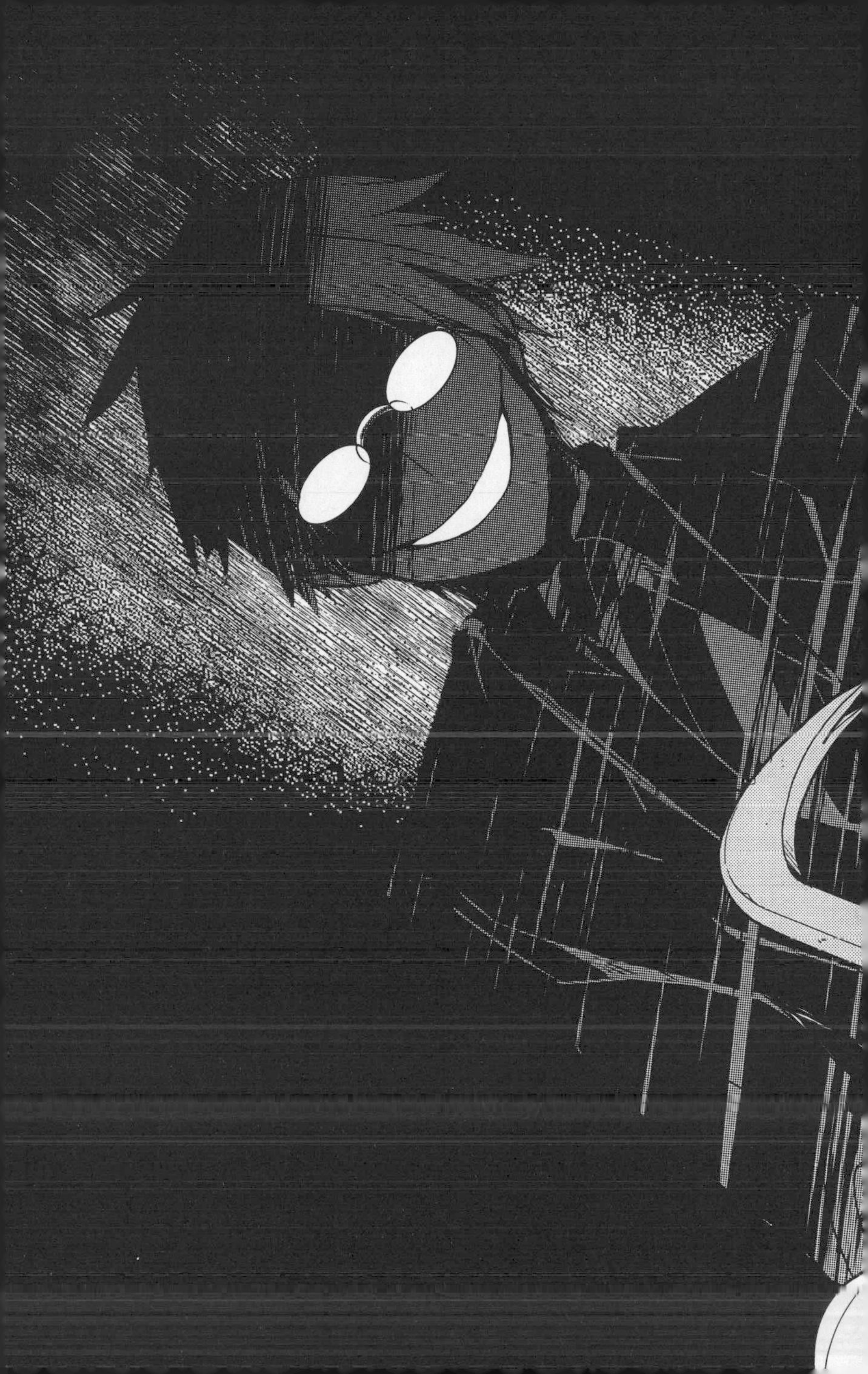

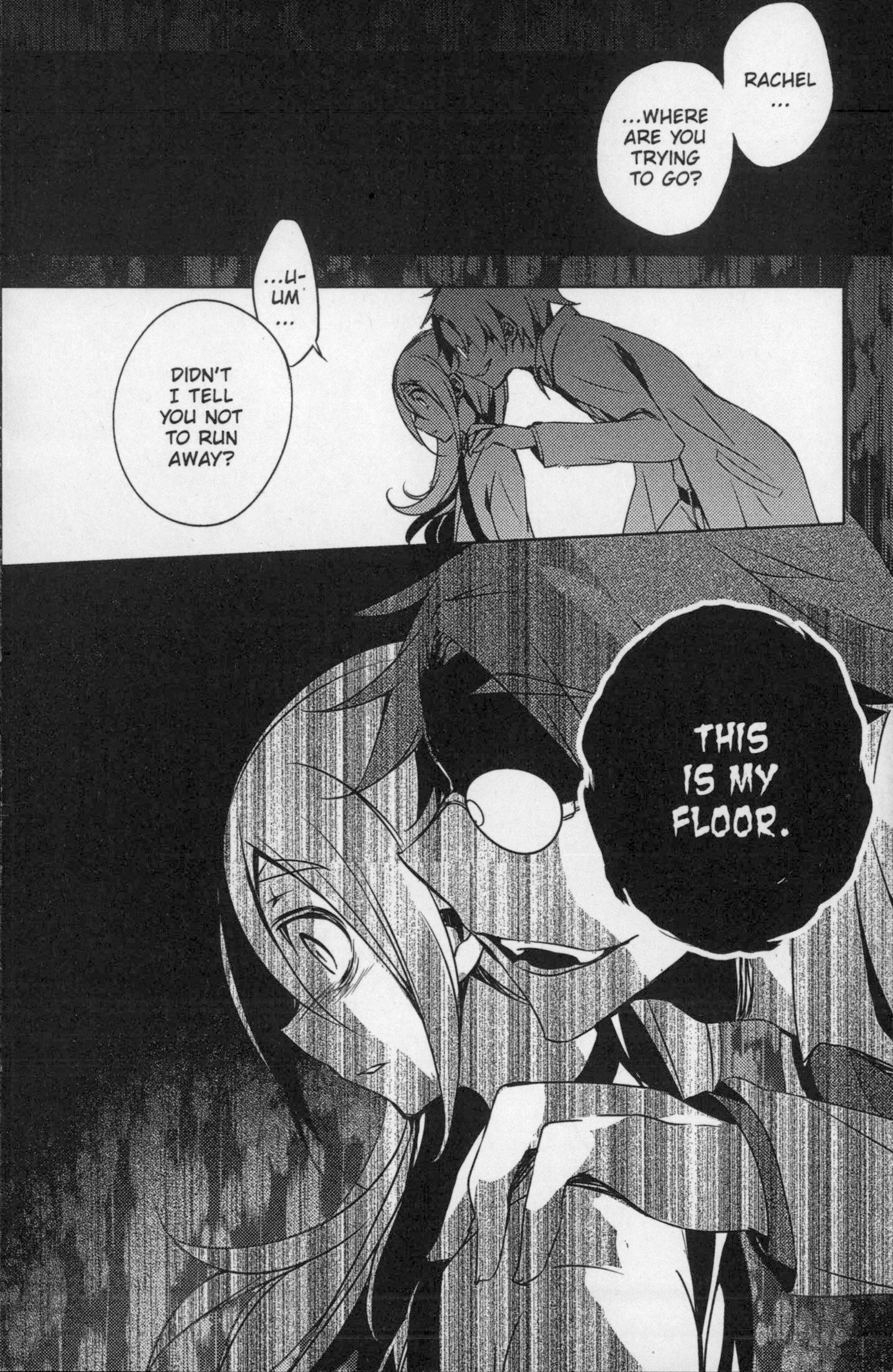
RACHEL ...
...WHERE ARE YOU TRYING TO GO?
...U-UM ...
DIDN'T I TELL YOU NOT TO RUN AWAY?
THIS IS MY FLOOR.

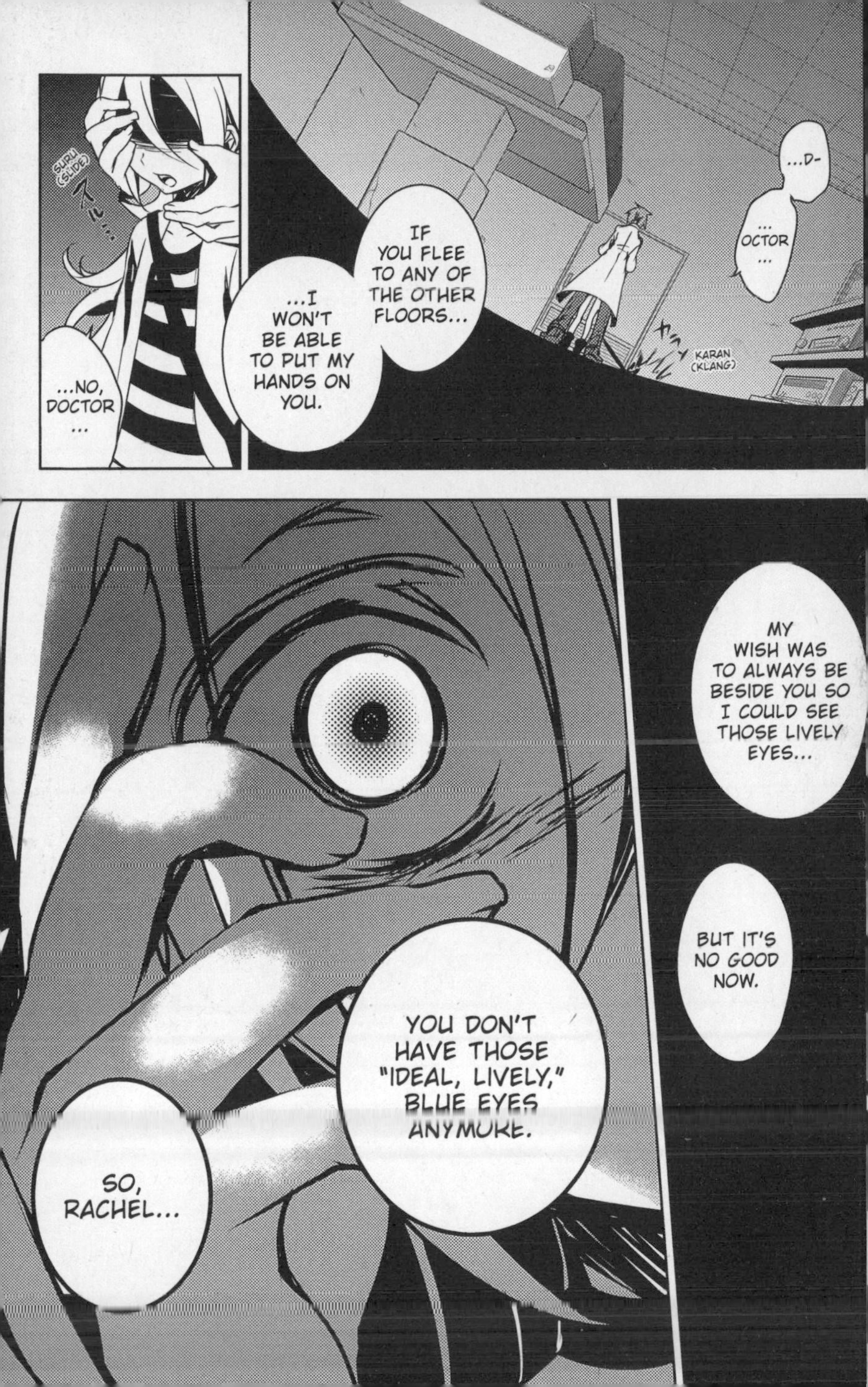
...D-
...OCTOR...
KARAN (KLANG)
IF YOU FLEE TO ANY OF THE OTHER FLOORS...
...I WON'T BE ABLE TO PUT MY HANDS ON YOU.
SURU (SLIDE)
...NO, DOCTOR...
MY WISH WAS TO ALWAYS BE BESIDE YOU SO I COULD SEE THOSE LIVELY EYES...
BUT IT'S NO GOOD NOW.
YOU DON'T HAVE THOSE "IDEAL, LIVELY," BLUE EYES ANYMORE.
SO, RACHEL...

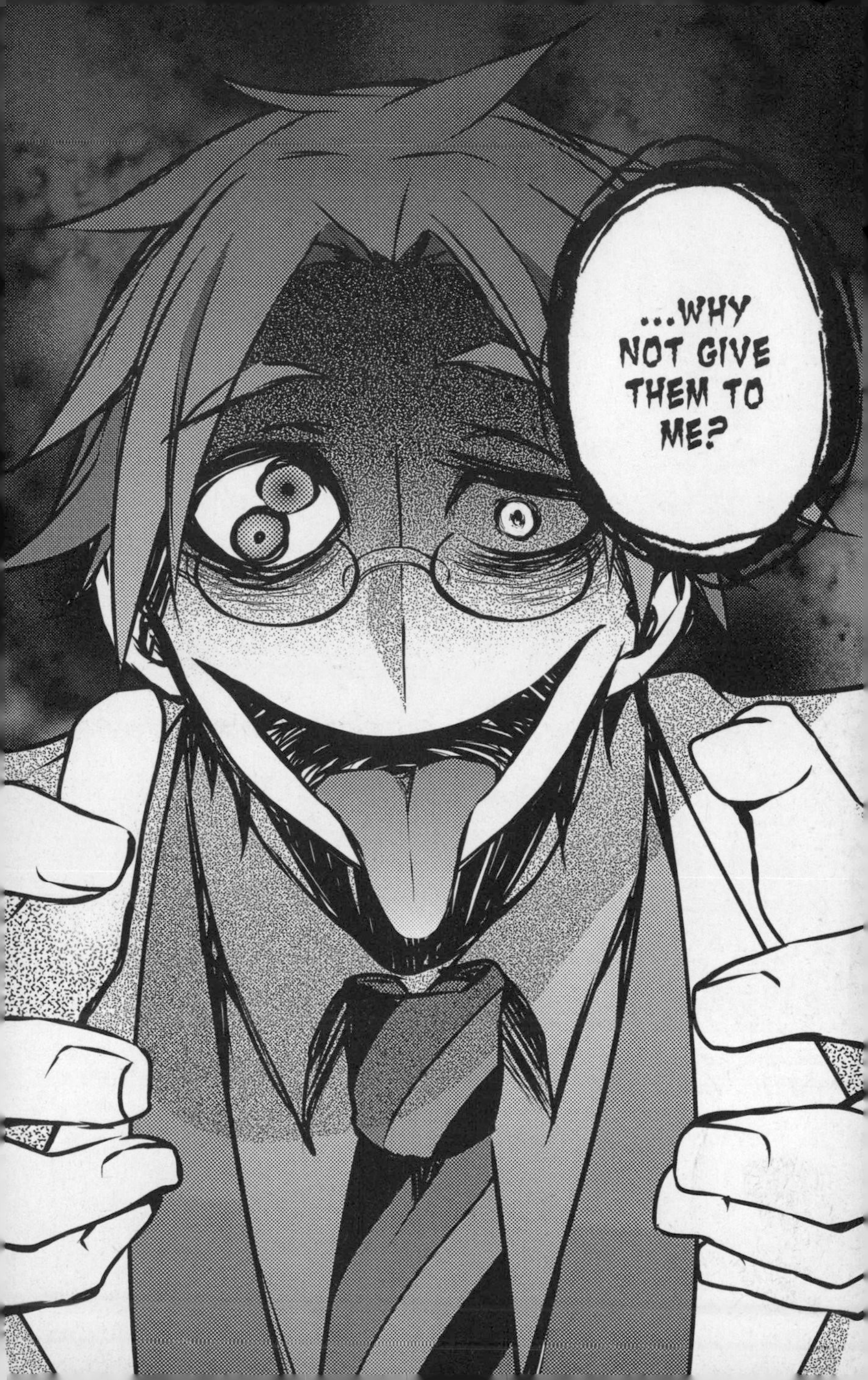
...WHY NOT GIVE THEM TO ME?

Angels of DEATH

INSIDE STORY OF PRODUCTION VOL.2

BY MAKOTO SANADA

As *Angels of Death* is my second work, I decided to try a lot of new things. For example, I tried to show each individual's personality in the pixel art for their walking animations, and I tried to add more action pixel art. (Though, I could still improve in a lot of ways, so I want to keep working hard at it.)

The story also incorporates game elements on each individual floor beyond searching for the correct way to proceed. This, of course, was meant to make the game more fun to play, but it was also an attempt to make players want to complete the entire game.

In particular, I even had my editor at *Niconico Game Magazine* play the scene included in this volume where Rachel is chased by Zack multiple times as I adjusted it over and over.

I did this because Zack is extremely fast, and while I wanted players to feel overwhelmed and afraid of him, on the other hand, they would end up at the game-over screen an unreasonable number of times if he was too fast.

As such, I paid attention to Zack's speed and the number of seconds you have to escape so players would feel excited while also being able to get away. After all of this testing, the game is made so you might groan, "Why is Zack so fast?" but still be able to beat the scene in two tries, give or take.

Part of what drove me to this was my desire to make the experience enjoyable for as many people as possible. I hope players will have fun as they progress through the campaign.

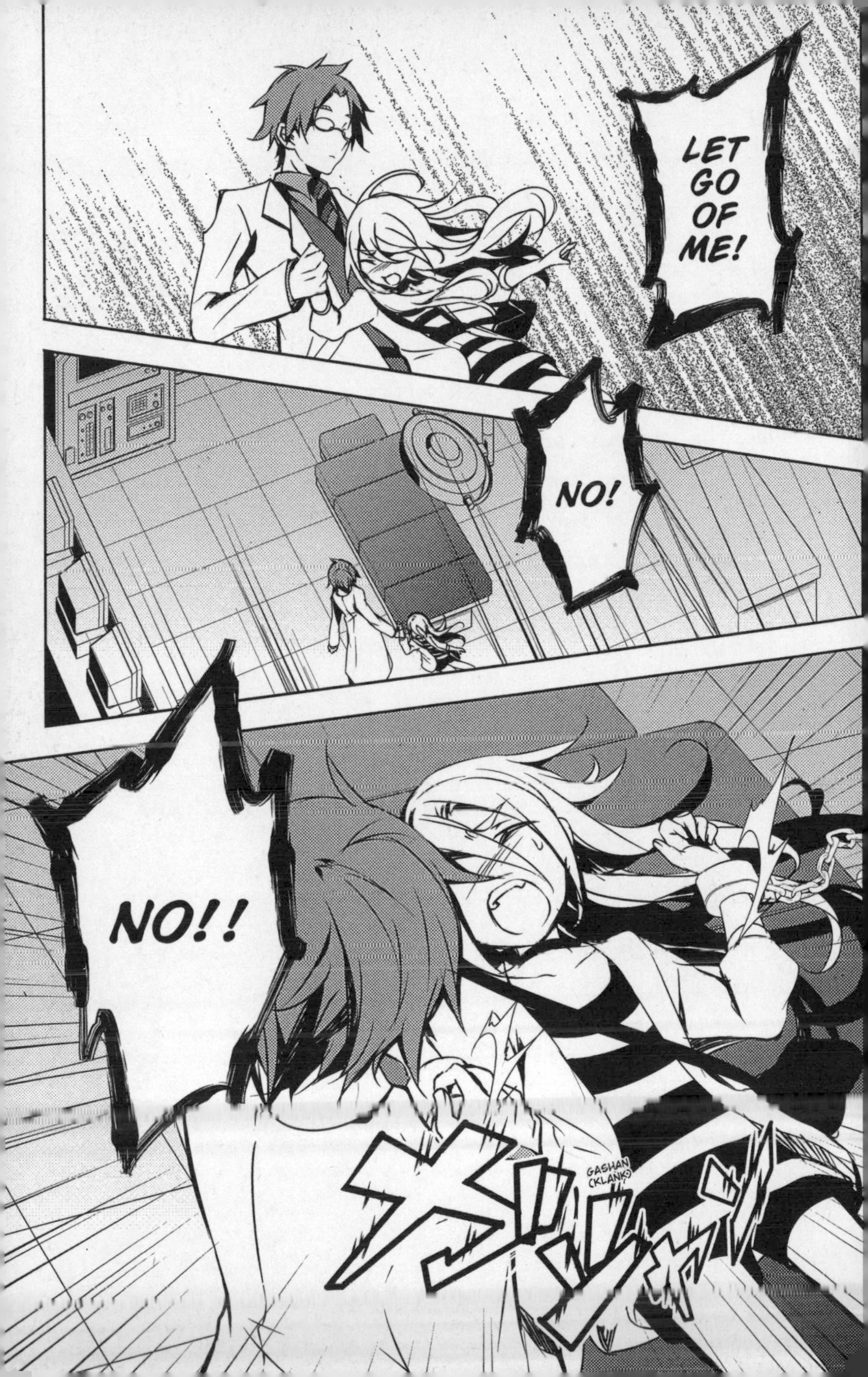
LET GO OF ME!
NO!
NO!!
GASHAN (KLANK)

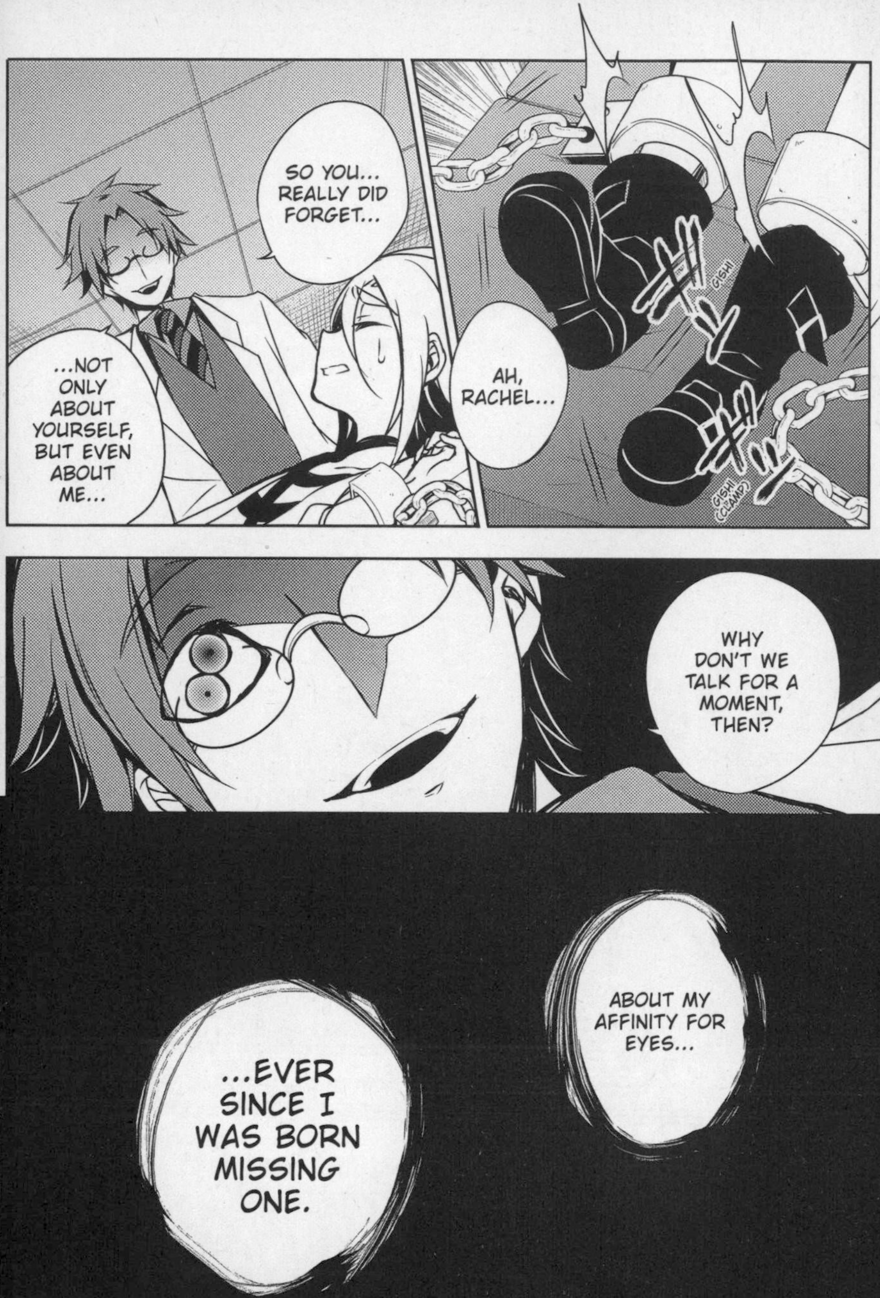
GISHI
GISHI (CLAMP)
SO YOU... REALLY DID FORGET...
AH, RACHEL...
...NOT ONLY ABOUT YOURSELF, BUT EVEN ABOUT ME...
WHY DON'T WE TALK FOR A MOMENT, THEN?
ABOUT MY AFFINITY FOR EYES...
...EVER SINCE I WAS BORN MISSING ONE.

[Chapter 3]
Chance Meeting

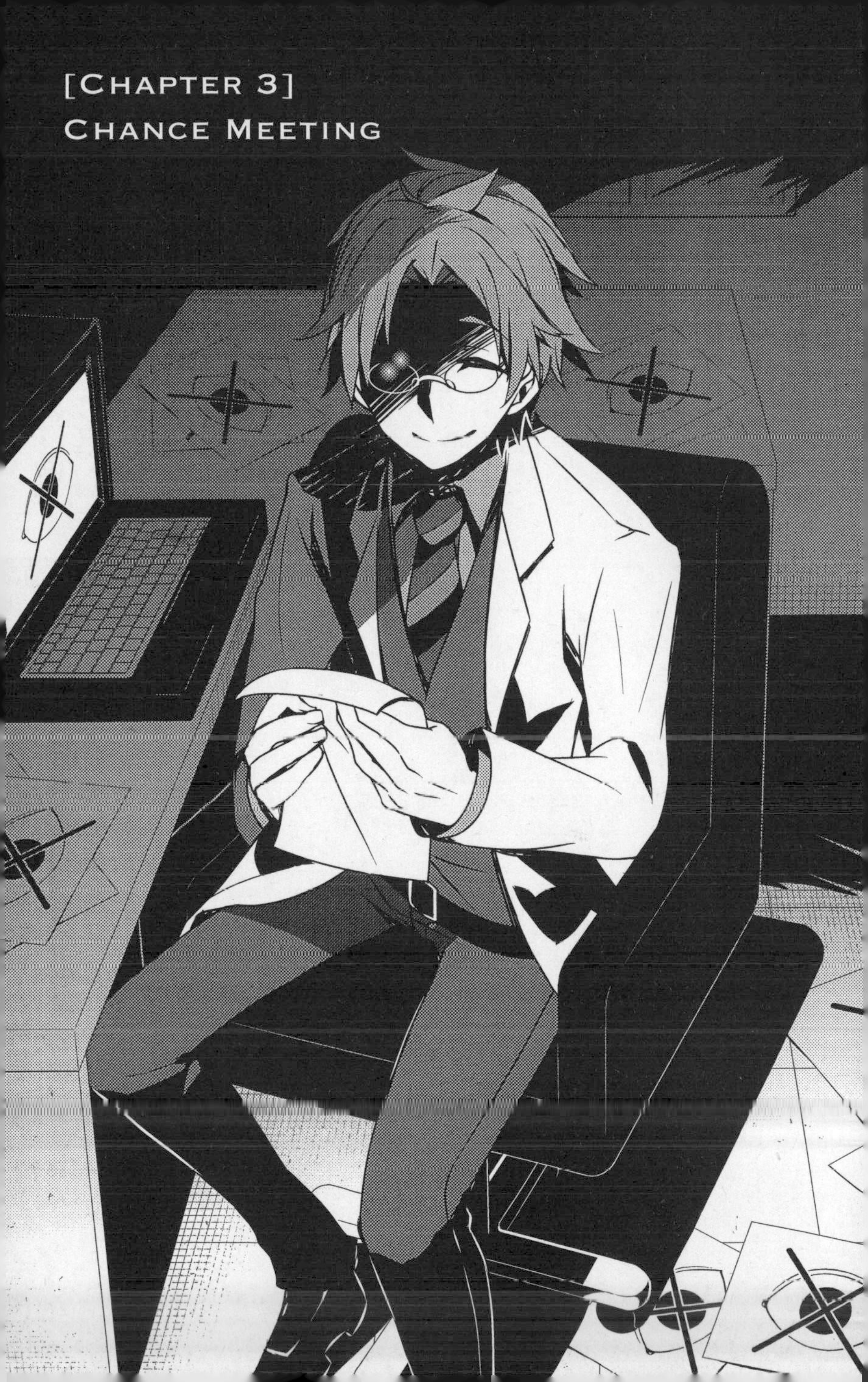

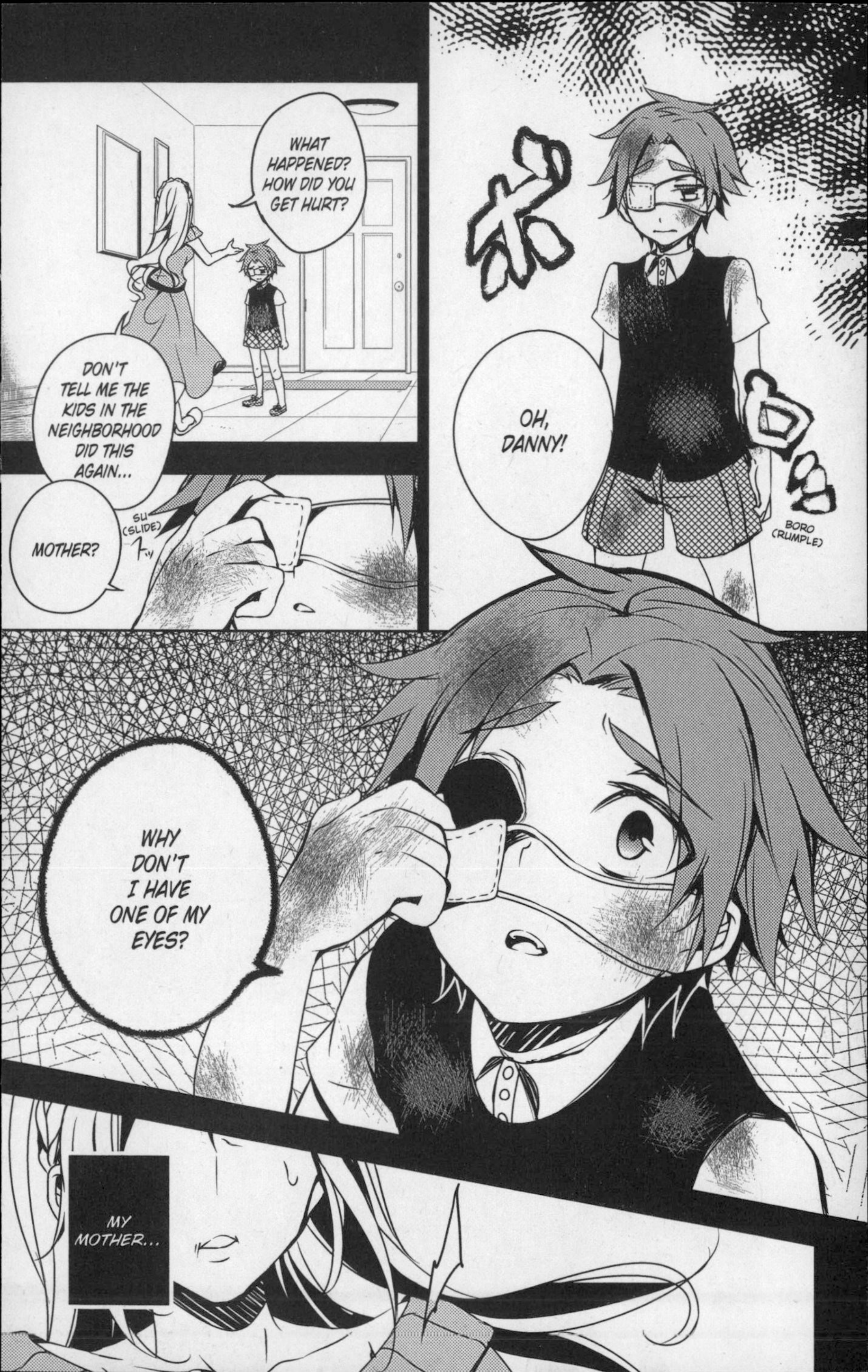
OH, DANNY!
BORO (RUMPLE)
WHAT HAPPENED? HOW DID YOU GET HURT?
DON'T TELL ME THE KIDS IN THE NEIGHBORHOOD DID THIS AGAIN...
SU (SLIDE)
MOTHER?
WHY DON'T I HAVE ONE OF MY EYES?
MY MOTHER...

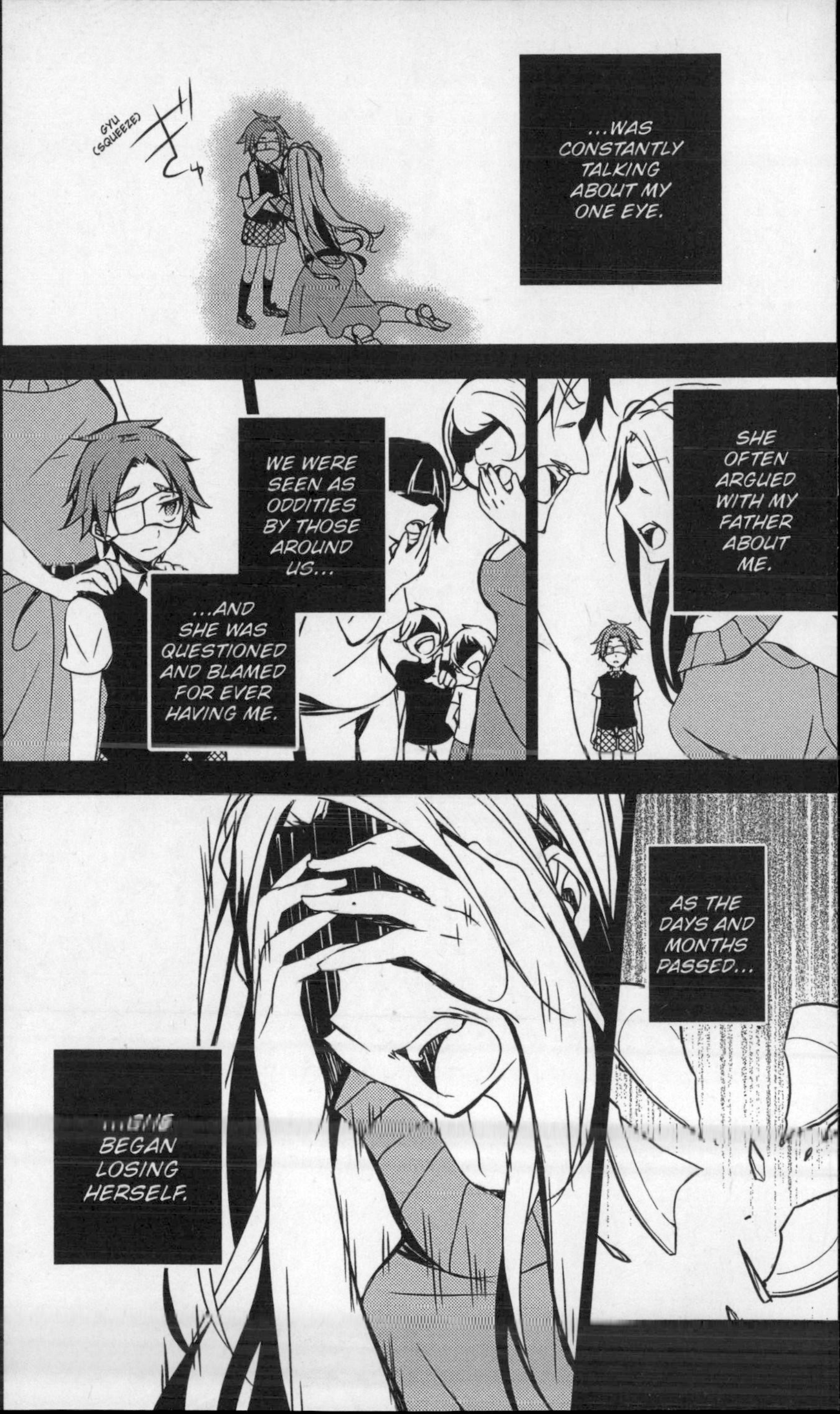
...WAS CONSTANTLY TALKING ABOUT MY ONE EYE.
GYU (SQUEEZE)
SHE OFTEN ARGUED WITH MY FATHER ABOUT ME.
WE WERE SEEN AS ODDITIES BY THOSE AROUND US...
...AND SHE WAS QUESTIONED AND BLAMED FOR EVER HAVING ME.
AS THE DAYS AND MONTHS PASSED...
...SHE BEGAN LOSING HERSELF.

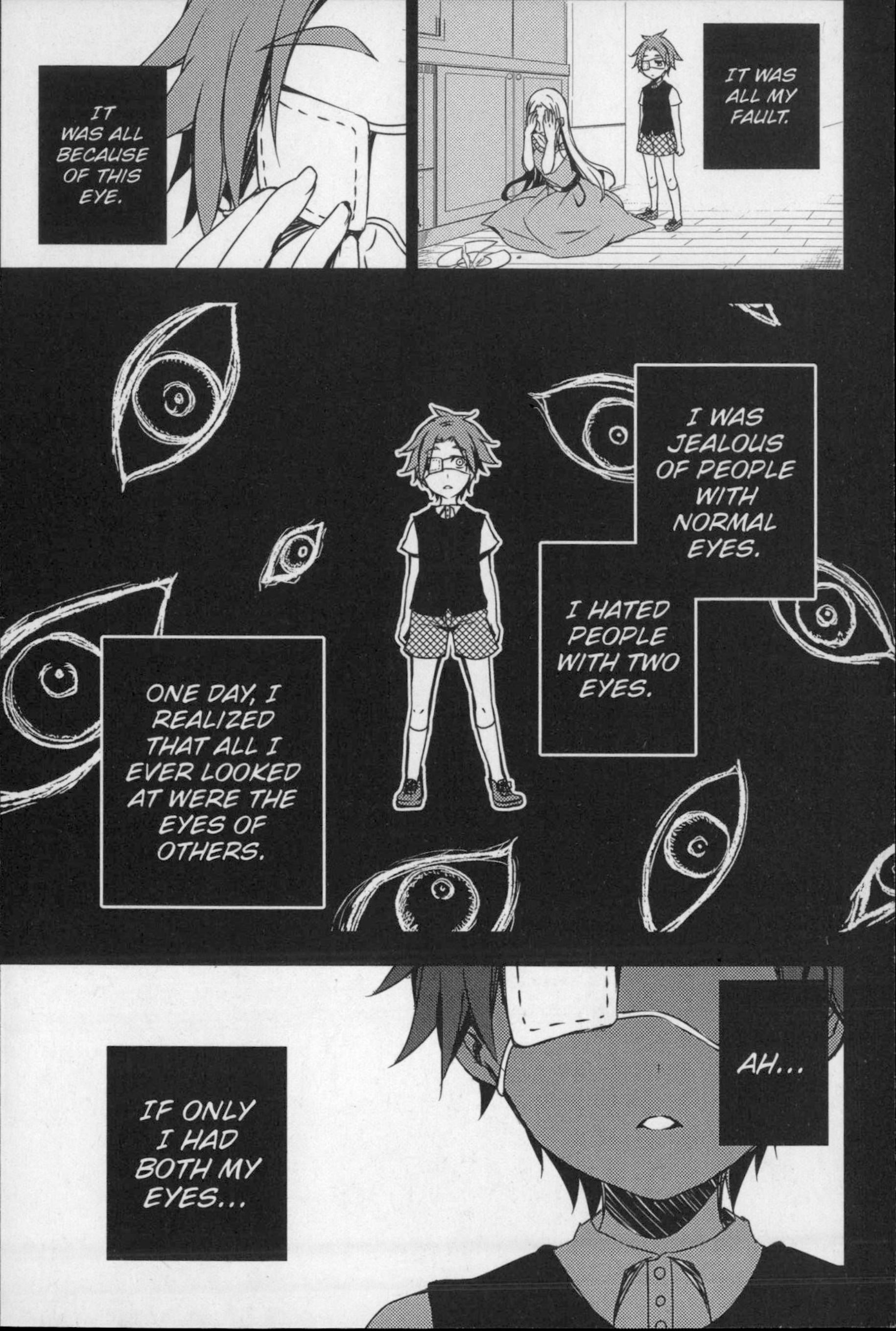
IT WAS ALL MY FAULT.
IT WAS ALL BECAUSE OF THIS EYE.
I WAS JEALOUS OF PEOPLE WITH NORMAL EYES.
I HATED PEOPLE WITH TWO EYES.
ONE DAY, I REALIZED THAT ALL I EVER LOOKED AT WERE THE EYES OF OTHERS.
AH...
IF ONLY I HAD BOTH MY EYES...

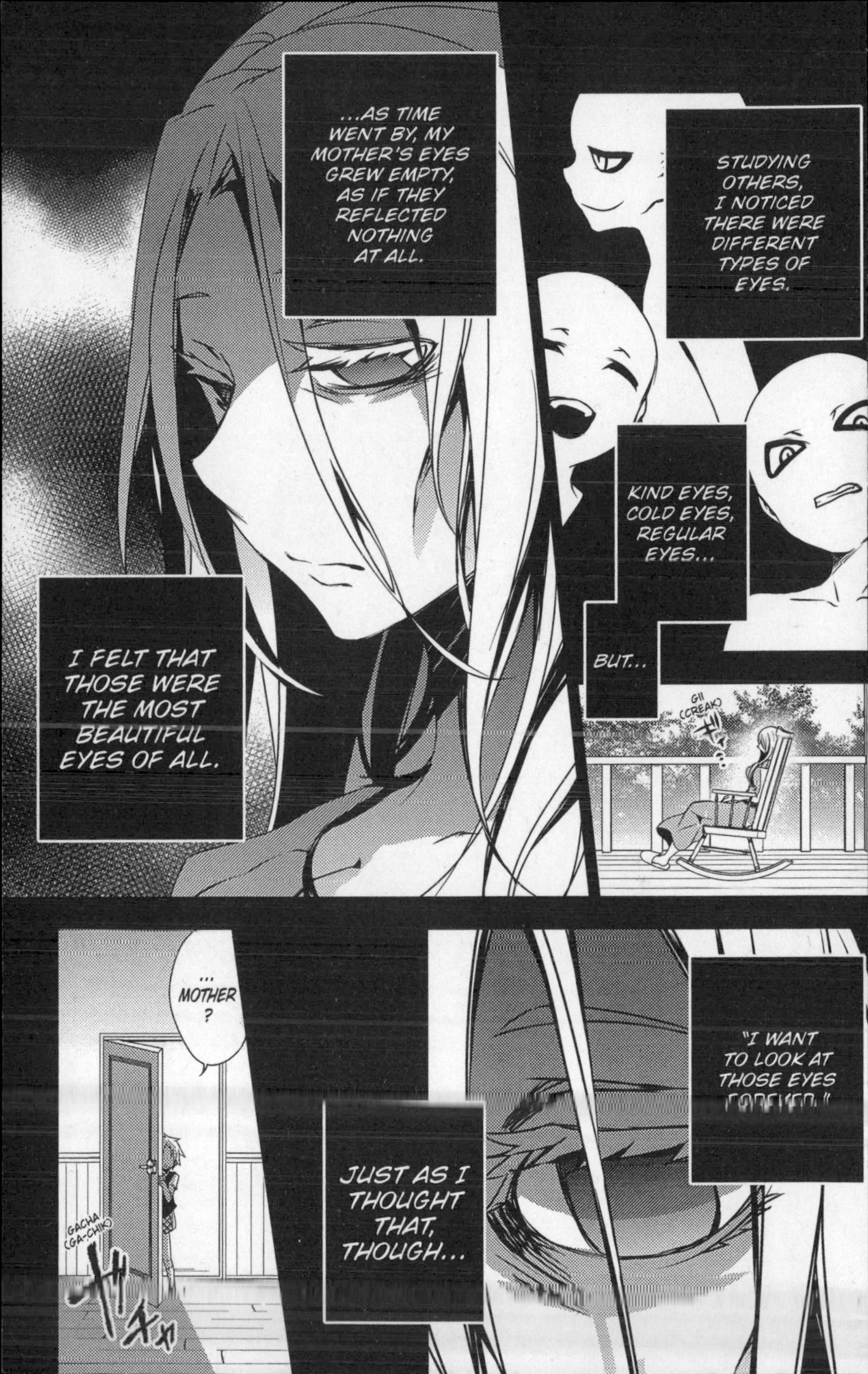
...AS TIME WENT BY, MY MOTHER'S EYES GREW EMPTY, AS IF THEY REFLECTED NOTHING AT ALL.
STUDYING OTHERS, I NOTICED THERE WERE DIFFERENT TYPES OF EYES.
KIND EYES, COLD EYES, REGULAR EYES...
BUT...
GII (CREAK)
I FELT THAT THOSE WERE THE MOST BEAUTIFUL EYES OF ALL.
"I WANT TO LOOK AT THOSE EYES FOREVER."
JUST AS I THOUGHT THAT, THOUGH...
...MOTHER?
GACHA (GA-CHIK)

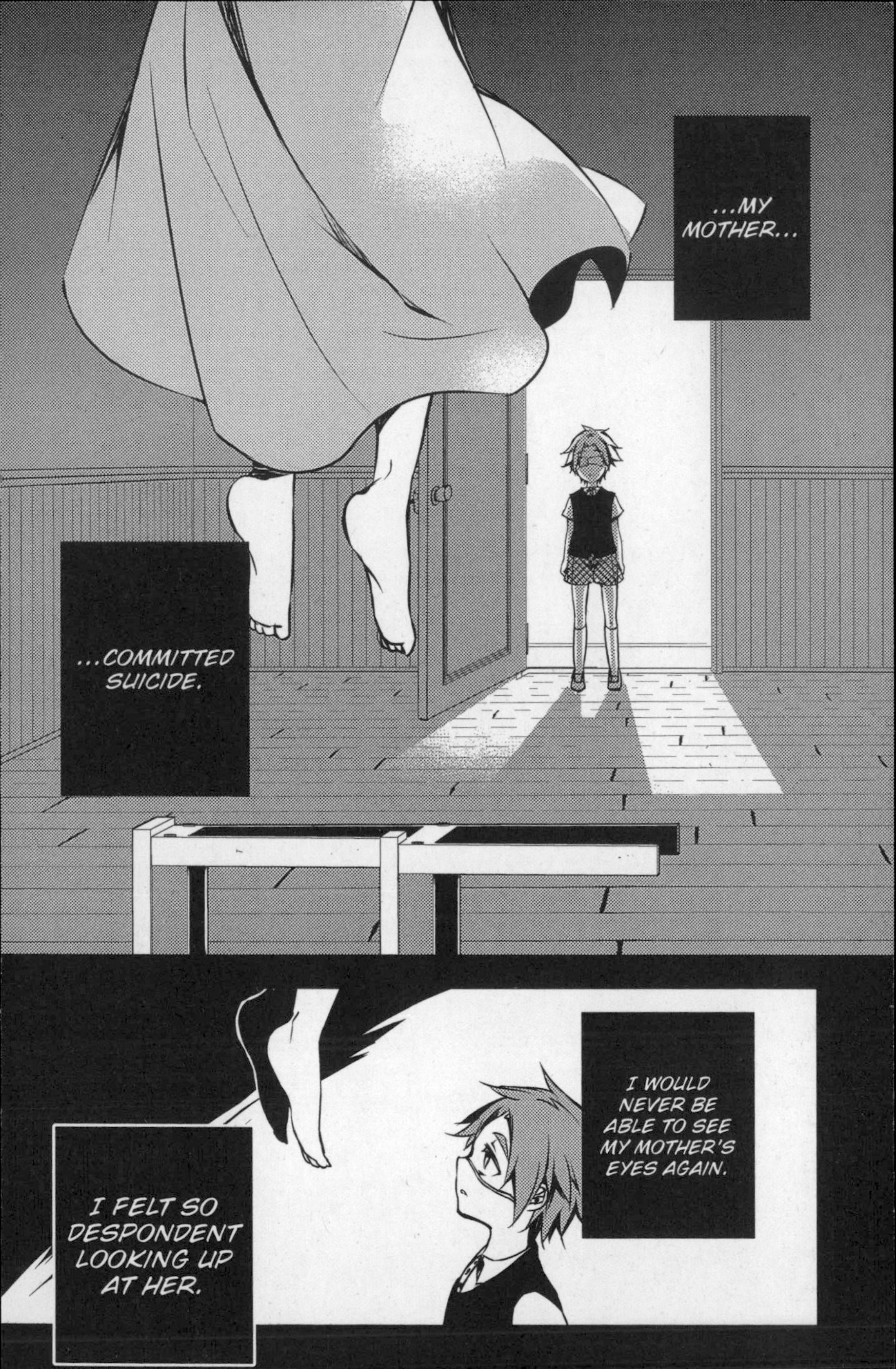
...MY MOTHER...
...COMMITTED SUICIDE.
I WOULD NEVER BE ABLE TO SEE MY MOTHER'S EYES AGAIN.
I FELT SO DESPONDENT LOOKING UP AT HER.

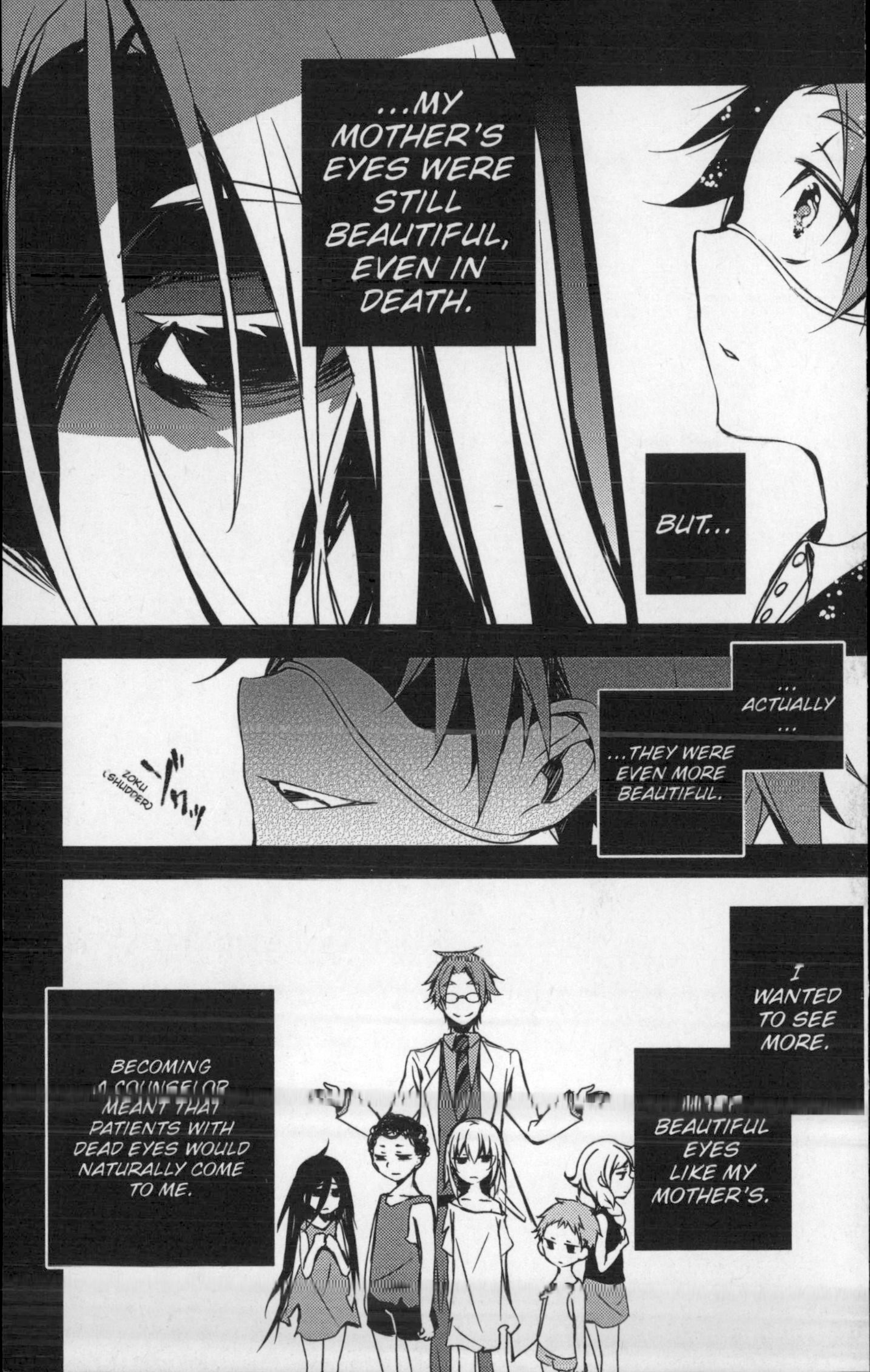
...MY MOTHER'S EYES WERE STILL BEAUTIFUL, EVEN IN DEATH.
BUT...
...ACTUALLY...
...THEY WERE EVEN MORE BEAUTIFUL.
ZOKU (SHUDDER)
I WANTED TO SEE MORE.
BEAUTIFUL EYES LIKE MY MOTHER'S.
BECOMING A COUNSELOR MEANT THAT PATIENTS WITH DEAD EYES WOULD NATURALLY COME TO ME.

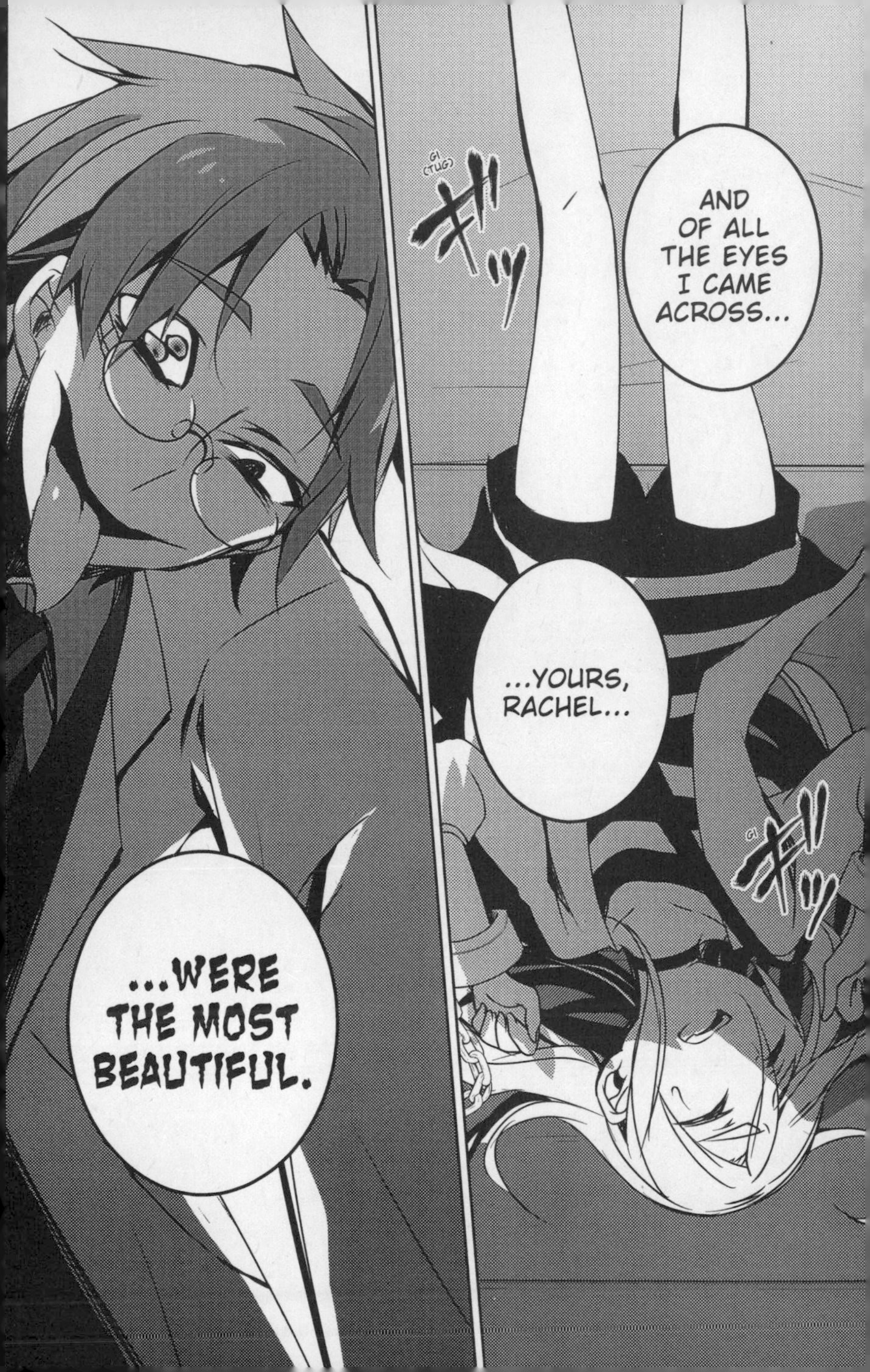
AND OF ALL THE EYES I CAME ACROSS...
GI (TUG)
...YOURS, RACHEL...
GI
...WERE THE MOST BEAUTIFUL.

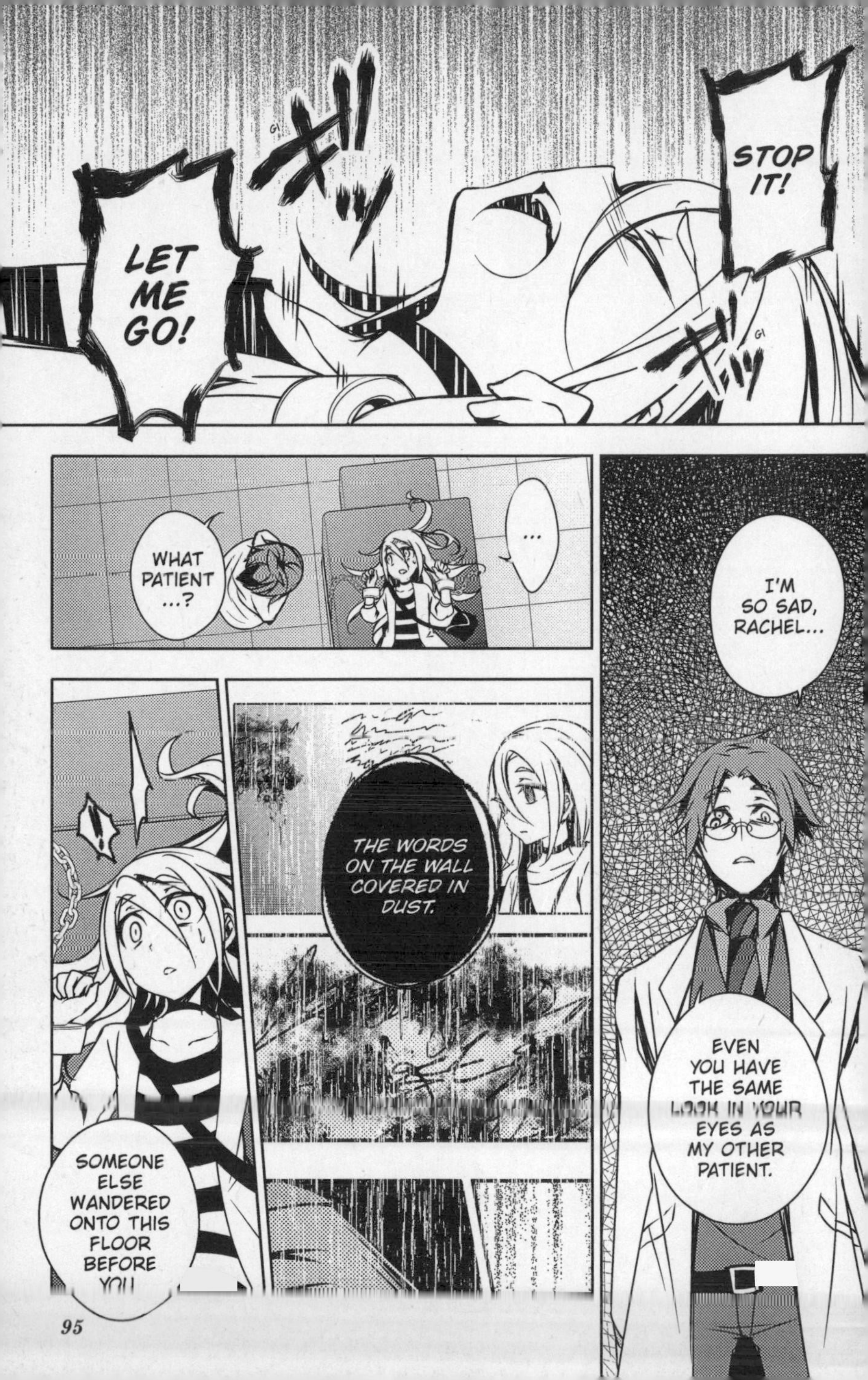
STOP IT!
GI
LET ME GO!
GI
I'M SO SAD, RACHEL...
EVEN YOU HAVE THE SAME LOOK IN YOUR EYES AS MY OTHER PATIENT.
...
WHAT PATIENT ...?
THE WORDS ON THE WALL COVERED IN DUST.
SOMEONE ELSE WANDERED ONTO THIS FLOOR BEFORE YOU

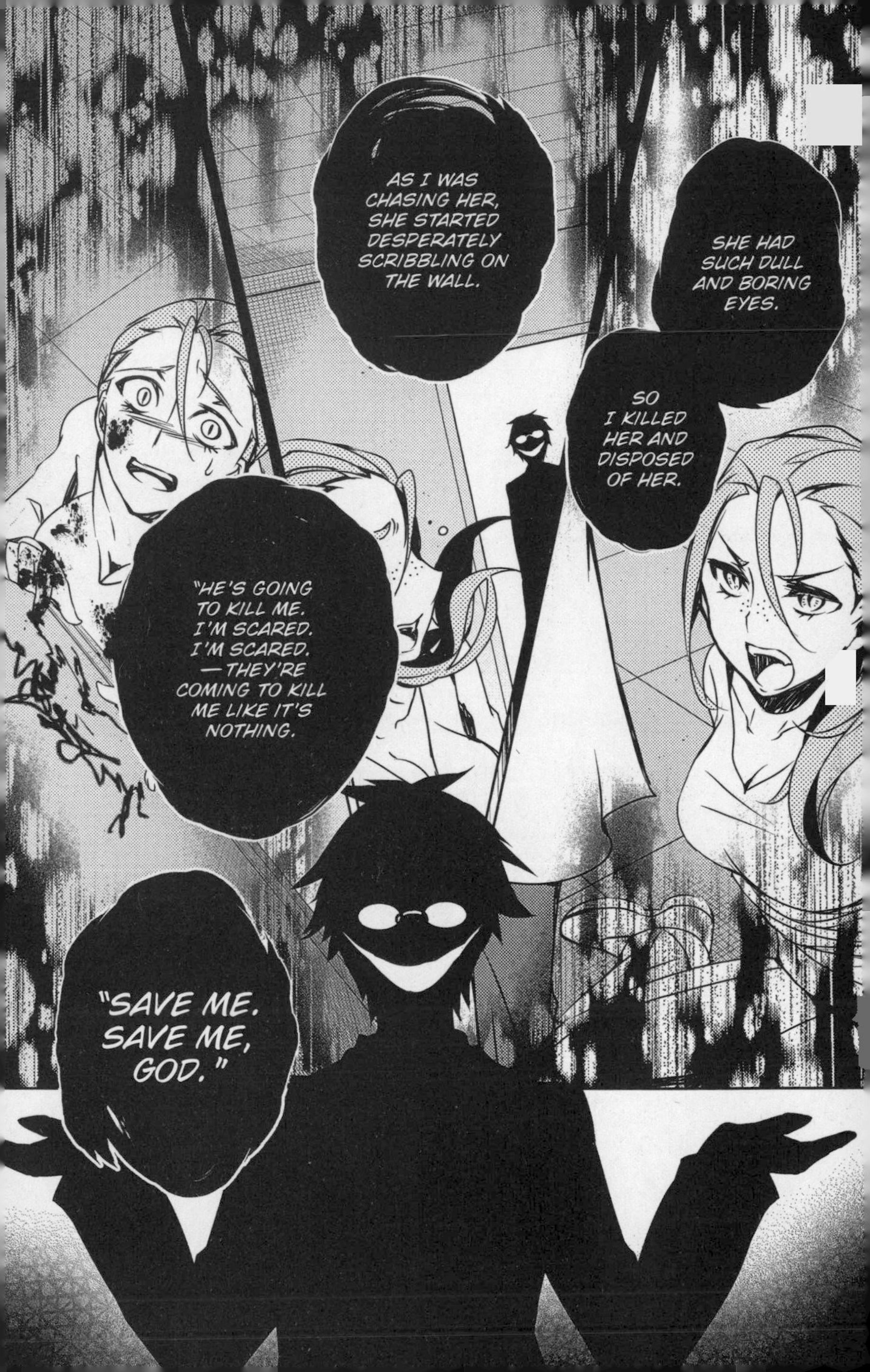
AS I WAS CHASING HER, SHE STARTED DESPERATELY SCRIBBLING ON THE WALL.
"HE'S GOING TO KILL ME. I'M SCARED. I'M SCARED. —THEY'RE COMING TO KILL ME LIKE IT'S NOTHING.
"SAVE ME. SAVE ME, GOD."
SHE HAD SUCH DULL AND BORING EYES.
SO I KILLED HER AND DISPOSED OF HER.

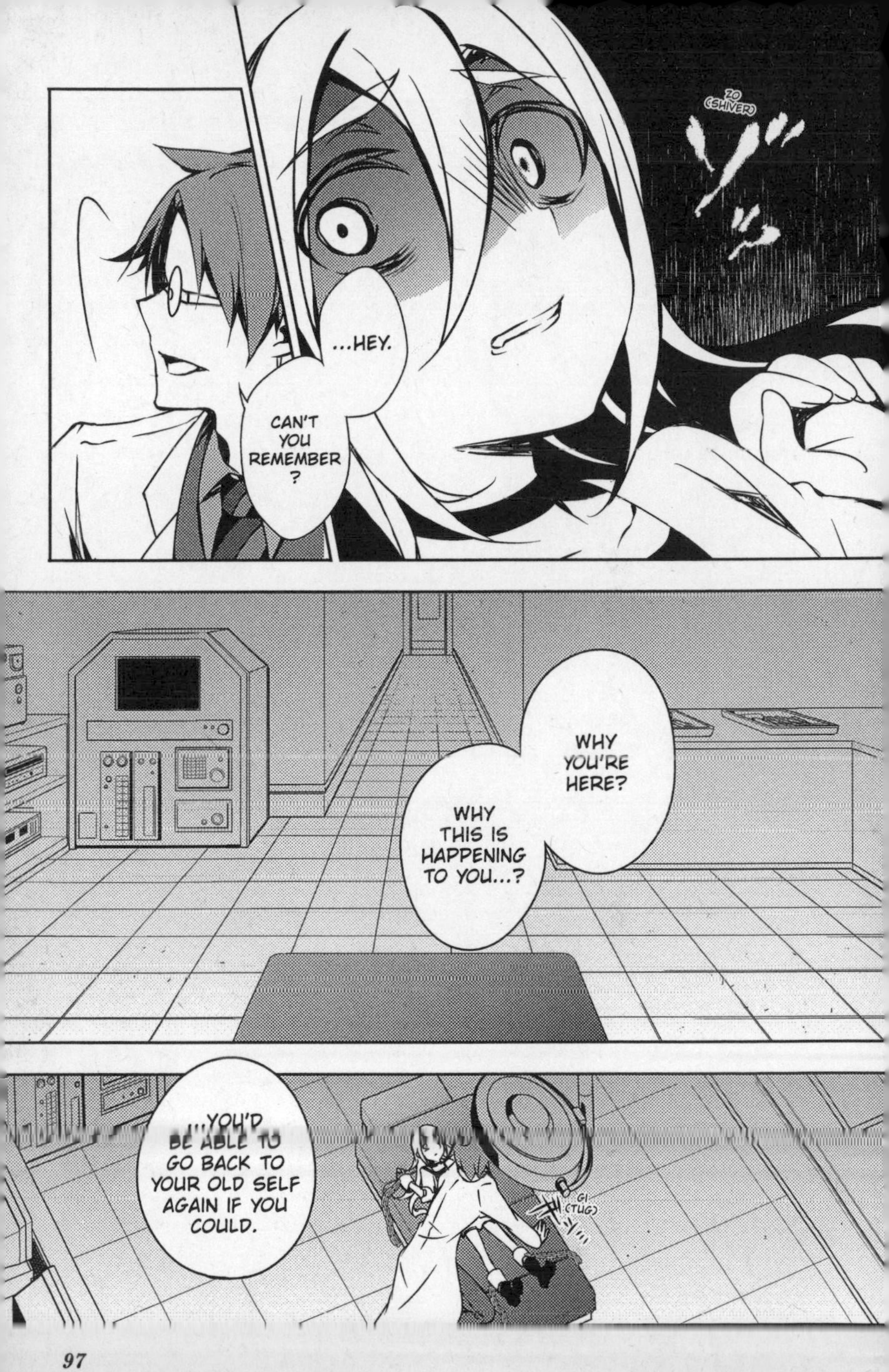
ZO (SHIVER)
...HEY.
CAN'T YOU REMEMBER?
WHY YOU'RE HERE?
WHY THIS IS HAPPENING TO YOU...?
GI (TUG)
...YOU'D BE ABLE TO GO BACK TO YOUR OLD SELF AGAIN IF YOU COULD.

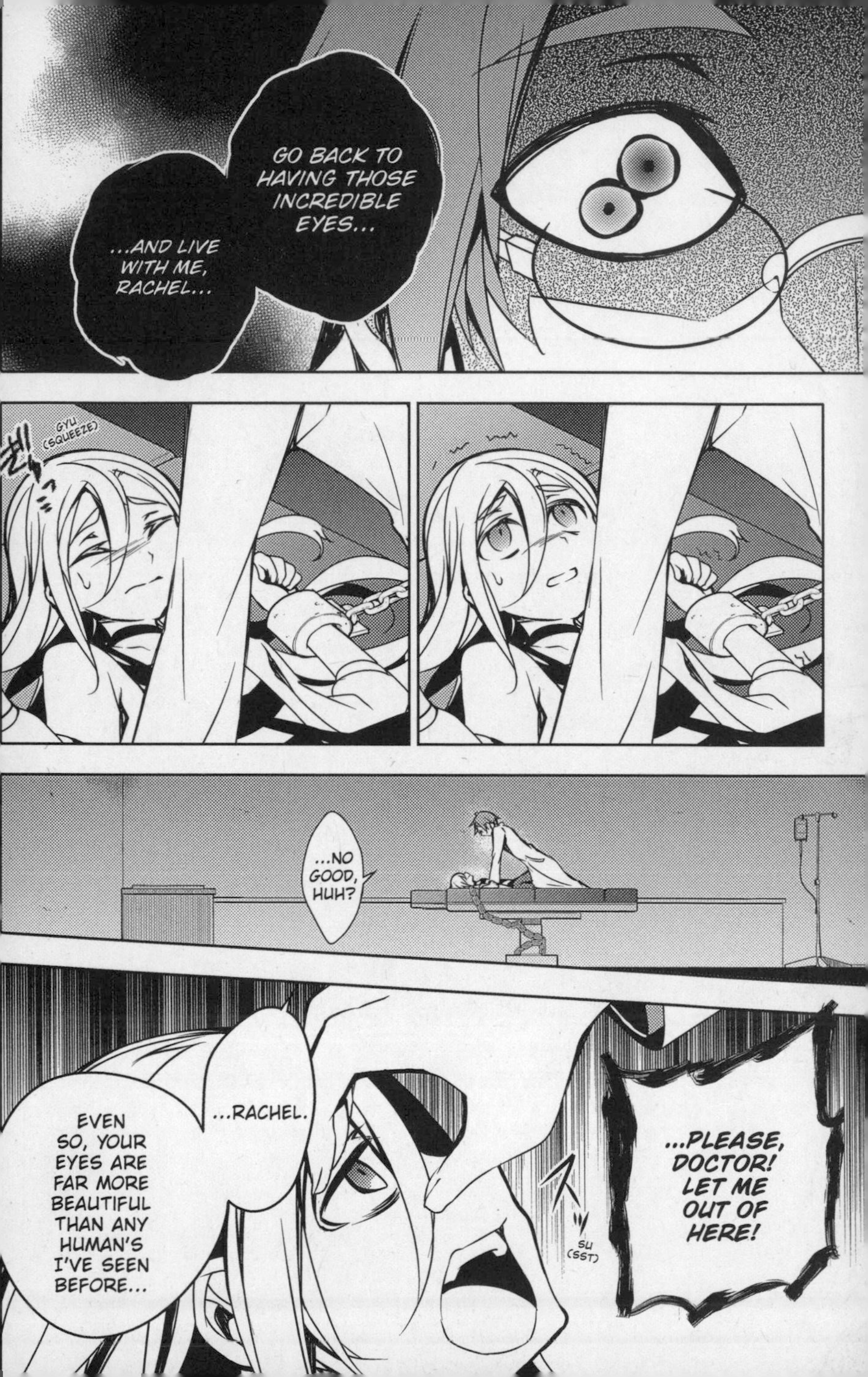
GO BACK TO HAVING THOSE INCREDIBLE EYES...
...AND LIVE WITH ME, RACHEL...
GYU (SQUEEZE)
...NO GOOD, HUH?
...PLEASE, DOCTOR! LET ME OUT OF HERE!
SU (SST)
...RACHEL.
EVEN SO, YOUR EYES ARE FAR MORE BEAUTIFUL THAN ANY HUMAN'S I'VE SEEN BEFORE...

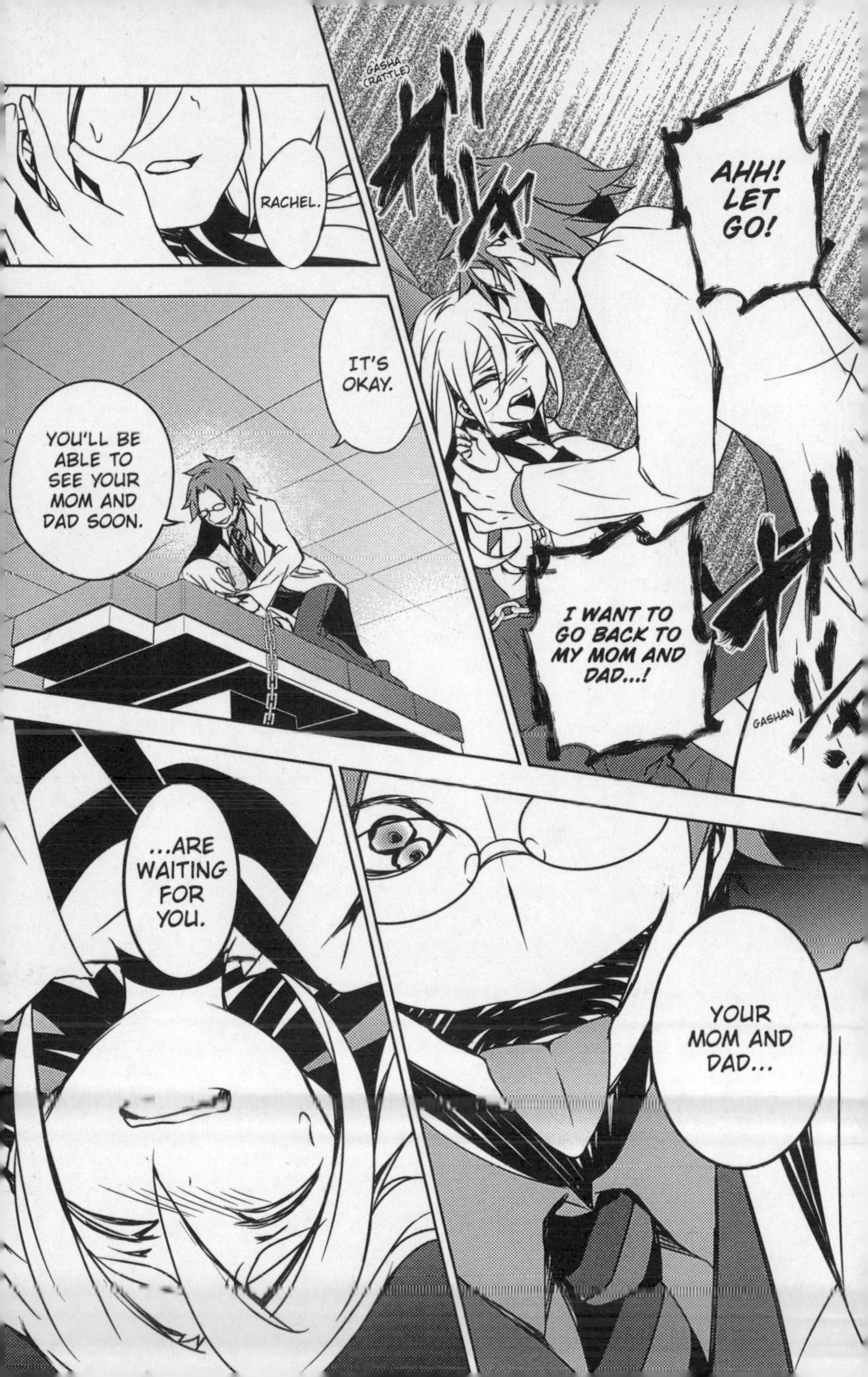
GASHA (RATTLE)
AHH! LET GO!
I WANT TO GO BACK TO MY MOM AND DAD...!
GASHAN
RACHEL.
IT'S OKAY.
YOU'LL BE ABLE TO SEE YOUR MOM AND DAD SOON.
YOUR MOM AND DAD...
...ARE WAITING FOR YOU.

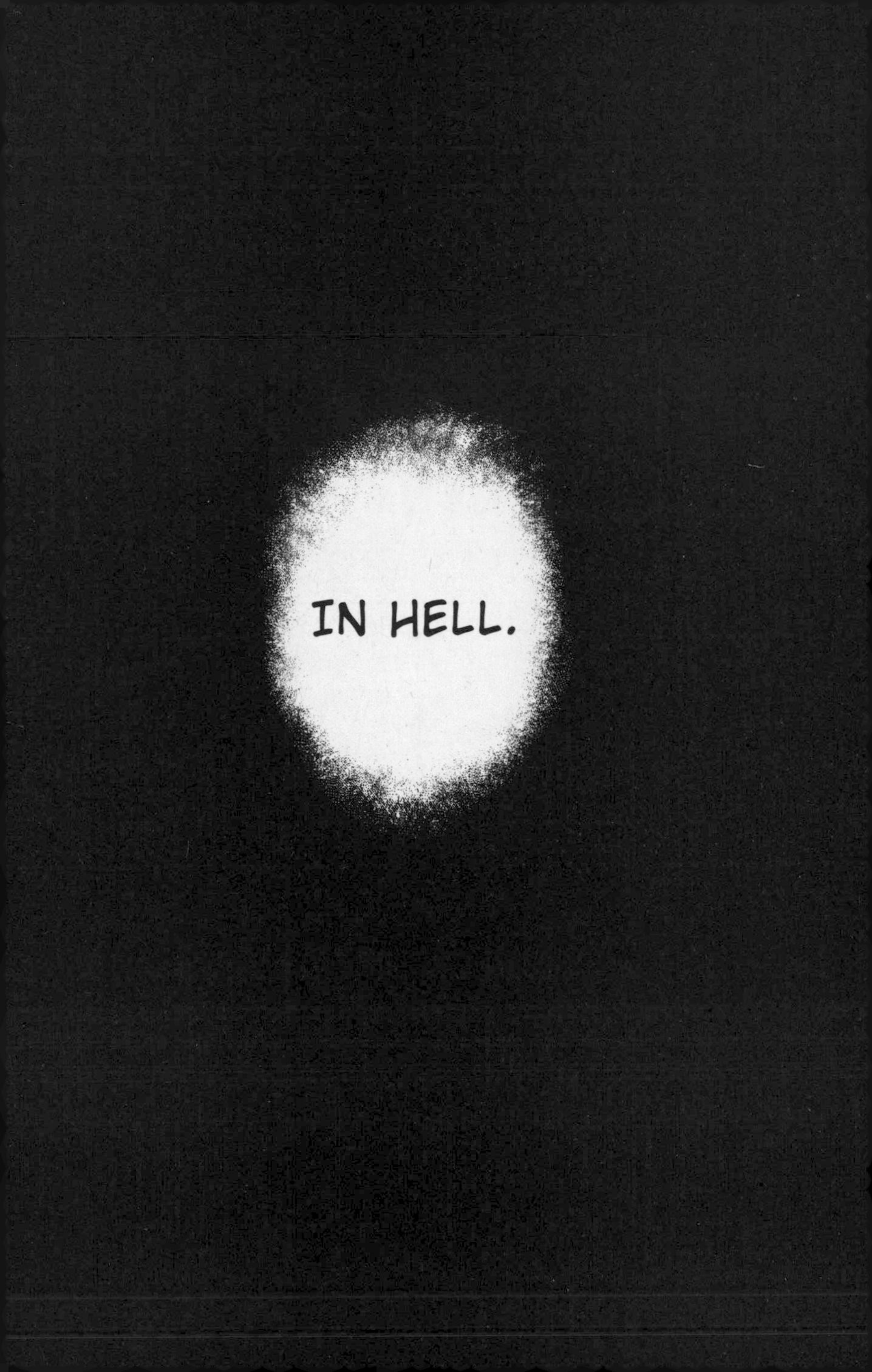
IN HELL.

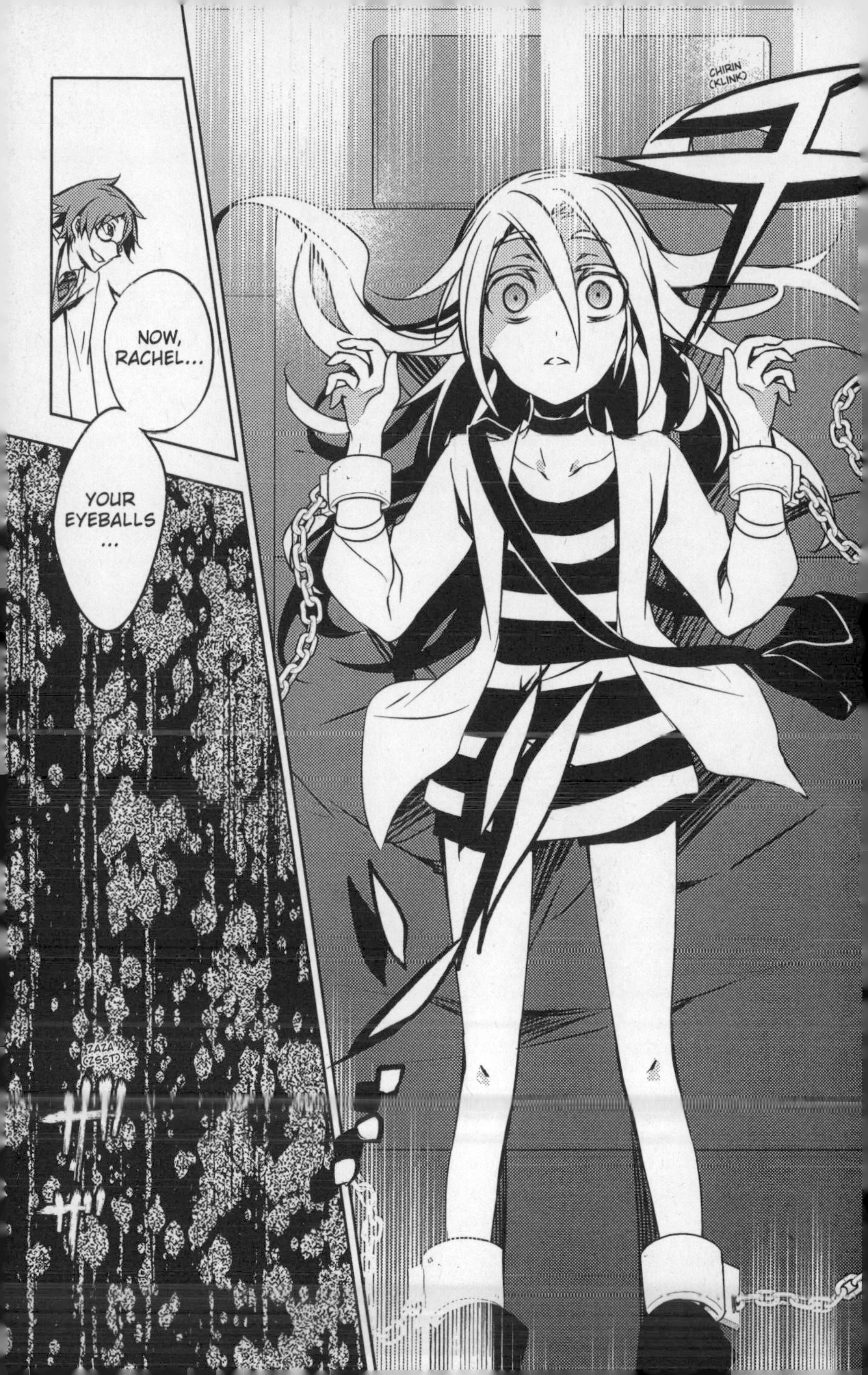
CHIRIN (KLINK)
NOW, RACHEL...
YOUR EYEBALLS ...
ZAZA (ZSST)

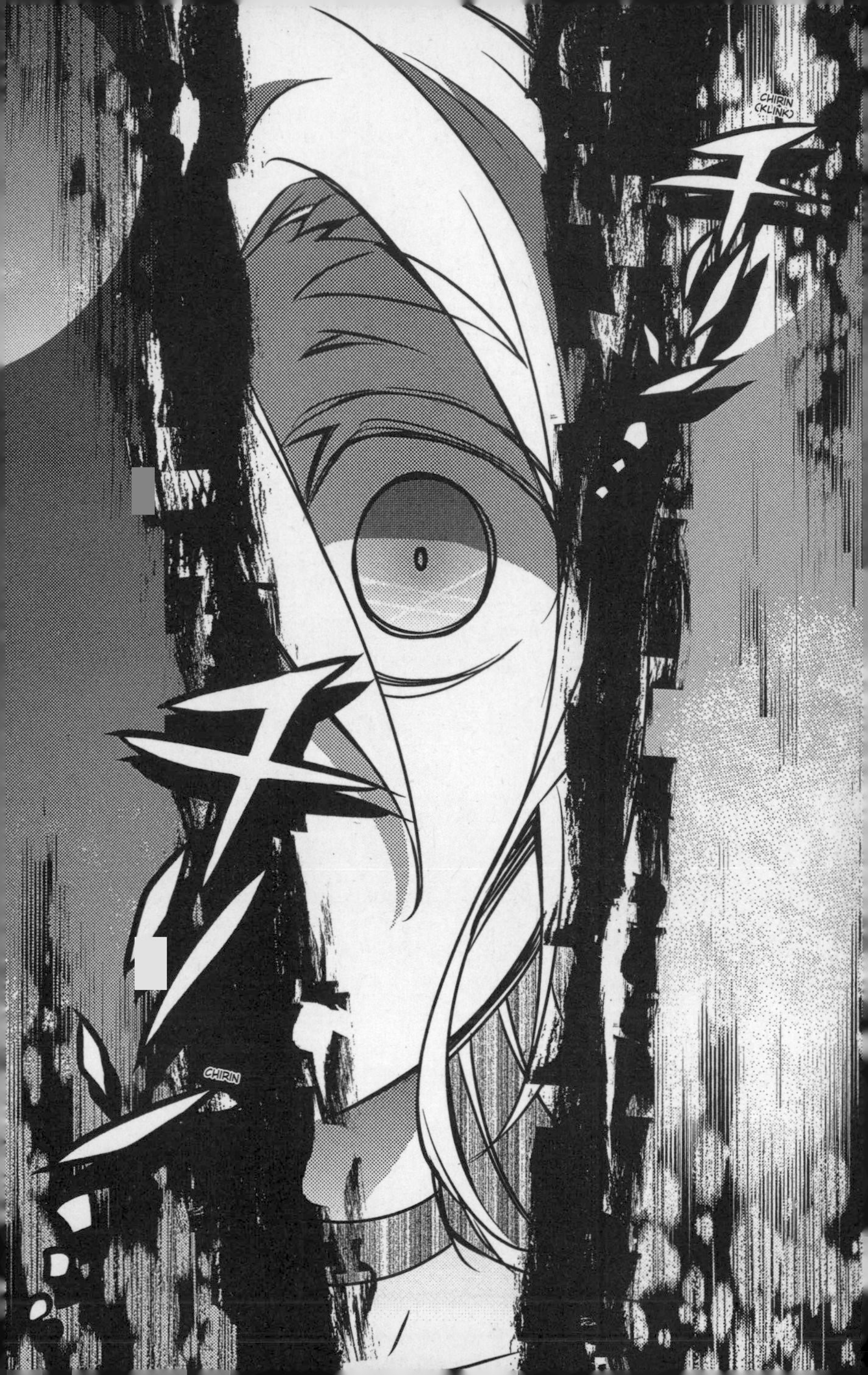
CHIRIN (KLINK)
CHIRIN

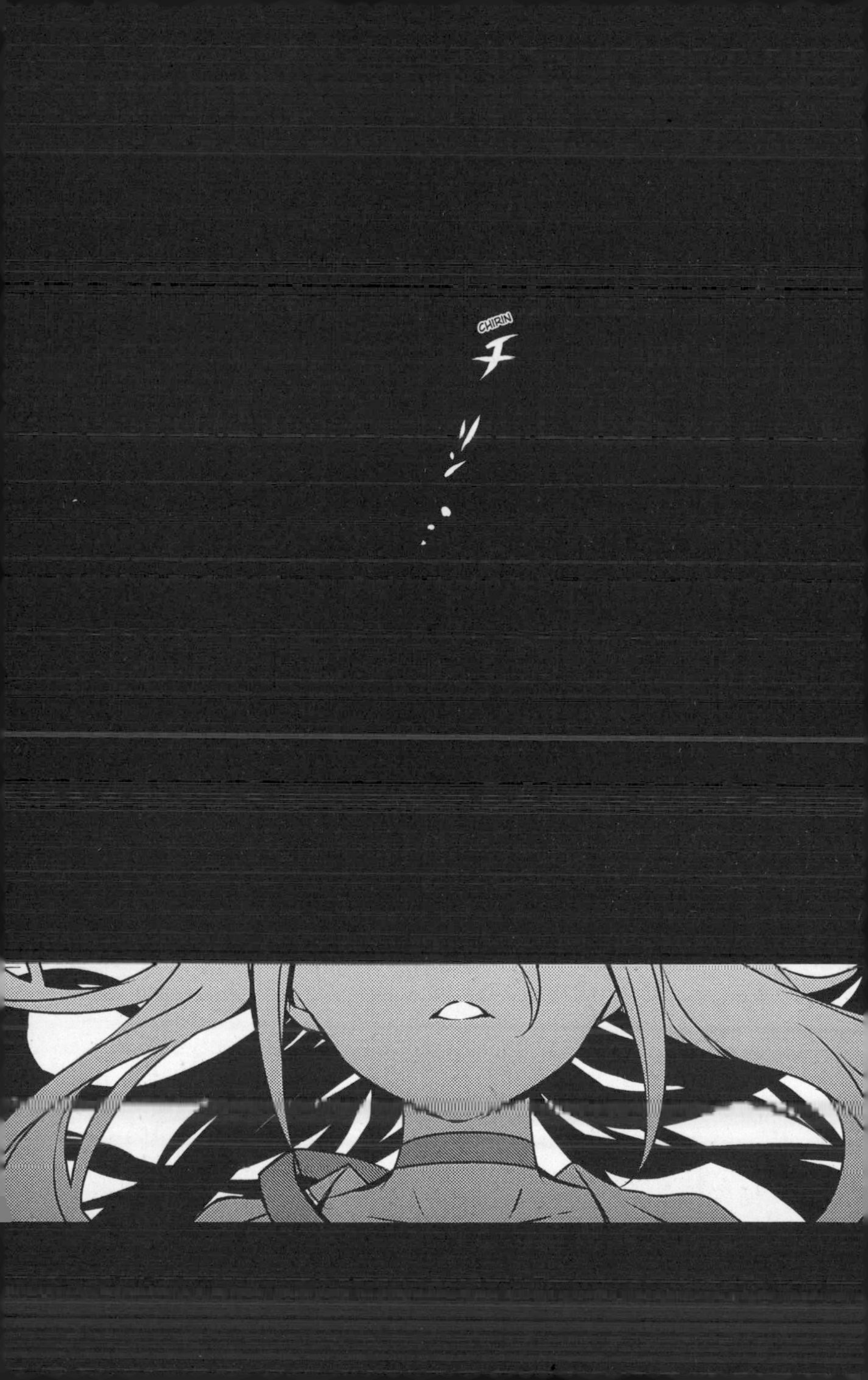
CHIRIN
チリ…

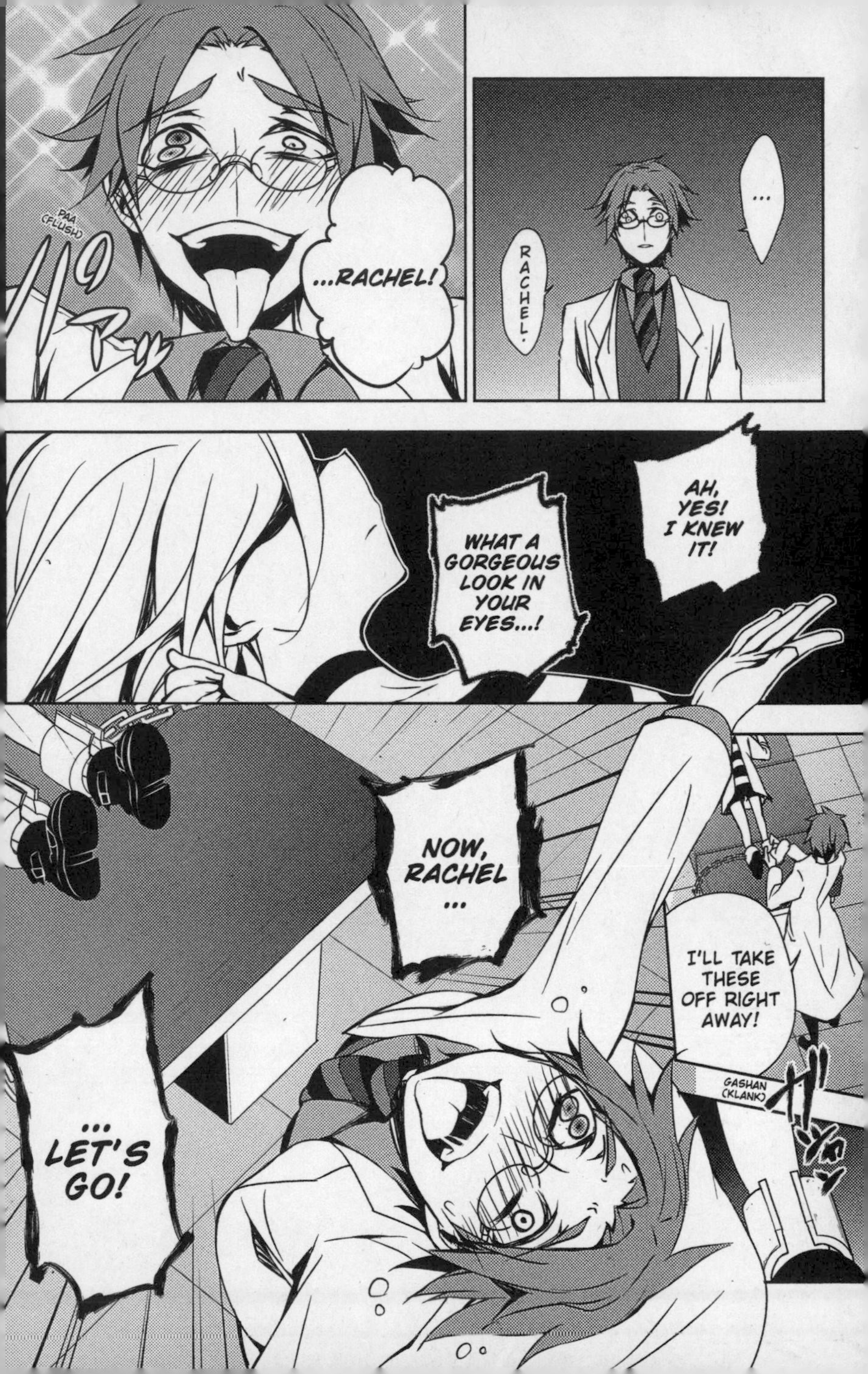
...
RACHEL.
...RACHEL!
PAA (FLUSH)
AH, YES! I KNEW IT!
WHAT A GORGEOUS LOOK IN YOUR EYES...!
NOW, RACHEL ...
I'LL TAKE THESE OFF RIGHT AWAY!
GASHAN (KLANK)
... LET'S GO!

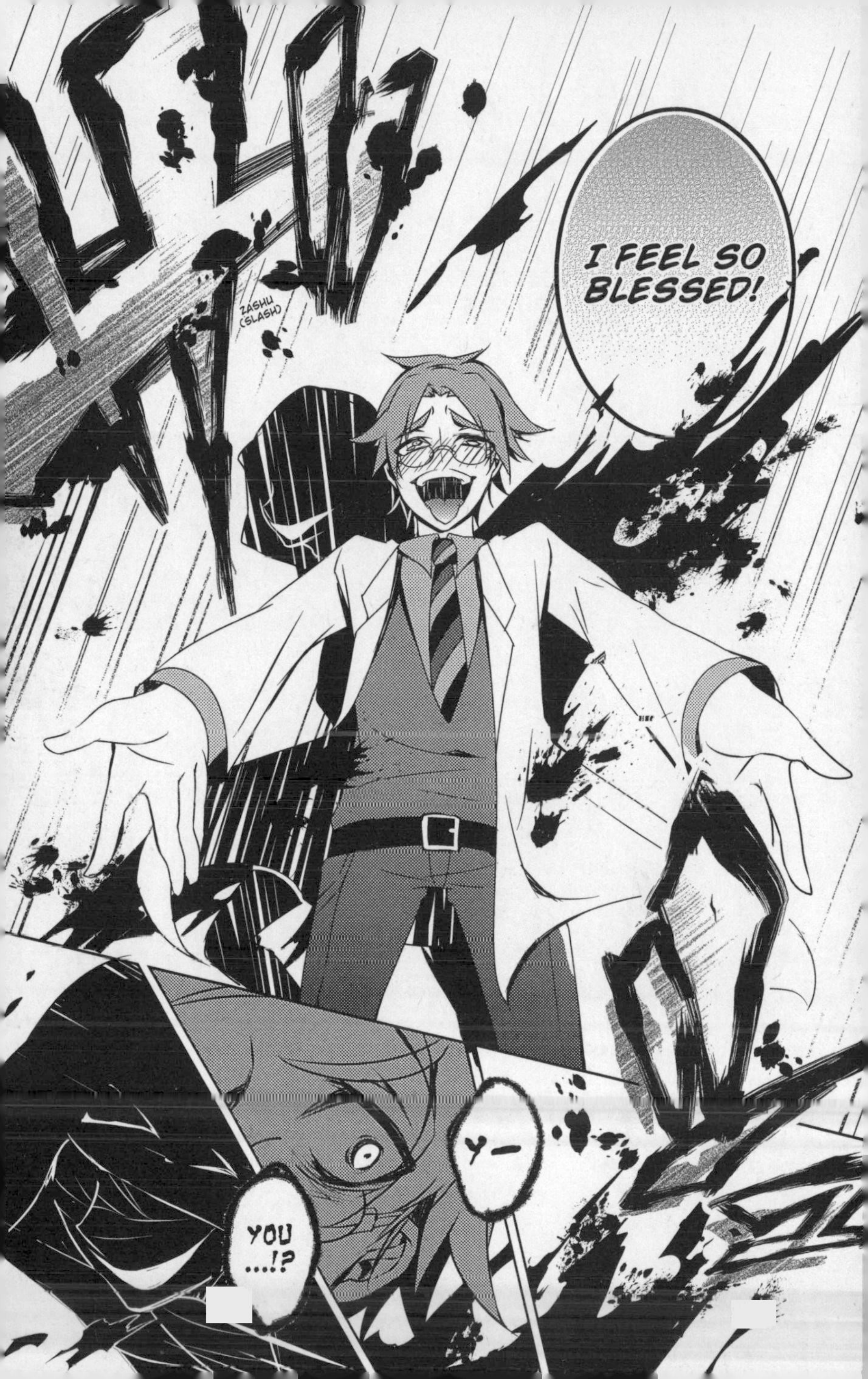
I FEEL SO BLESSED!
ZASHU (SLASH)
Y—
YOU ...!?

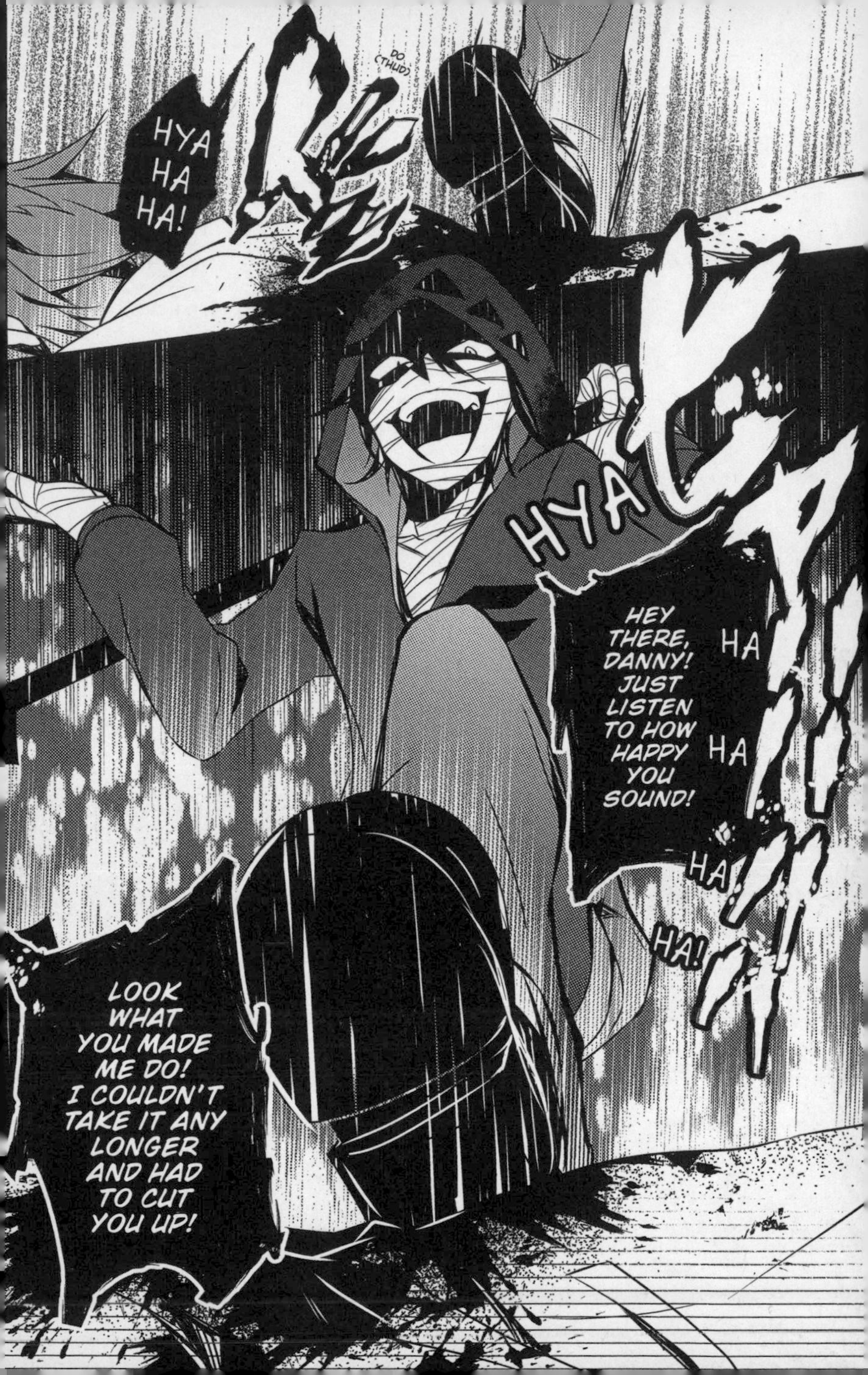
DO (THUD)
HYA HA HA!
HYA
HA HA HA HA!
HEY THERE, DANNY! JUST LISTEN TO HOW HAPPY YOU SOUND!
LOOK WHAT YOU MADE ME DO! I COULDN'T TAKE IT ANY LONGER AND HAD TO CUT YOU UP!

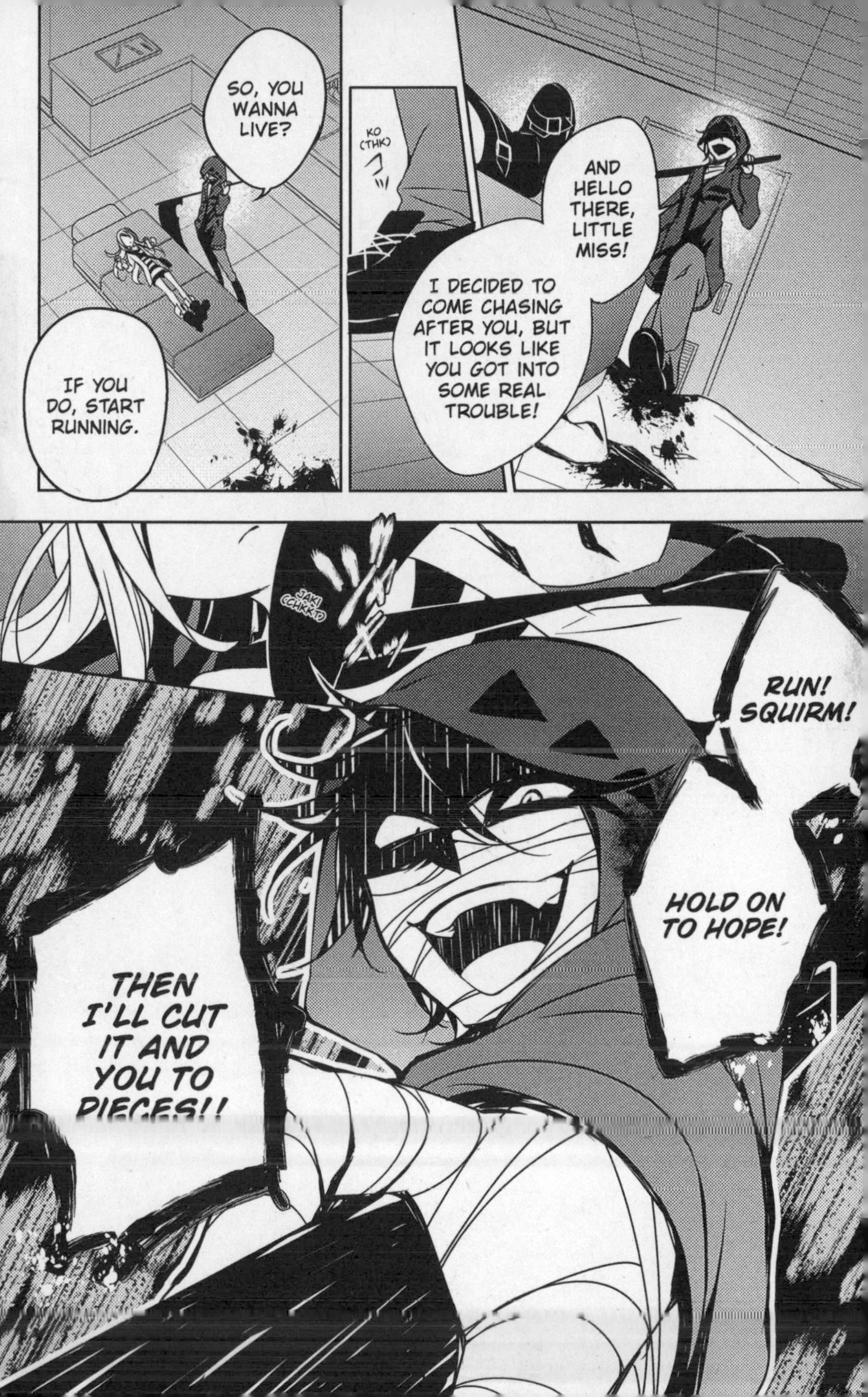
AND HELLO THERE, LITTLE MISS!
KO (THK)
I DECIDED TO COME CHASING AFTER YOU, BUT IT LOOKS LIKE YOU GOT INTO SOME REAL TROUBLE!
SO, YOU WANNA LIVE?
IF YOU DO, START RUNNING.
JAKI (CHKKT)
RUN! SQUIRM!
HOLD ON TO HOPE!
THEN I'LL CUT IT AND YOU TO PIECES!!

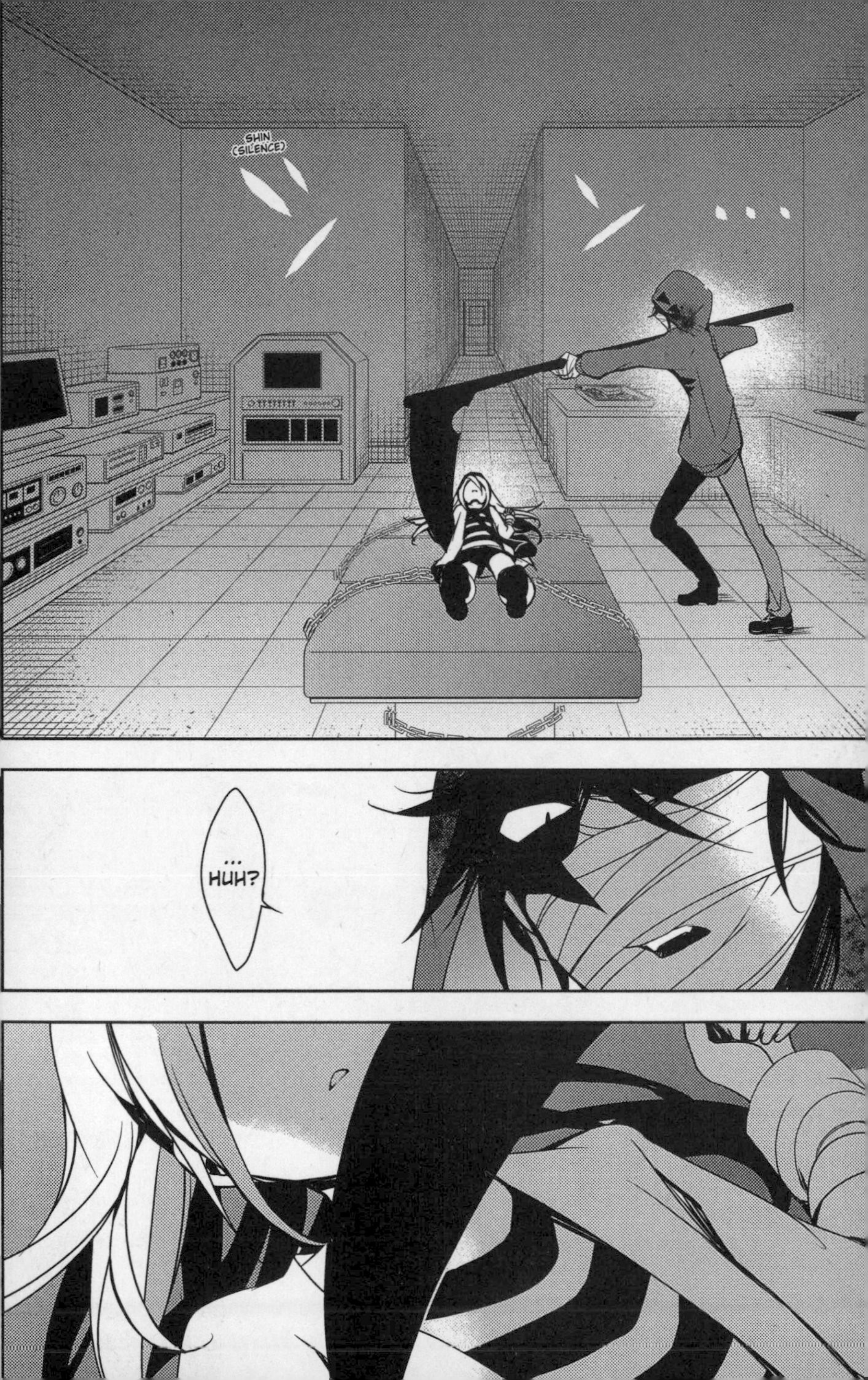
SHIN (SILENCE)
...HUH?

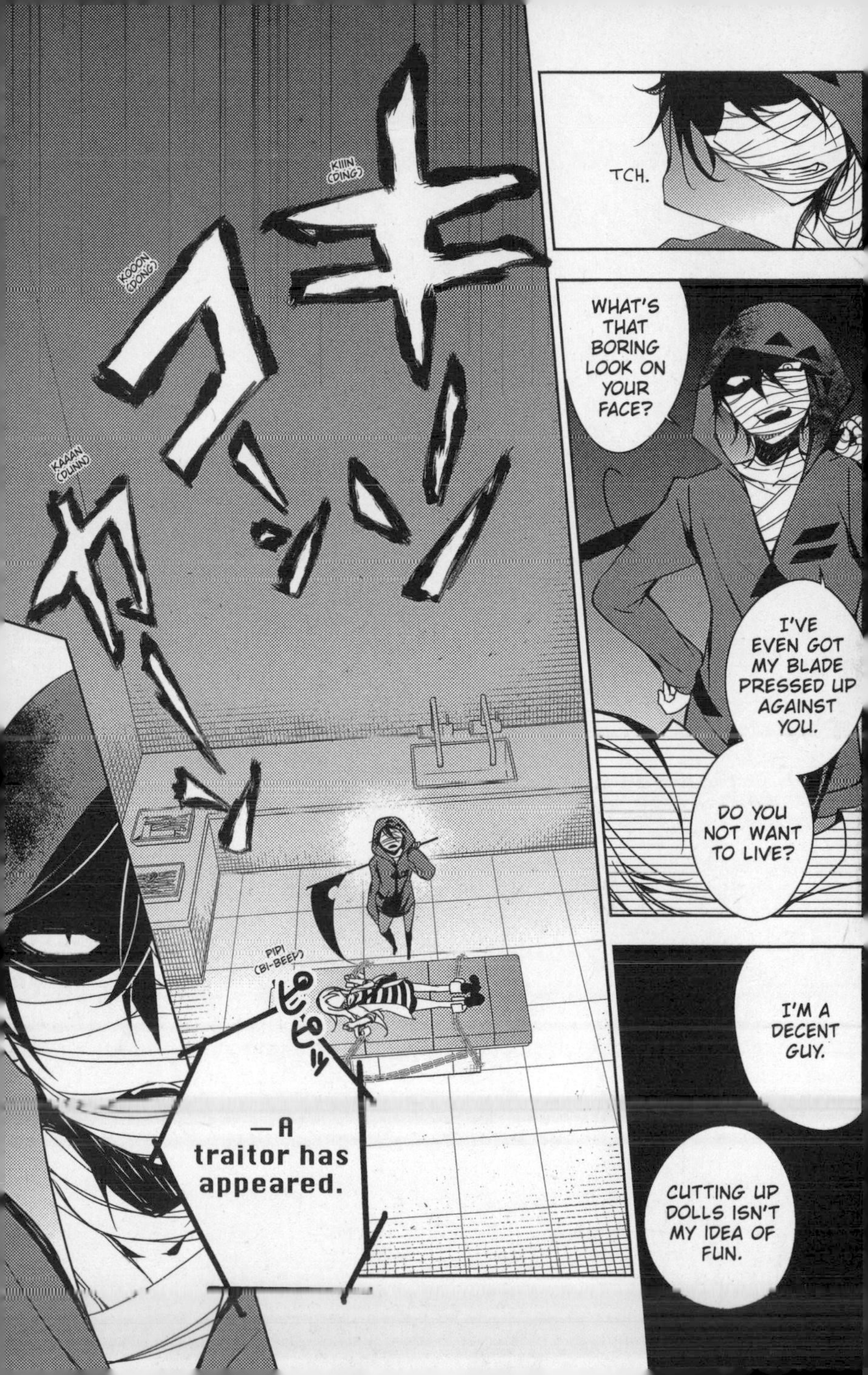
TCH.
WHAT'S THAT BORING LOOK ON YOUR FACE?
I'VE EVEN GOT MY BLADE PRESSED UP AGAINST YOU.
DO YOU NOT WANT TO LIVE?
I'M A DECENT GUY.
CUTTING UP DOLLS ISN'T MY IDEA OF FUN.
KIIN (DING)
KOOON (DONG)
KAAAN (DUNN)
PIPI (BI-BEEP)
—A traitor has appeared.

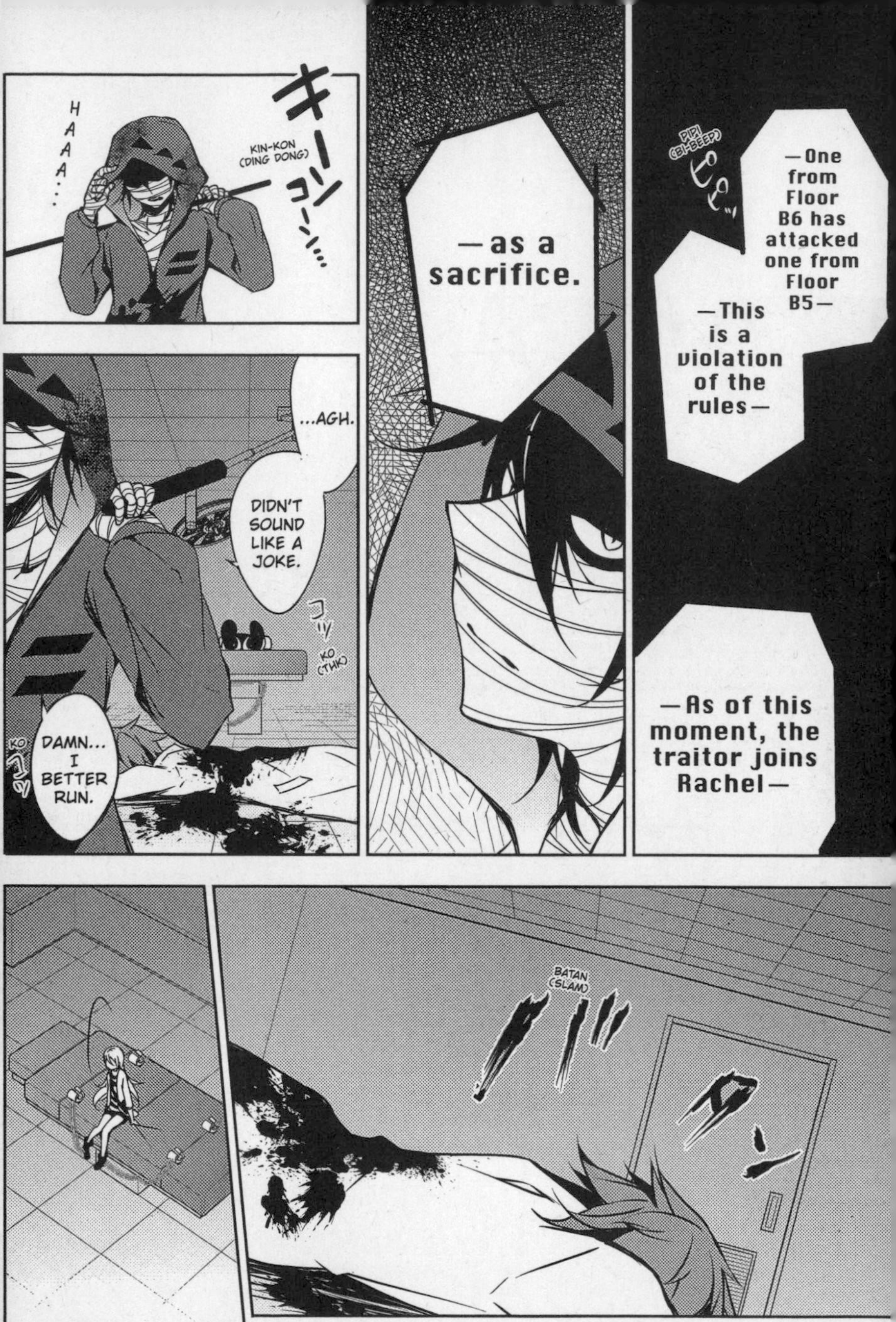
PIPI (BI-BEEP)
—One from Floor B6 has attacked one from Floor B5—
—This is a violation of the rules—
—As of this moment, the traitor joins Rachel—
—as a sacrifice.
KIN-KON (DING DONG)
HAAAA...
...AGH.
DIDN'T SOUND LIKE A JOKE.
KO (THK)
DAMN... I BETTER RUN.
KO
BATAN (SLAM)

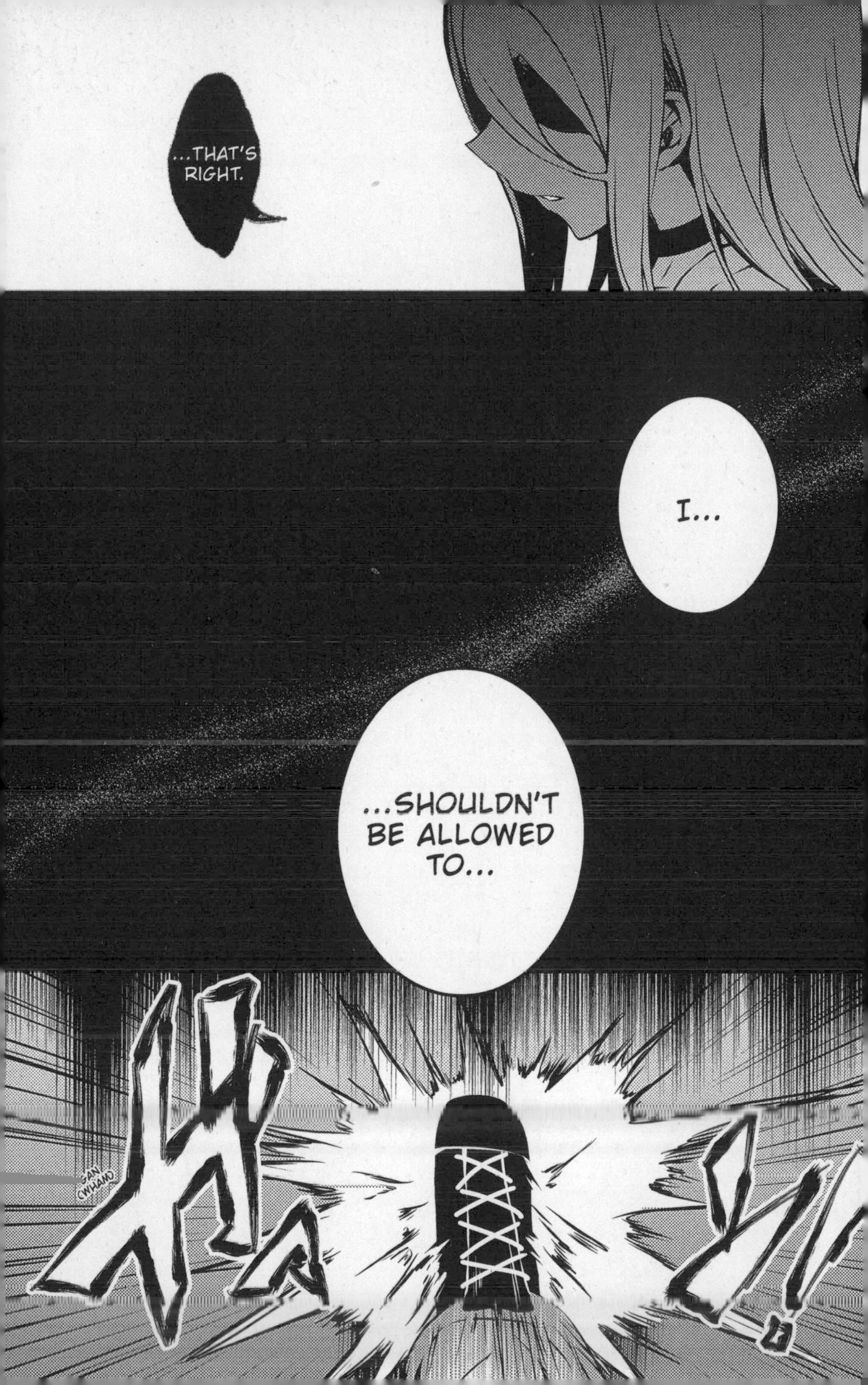
...THAT'S RIGHT.
I...
...SHOULDN'T BE ALLOWED TO...
GAN (WHAM)

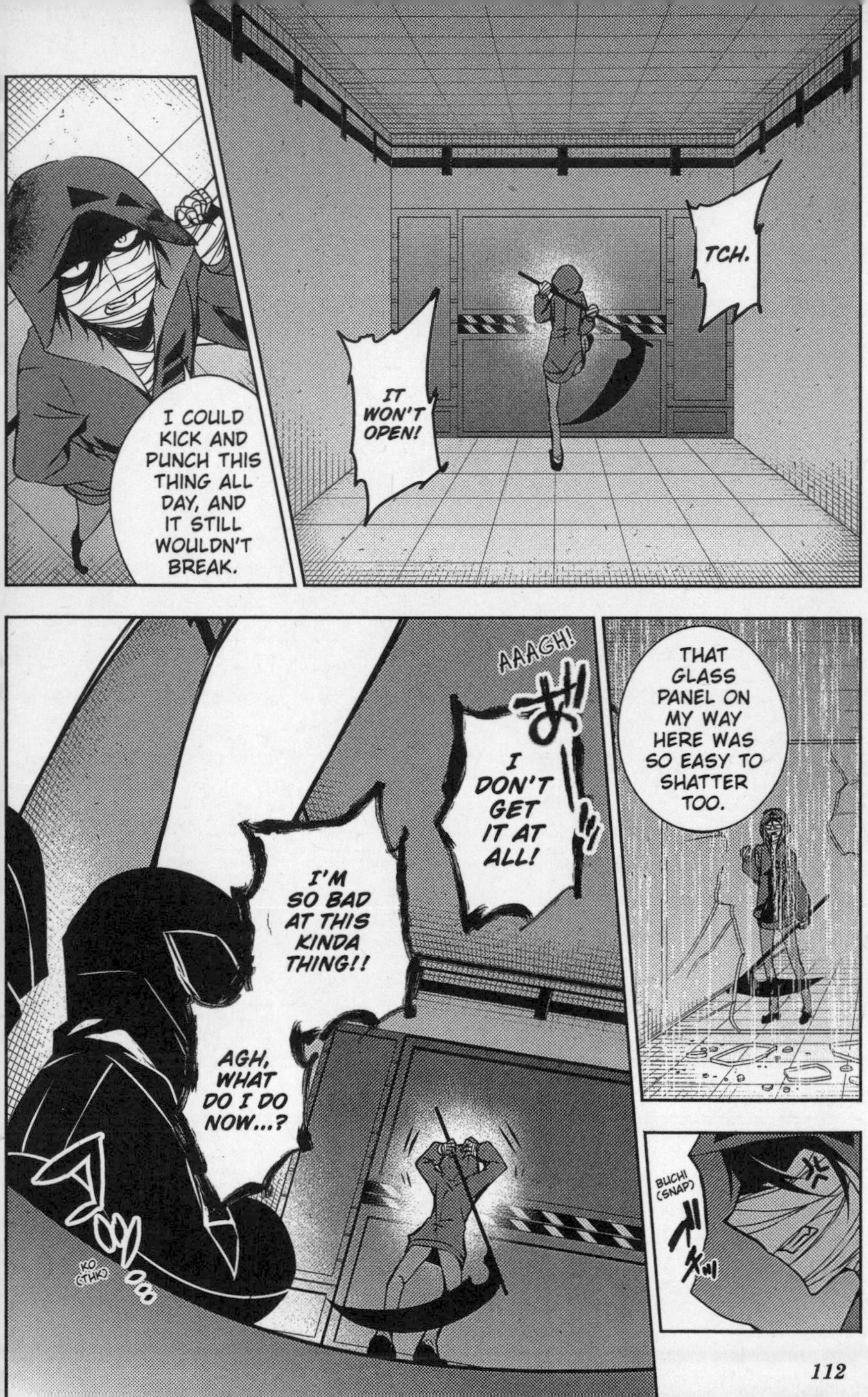
TCH.
IT WON'T OPEN!
I COULD KICK AND PUNCH THIS THING ALL DAY, AND IT STILL WOULDN'T BREAK.
THAT GLASS PANEL ON MY WAY HERE WAS SO EASY TO SHATTER TOO.
BUCHI (SNAP)
AAAGH!
I DON'T GET IT AT ALL!
I'M SO BAD AT THIS KINDA THING!!
AGH, WHAT DO I DO NOW...?
KO (THK)

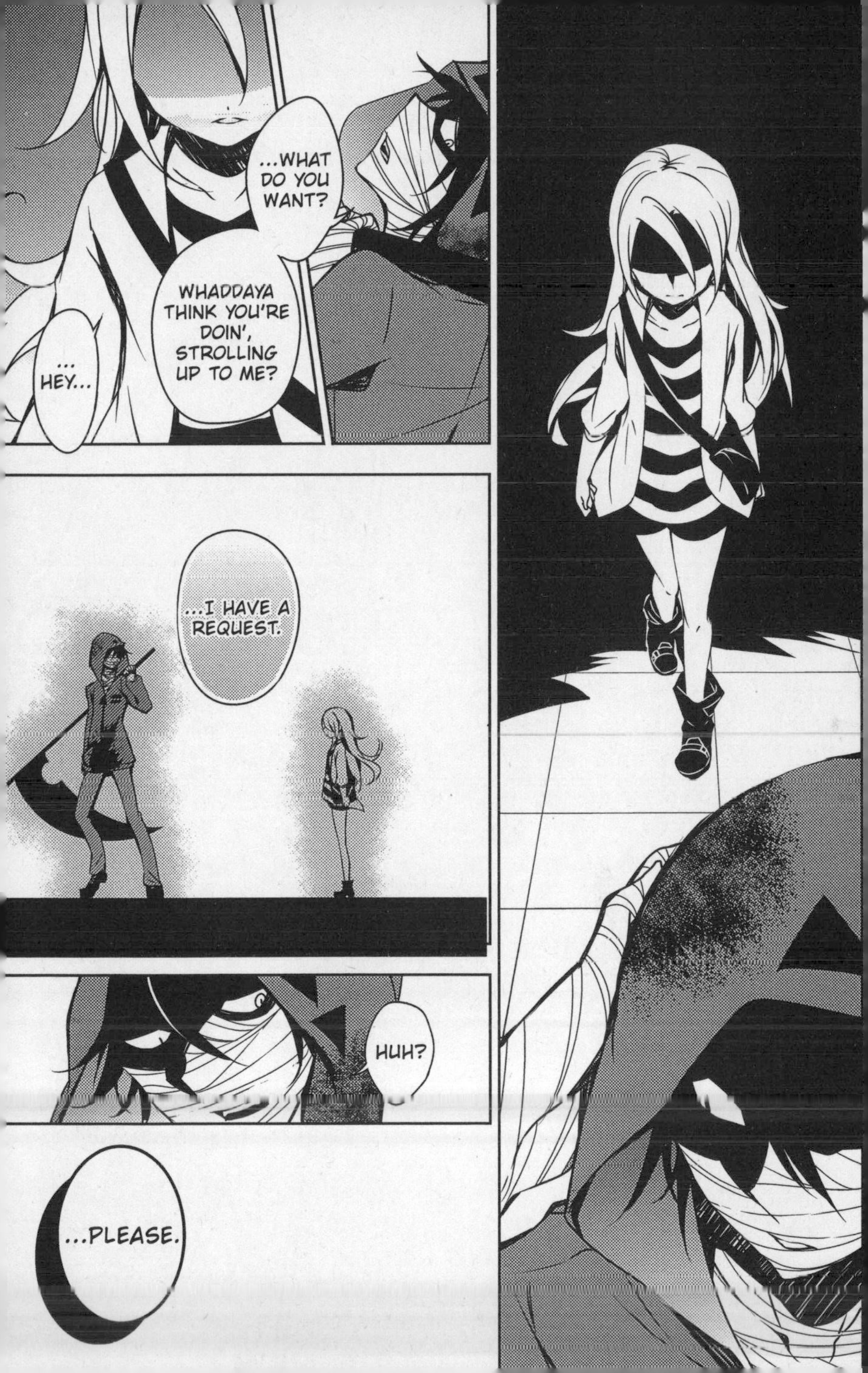
...WHAT DO YOU WANT?
WHADDAYA THINK YOU'RE DOIN', STROLLING UP TO ME?
... HEY...
...I HAVE A REQUEST.
HUH?
...PLEASE.

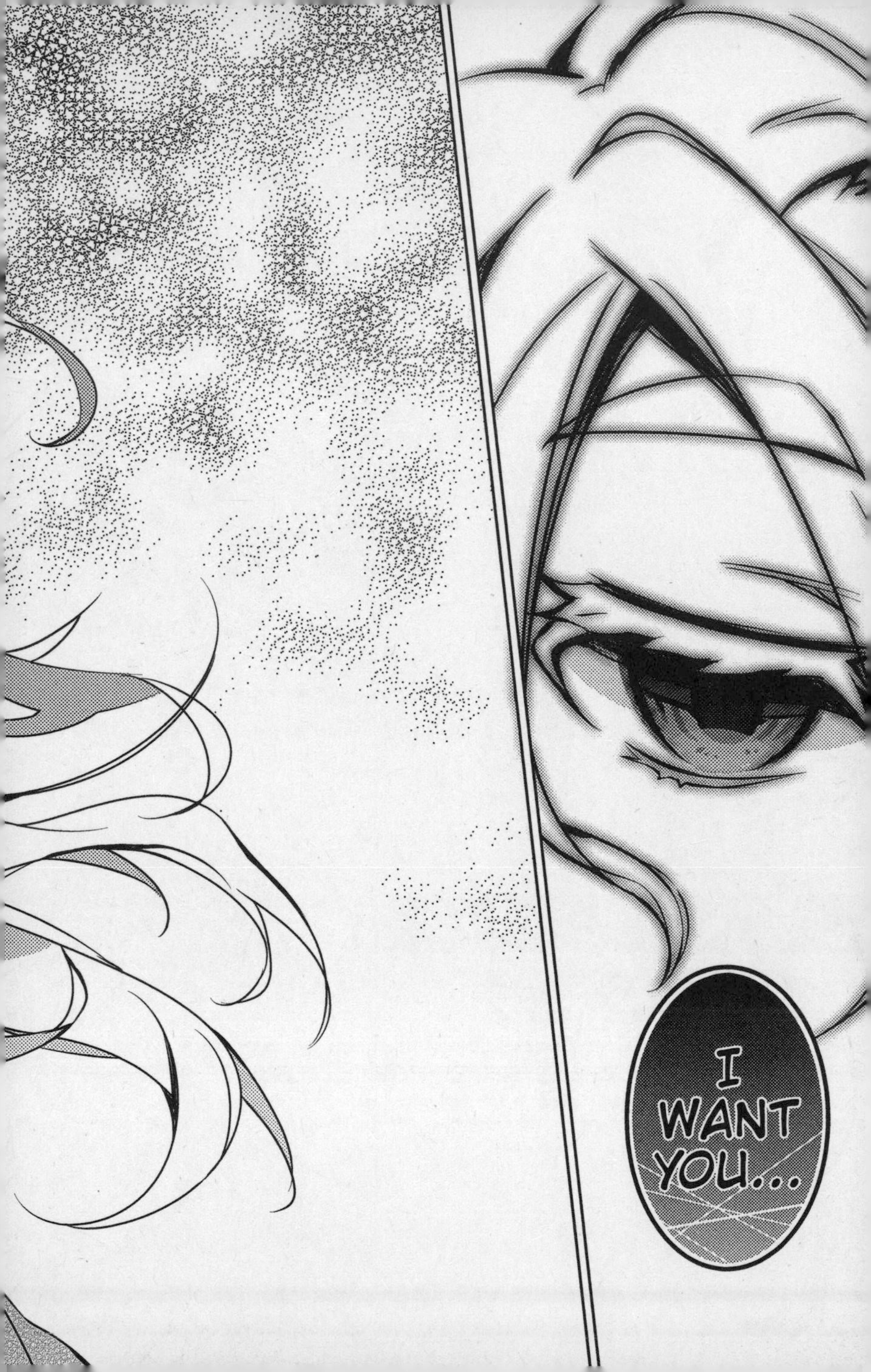
I WANT YOU...

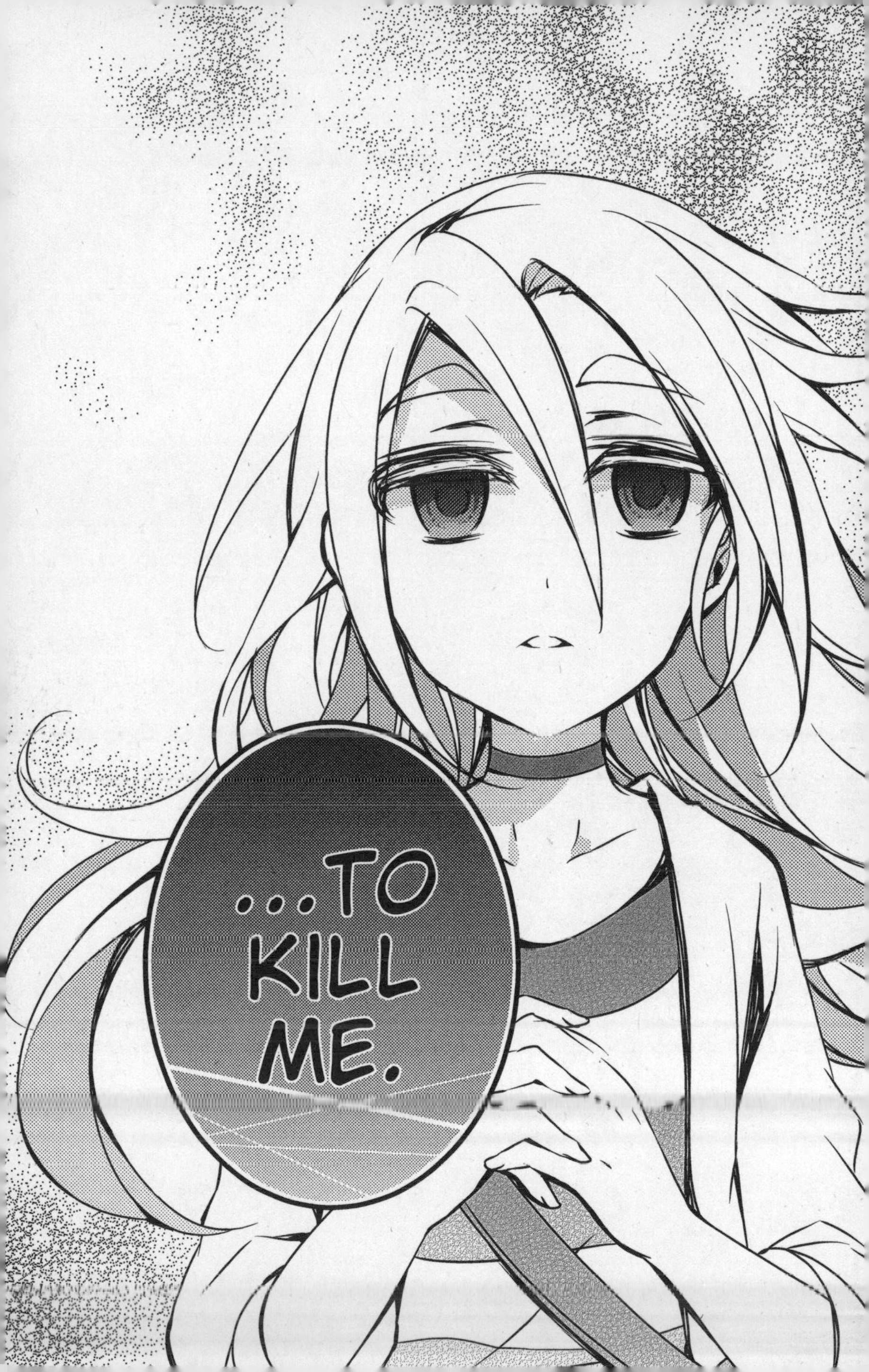
...TO KILL ME.

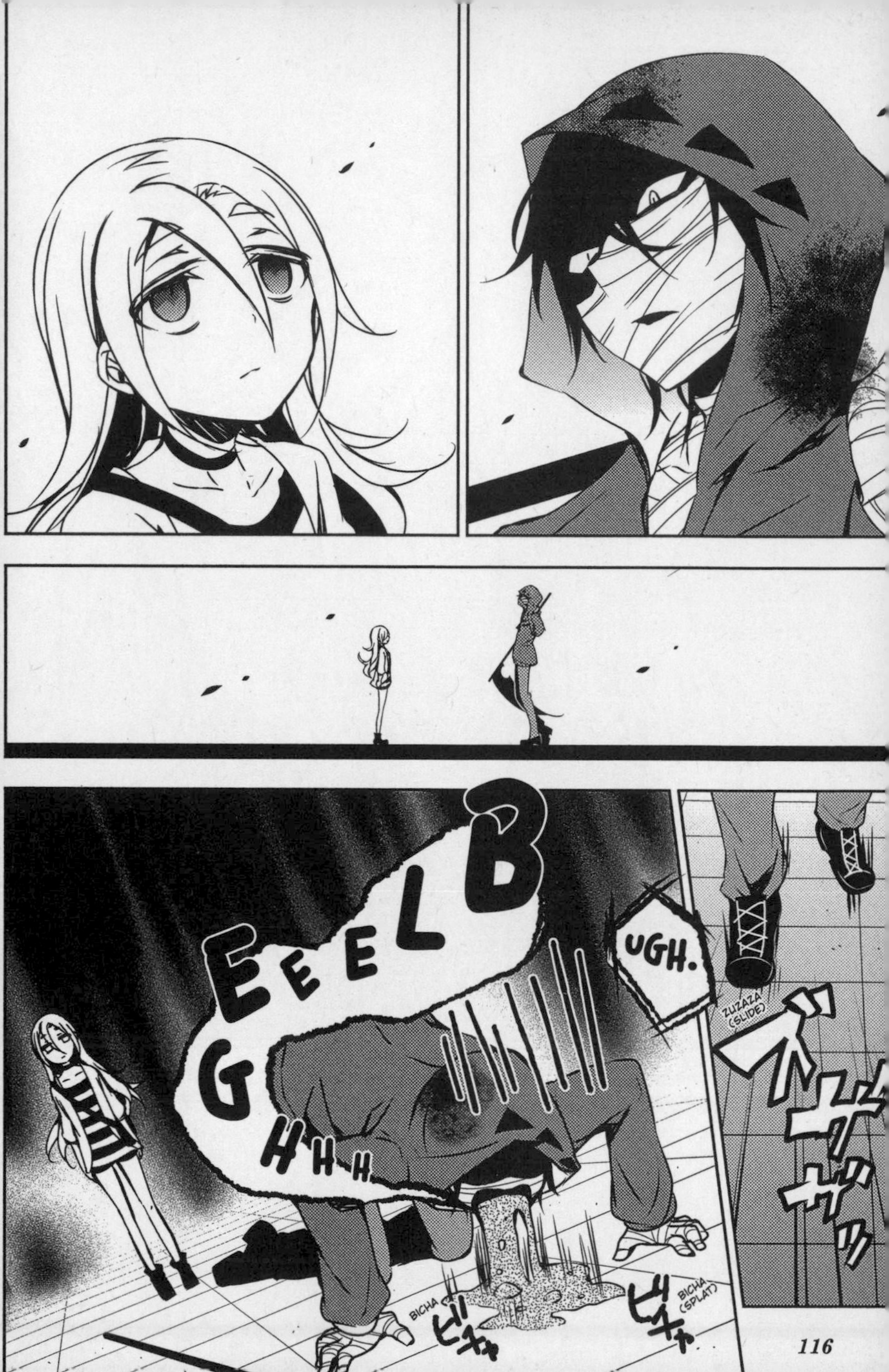
ZUZAZA (SLIDE)
ズザザッ
UGH.
BLEEEGHHH
BICHA (SPLAT)
ビチャ
BICHA
ビチャ

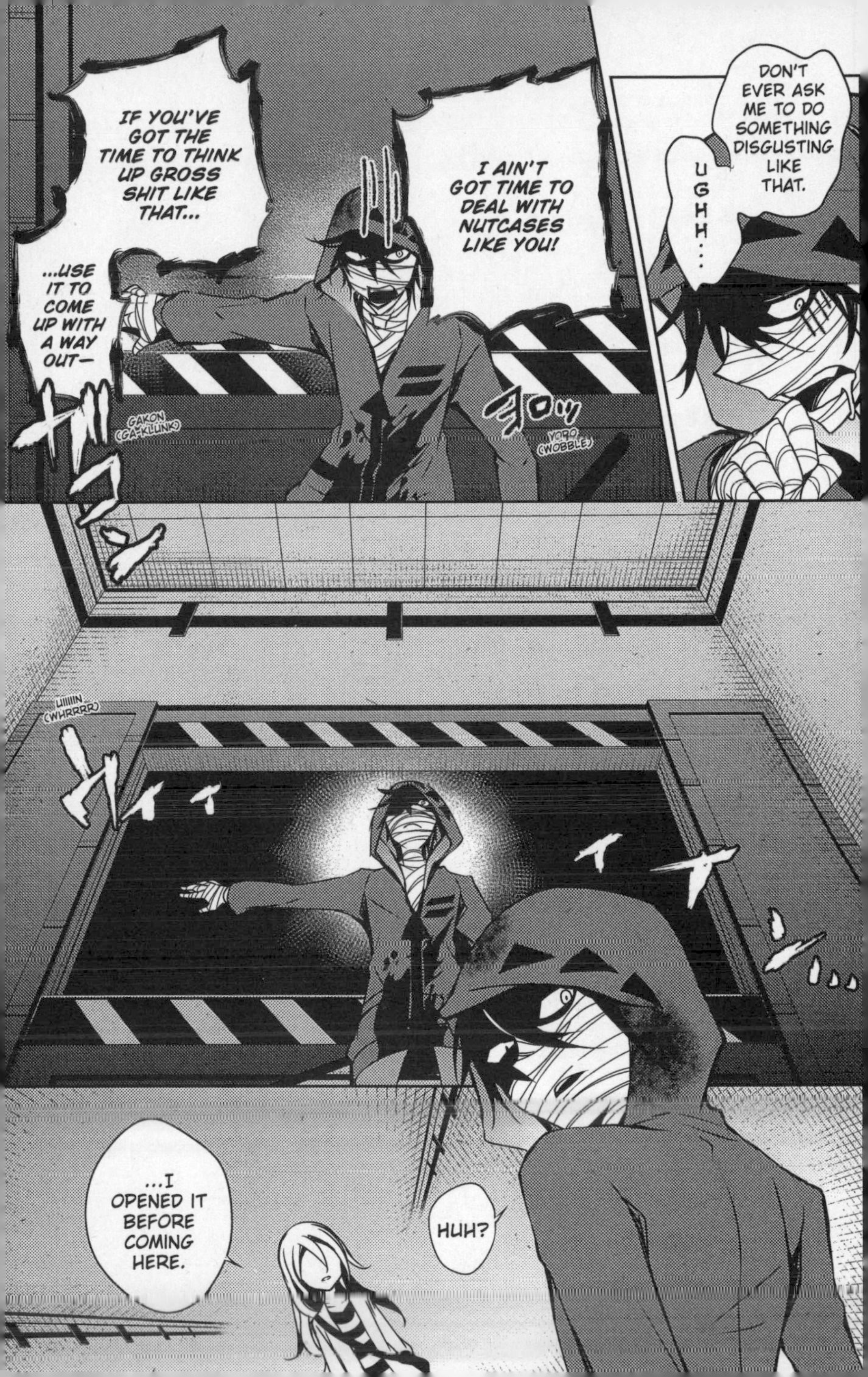
DON'T EVER ASK ME TO DO SOMETHING DISGUSTING LIKE THAT.
UGHH...
I AIN'T GOT TIME TO DEAL WITH NUTCASES LIKE YOU!
IF YOU'VE GOT THE TIME TO THINK UP GROSS SHIT LIKE THAT...
...USE IT TO COME UP WITH A WAY OUT—
YORO (WOBBLE)
GAKON (GA-KLUNK)
UIIIIN (WHRRRR)
HUH?
...I OPENED IT BEFORE COMING HERE.

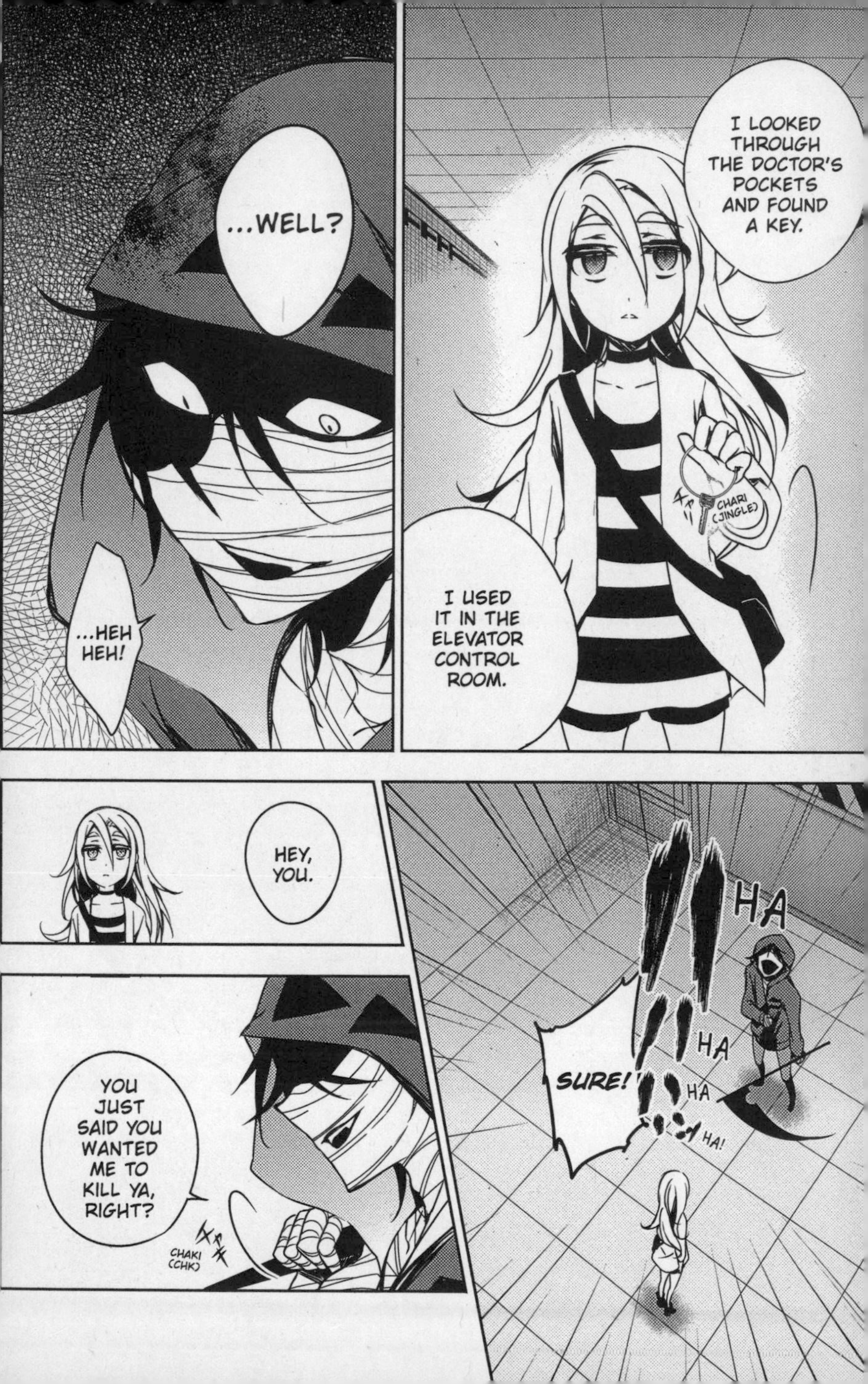
...WELL?
...HEH HEH!
I LOOKED THROUGH THE DOCTOR'S POCKETS AND FOUND A KEY.
CHARI (JINGLE)
I USED IT IN THE ELEVATOR CONTROL ROOM.
HEY, YOU.
YOU JUST SAID YOU WANTED ME TO KILL YA, RIGHT?
CHAKI (CHK)
SURE!
HA
HA
HA
HA!

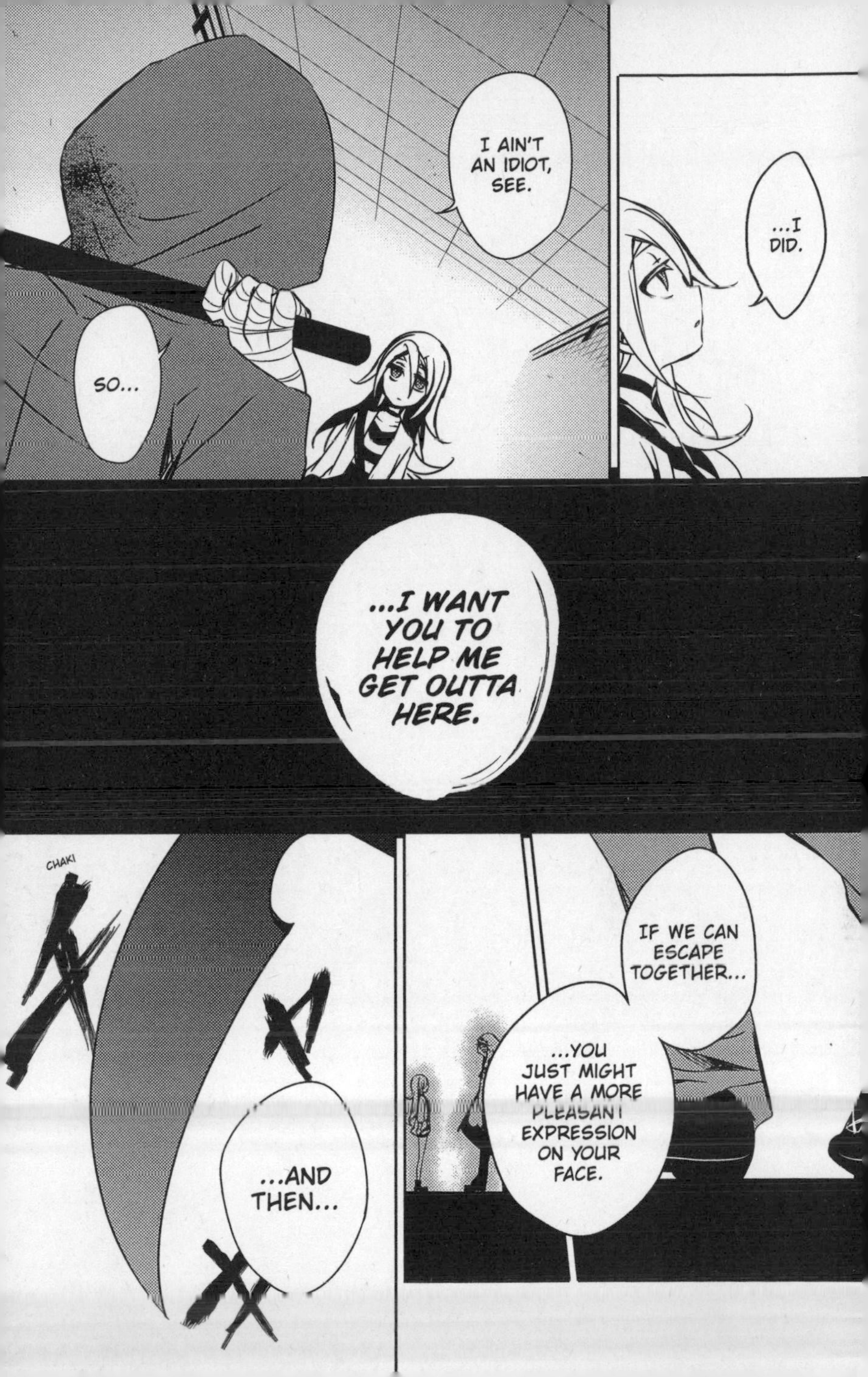
...I DID.
I AIN'T AN IDIOT, SEE.
SO...
...I WANT YOU TO HELP ME GET OUTTA HERE.
IF WE CAN ESCAPE TOGETHER...
...YOU JUST MIGHT HAVE A MORE PLEASANT EXPRESSION ON YOUR FACE.
CHAKI
...AND THEN...

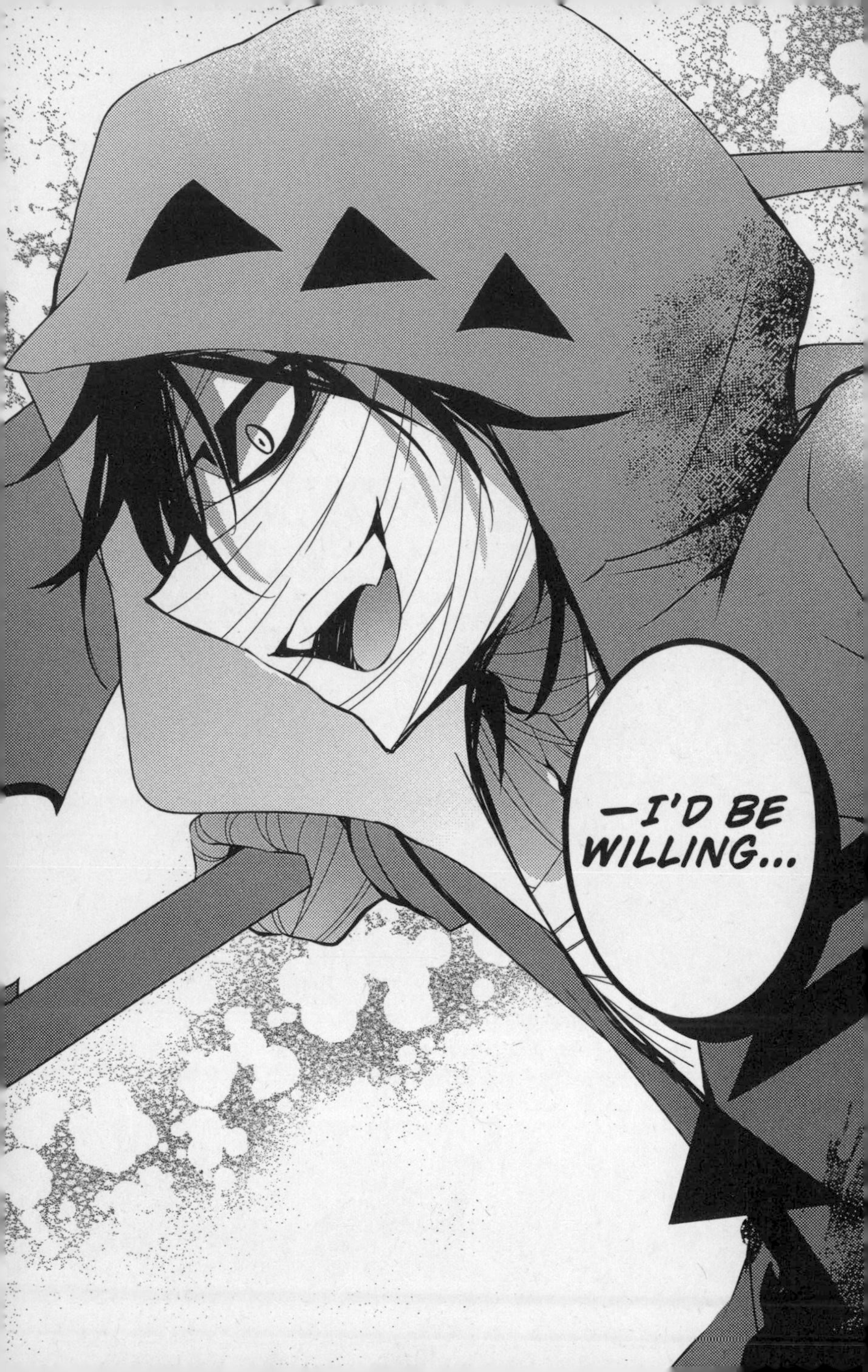
—I'D BE WILLING...

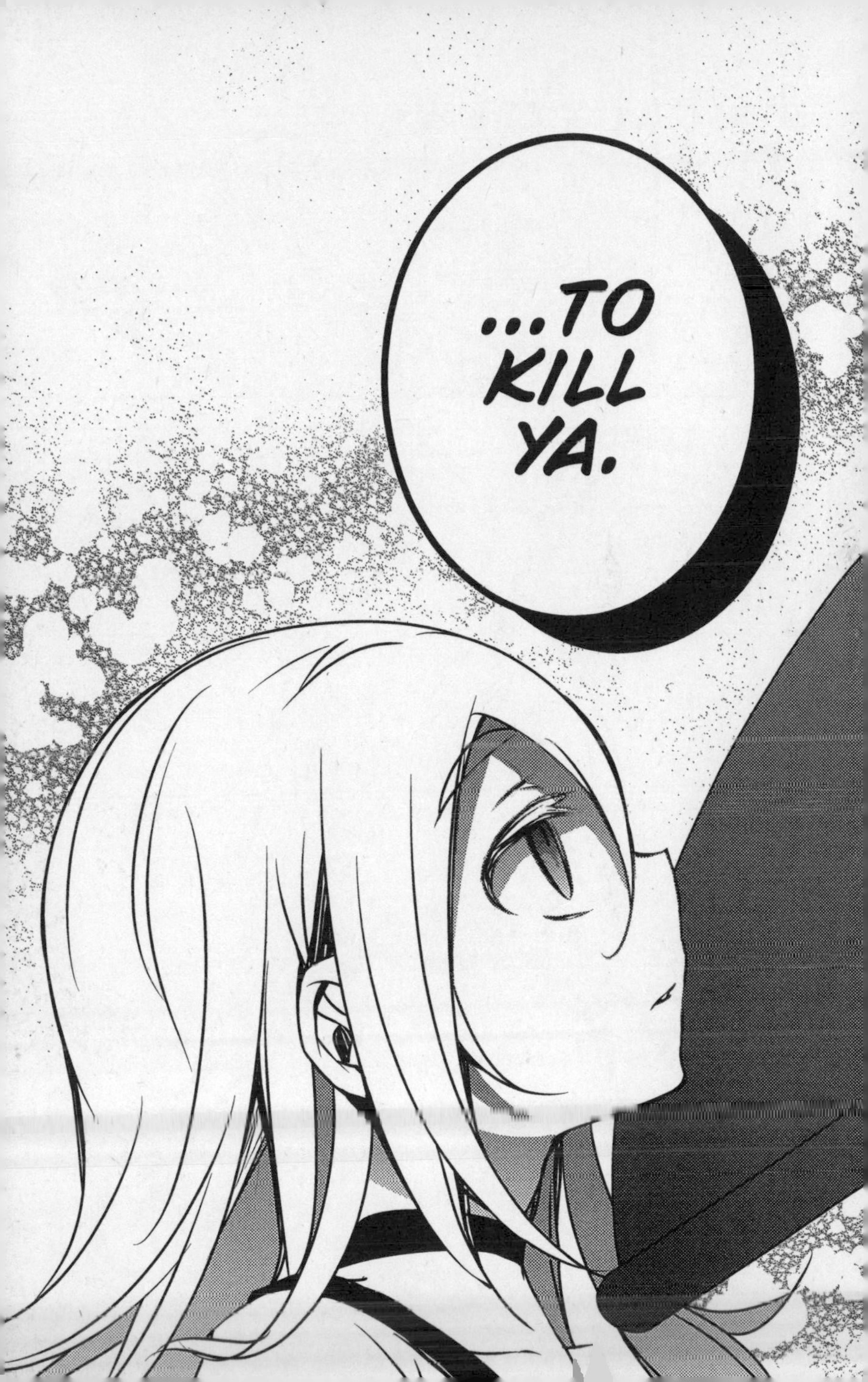
...TO KILL YA.

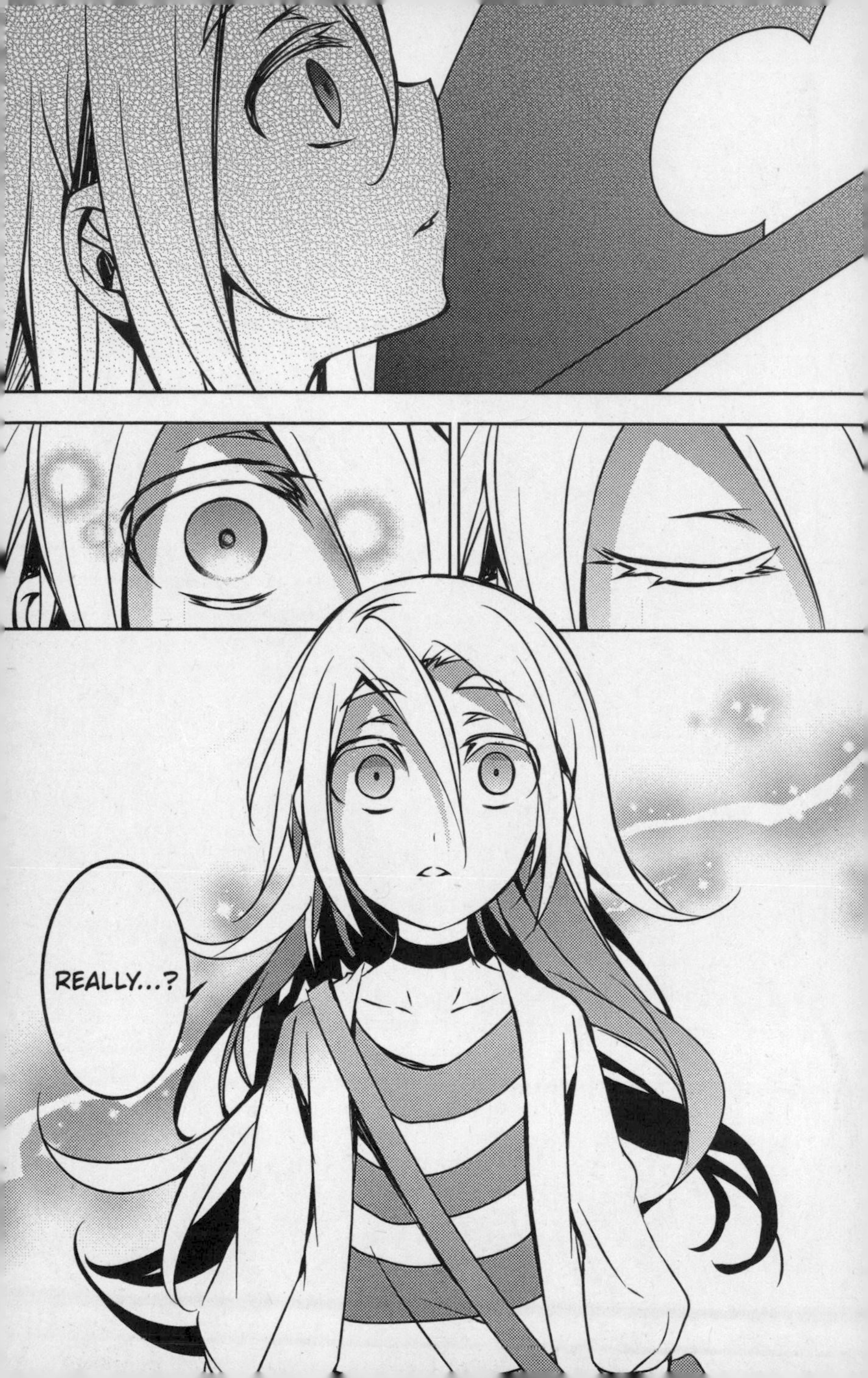
REALLY...?

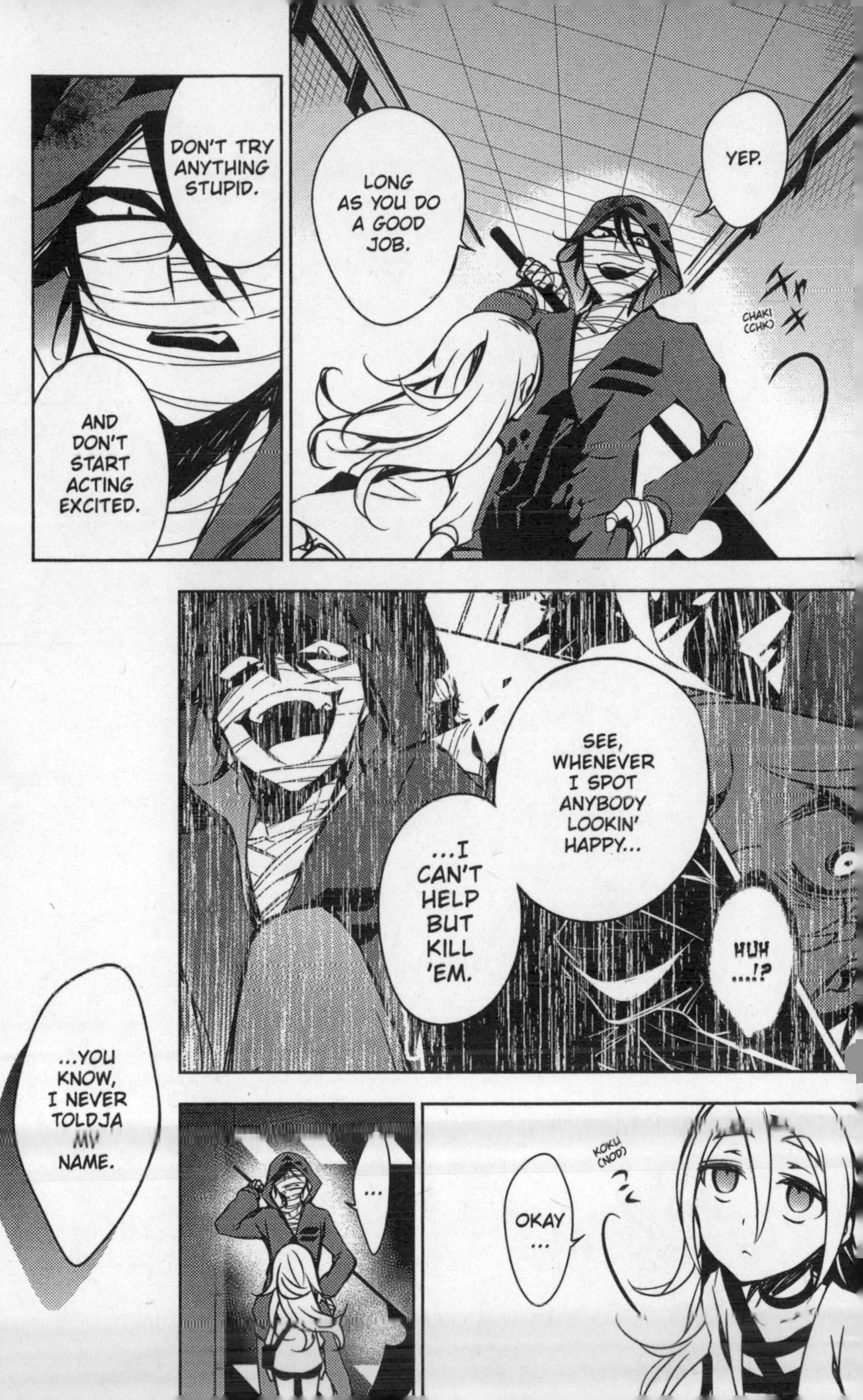
YEP.
LONG AS YOU DO A GOOD JOB.
CHAKI (CHK)
DON'T TRY ANYTHING STUPID.
AND DON'T START ACTING EXCITED.
SEE, WHENEVER I SPOT ANYBODY LOOKIN' HAPPY...
...I CAN'T HELP BUT KILL 'EM.
HUH ...!?
KOKU (NOD)
OKAY ...
...
...YOU KNOW, I NEVER TOLDJA MY NAME.

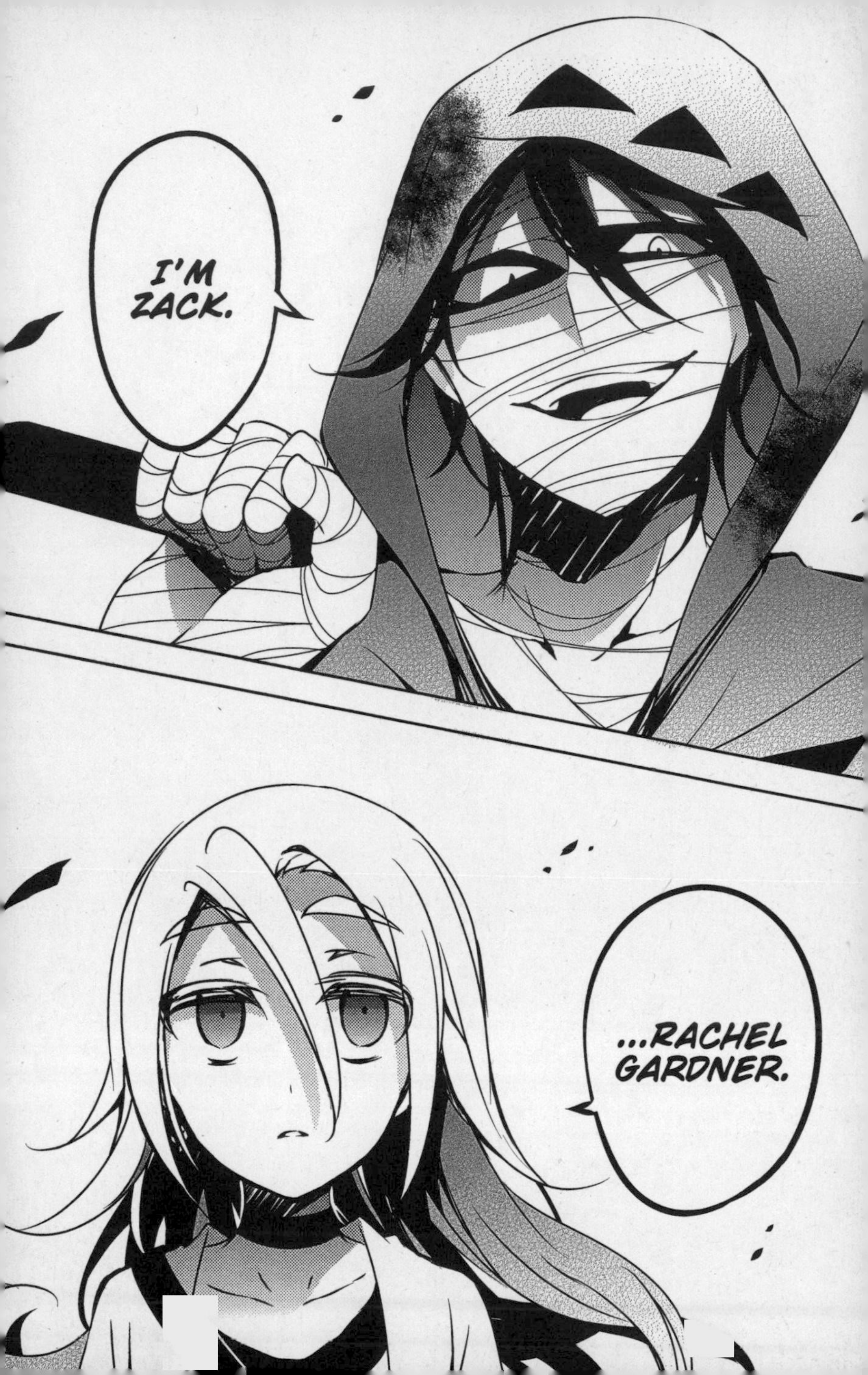
I'M ZACK.
...RACHEL GARDNER.

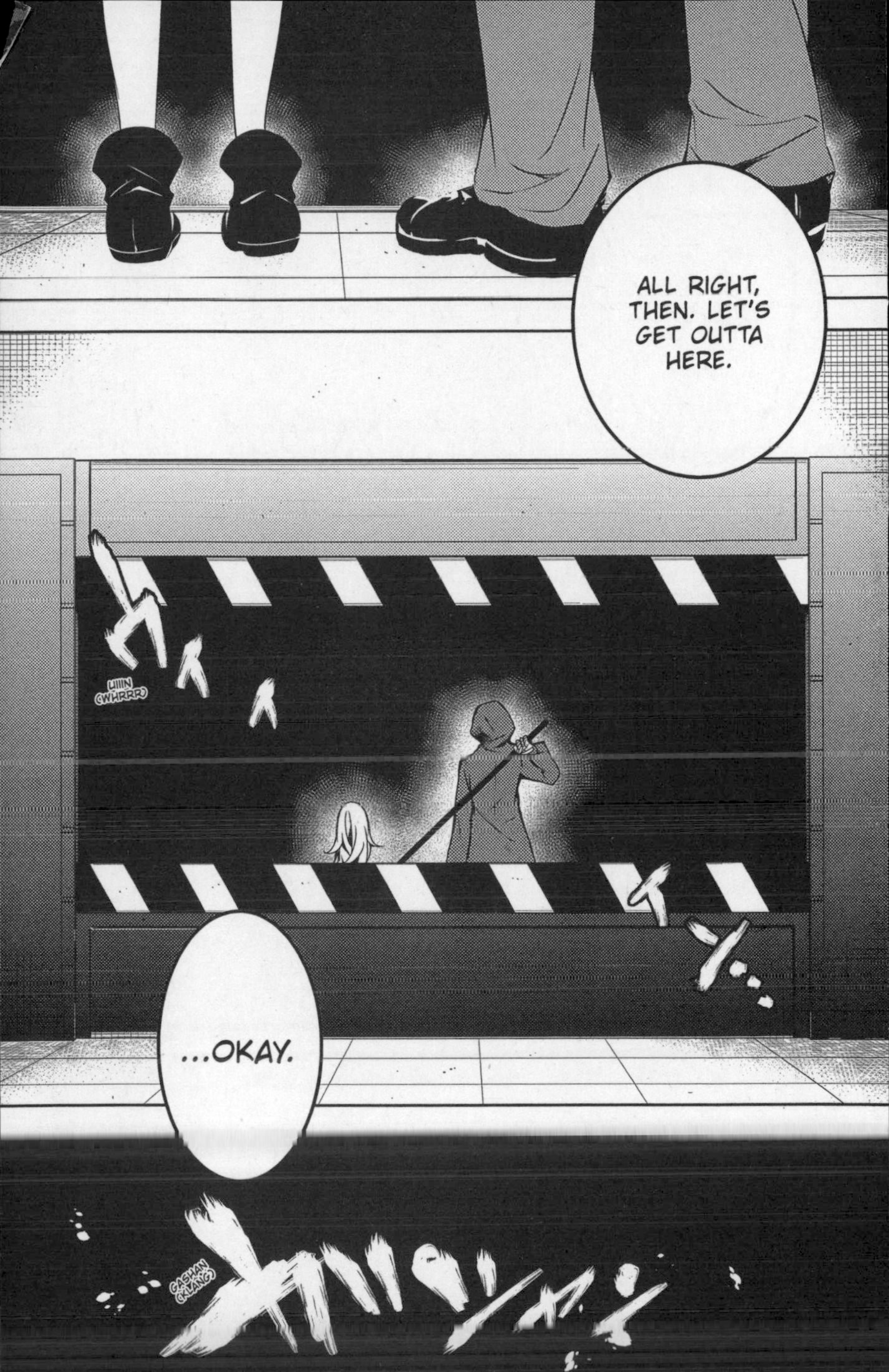
ALL RIGHT, THEN. LET'S GET OUTTA HERE.
UIIIN (WHRRR)
...OKAY.
GASHAN (KLANG)

INSIDE STORY OF PRODUCTION VOL.3

BY MAKOTO SANADA

Three characters appear in this first volume: Rachel, Zack, and Danny. We'll eventually end up meeting the residents of other floors, but these three were the most fully-formed characters at the time I was writing the initial plot for this story, even if they were somewhat vague. (Though, it seems obvious Rachel and Zack would be the most developed.)

The characters all have some degree of story to their past. Zack and Rachel's backstories are gradually revealed within the game, but unlike the game, the manga goes into Danny's past in detail, showing why he's so fixated on eyes and what made him so twisted.

After the game's production began and I started working on it, I started thinking that he may have ended up as the character with the deepest emotions in this title. Zack also talks a lot more than he did in the original plot, but Danny became even chattier than him. He also had more drawings of his face, as if to match that range of emotions. (Though, there were also the additional files for different eye graphics.)

My favorite line in the game's first episode is Danny's crazy and dangerous line: "My eyes are alexandrite."

[Chapter 4]
Destroyer

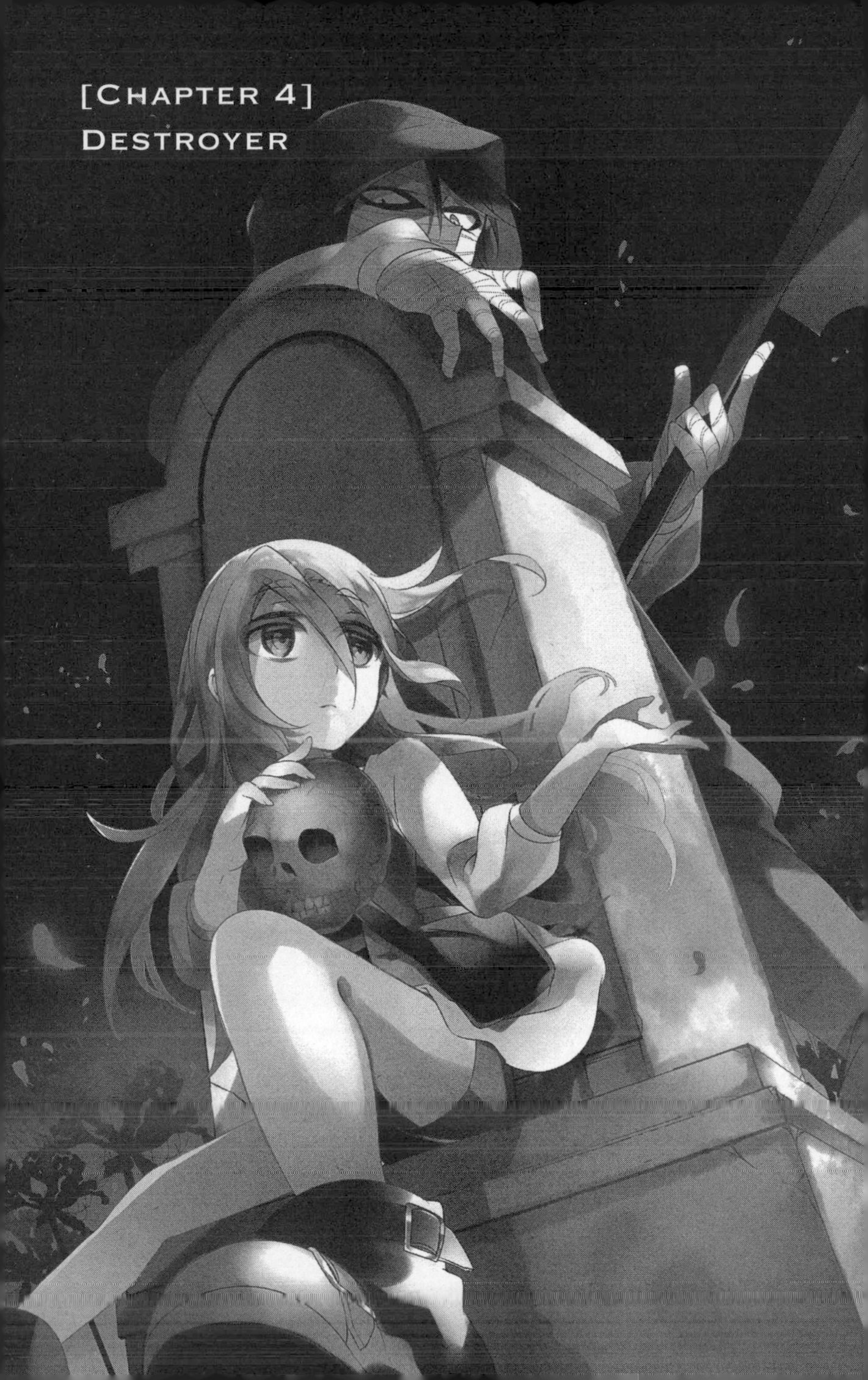

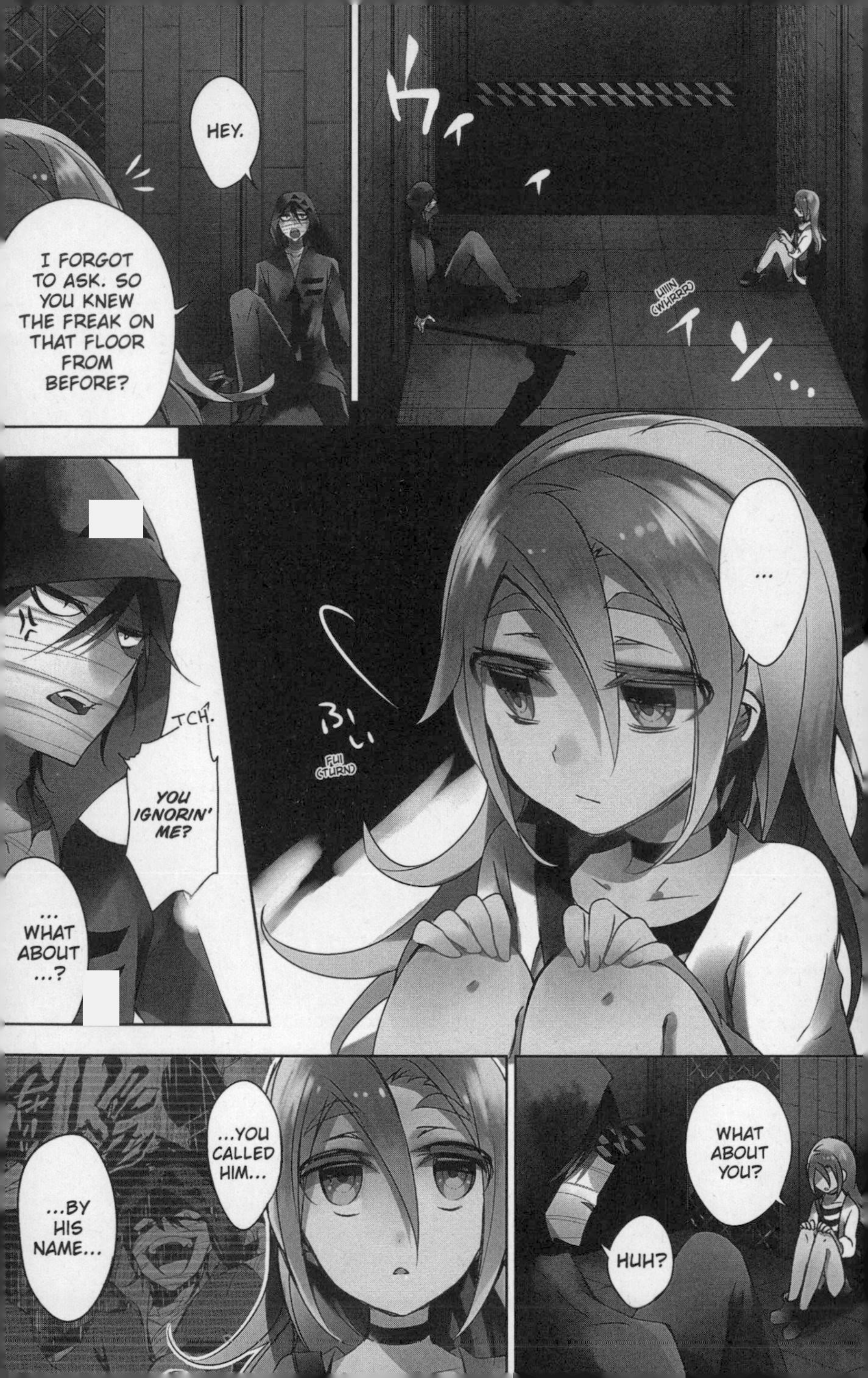
UIIIN (WHRRR)
HEY.
I FORGOT TO ASK. SO YOU KNEW THE FREAK ON THAT FLOOR FROM BEFORE?
...
FUI (TURN)
TCH.
YOU IGNORIN' ME?
...WHAT ABOUT ...?
WHAT ABOUT YOU?
HUH?
...YOU CALLED HIM...
...BY HIS NAME...

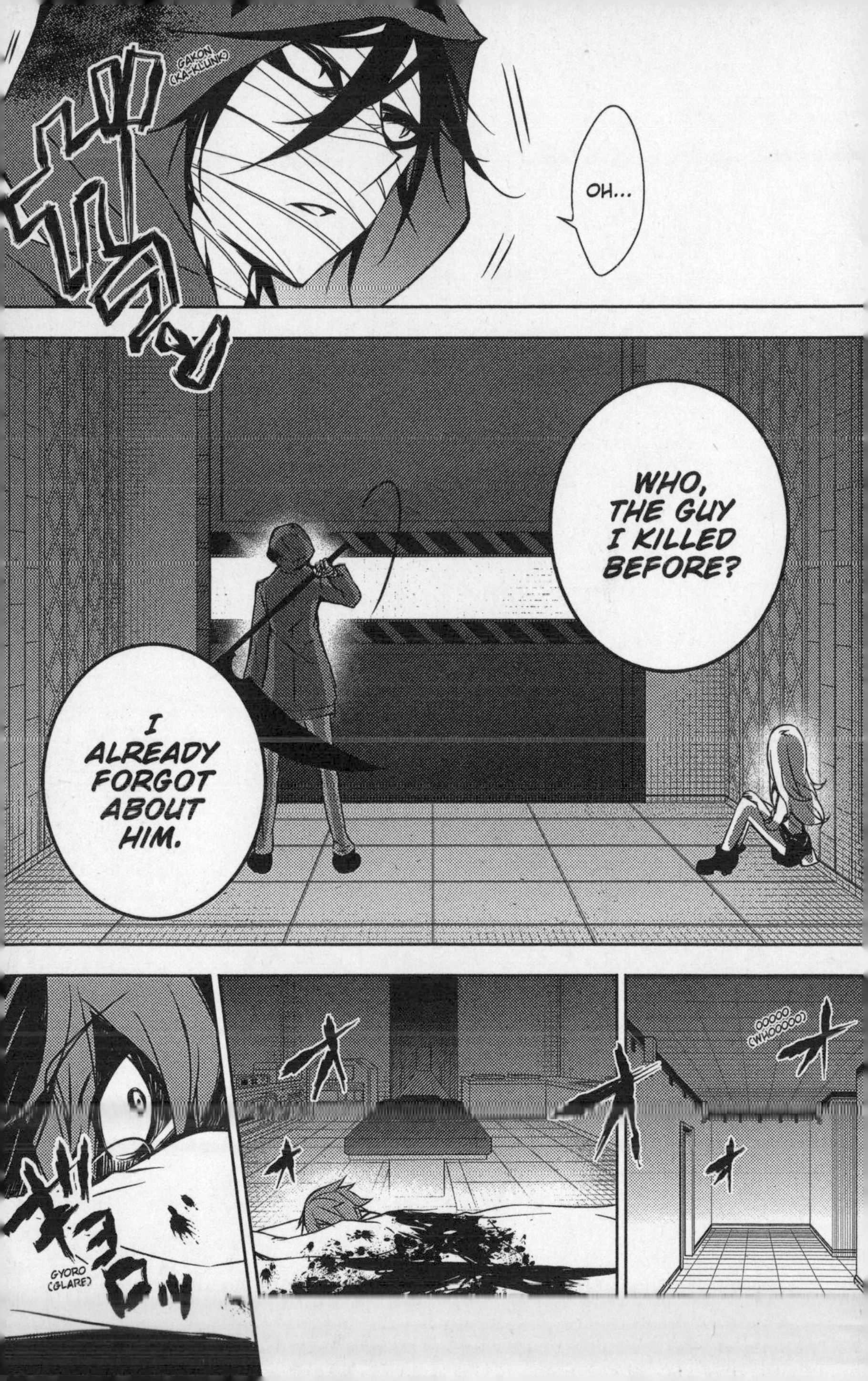
GAKON (KA-KLUNK)
OH...
WHO, THE GUY I KILLED BEFORE?
I ALREADY FORGOT ABOUT HIM.
OOOOO (WHOOOOO)
GYORO (GLARE)

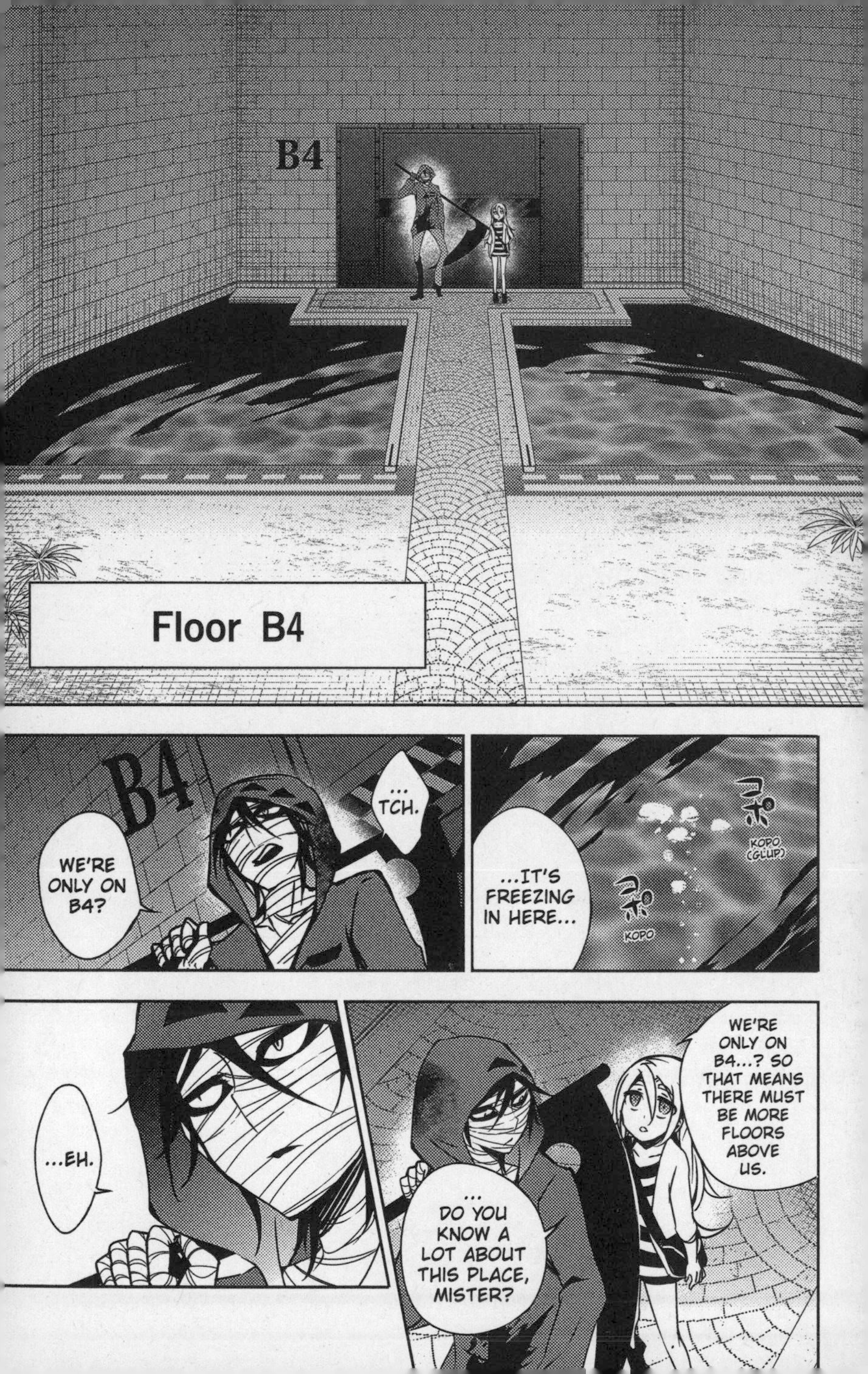
B4
Floor B4
KOPO (GLUP)
...IT'S FREEZING IN HERE...
KOPO
... TCH.
B4
WE'RE ONLY ON B4?
WE'RE ONLY ON B4...? SO THAT MEANS THERE MUST BE MORE FLOORS ABOVE US.
... DO YOU KNOW A LOT ABOUT THIS PLACE, MISTER?
...EH.

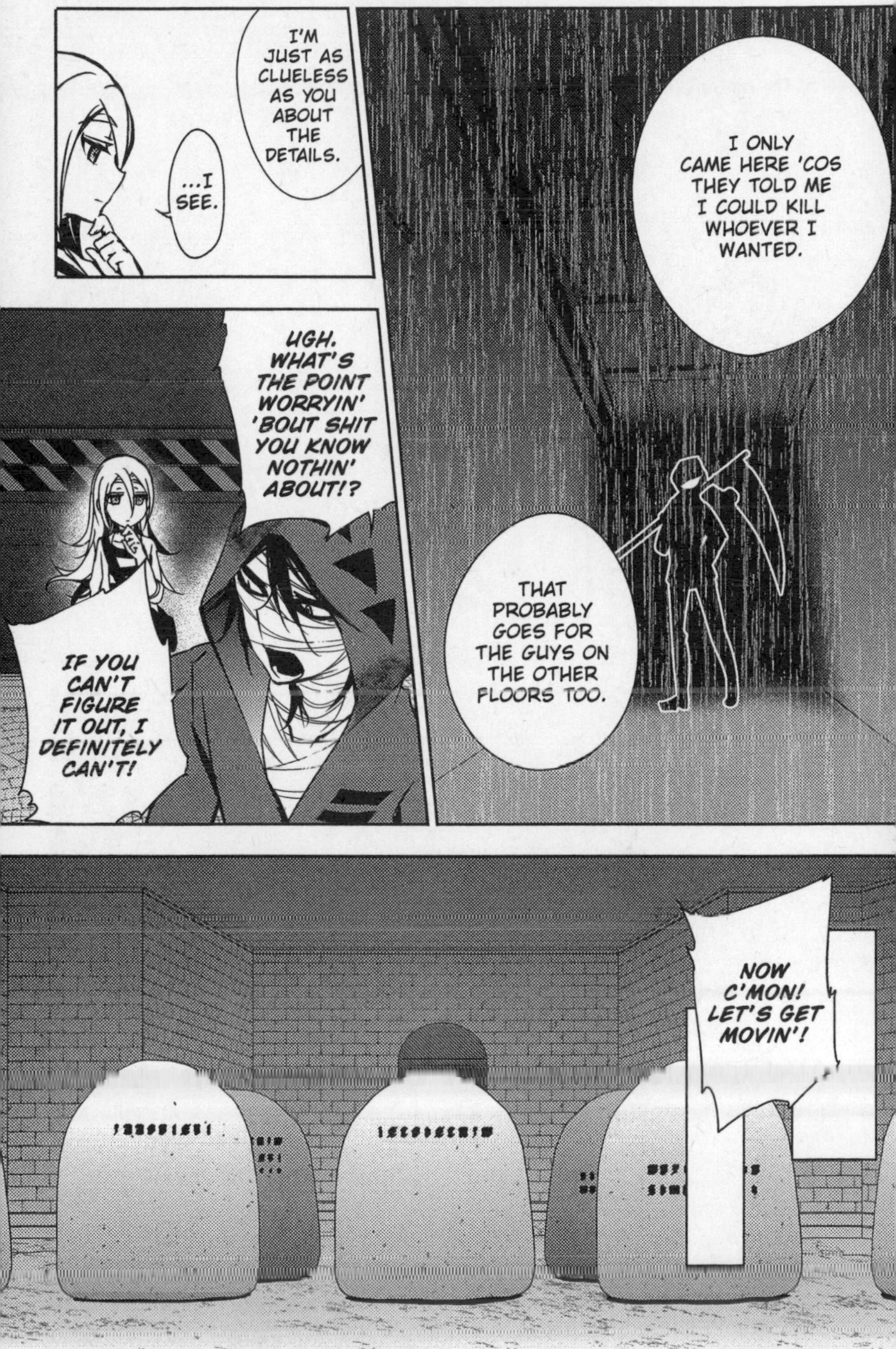
I ONLY CAME HERE 'COS THEY TOLD ME I COULD KILL WHOEVER I WANTED.
THAT PROBABLY GOES FOR THE GUYS ON THE OTHER FLOORS TOO.
I'M JUST AS CLUELESS AS YOU ABOUT THE DETAILS.
...I SEE.
UGH. WHAT'S THE POINT WORRYIN' 'BOUT SHIT YOU KNOW NOTHIN' ABOUT!?
IF YOU CAN'T FIGURE IT OUT, I DEFINITELY CAN'T!
NOW C'MON! LET'S GET MOVIN'!

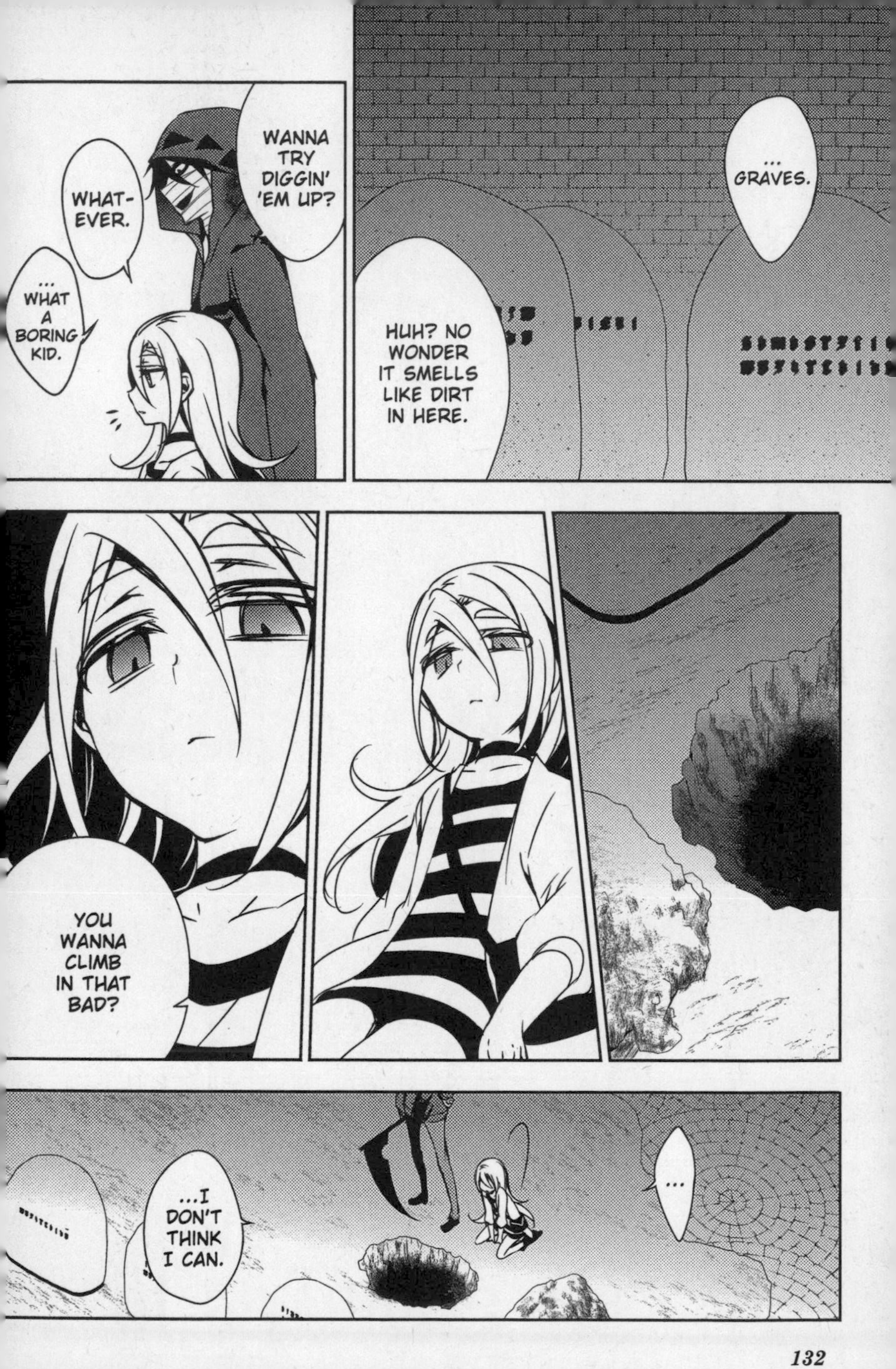
...GRAVES.
HUH? NO WONDER IT SMELLS LIKE DIRT IN HERE.
WANNA TRY DIGGIN' 'EM UP?
WHAT-EVER.
...WHAT A BORING KID.
YOU WANNA CLIMB IN THAT BAD?
...
...I DON'T THINK I CAN.

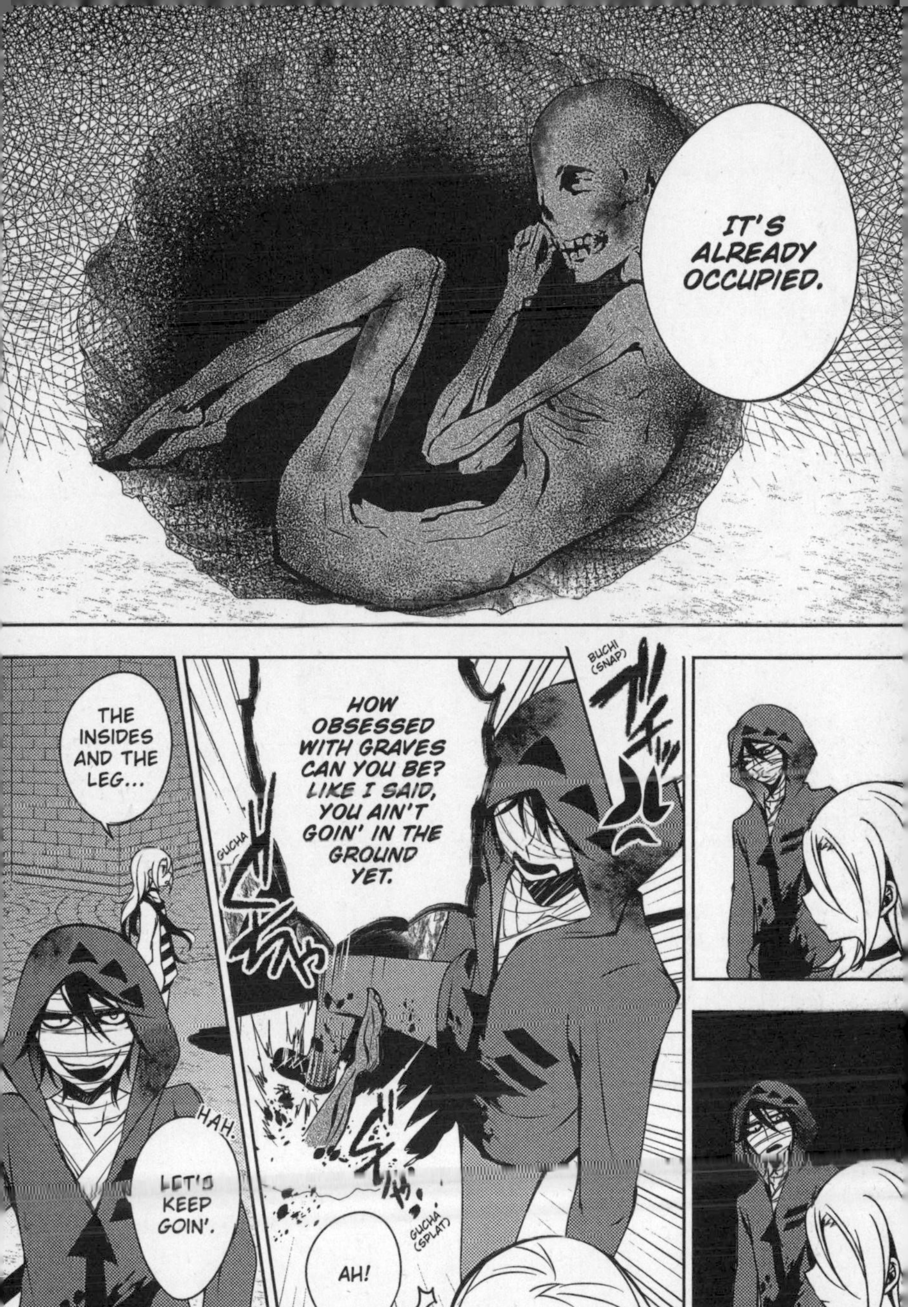
IT'S ALREADY OCCUPIED.
BUCHI (SNAP)
HOW OBSESSED WITH GRAVES CAN YOU BE? LIKE I SAID, YOU AIN'T GOIN' IN THE GROUND YET.
GUCHA
GUCHA (SPLAT)
AH!
THE INSIDES AND THE LEG...
HAH.
LET'S KEEP GOIN'.

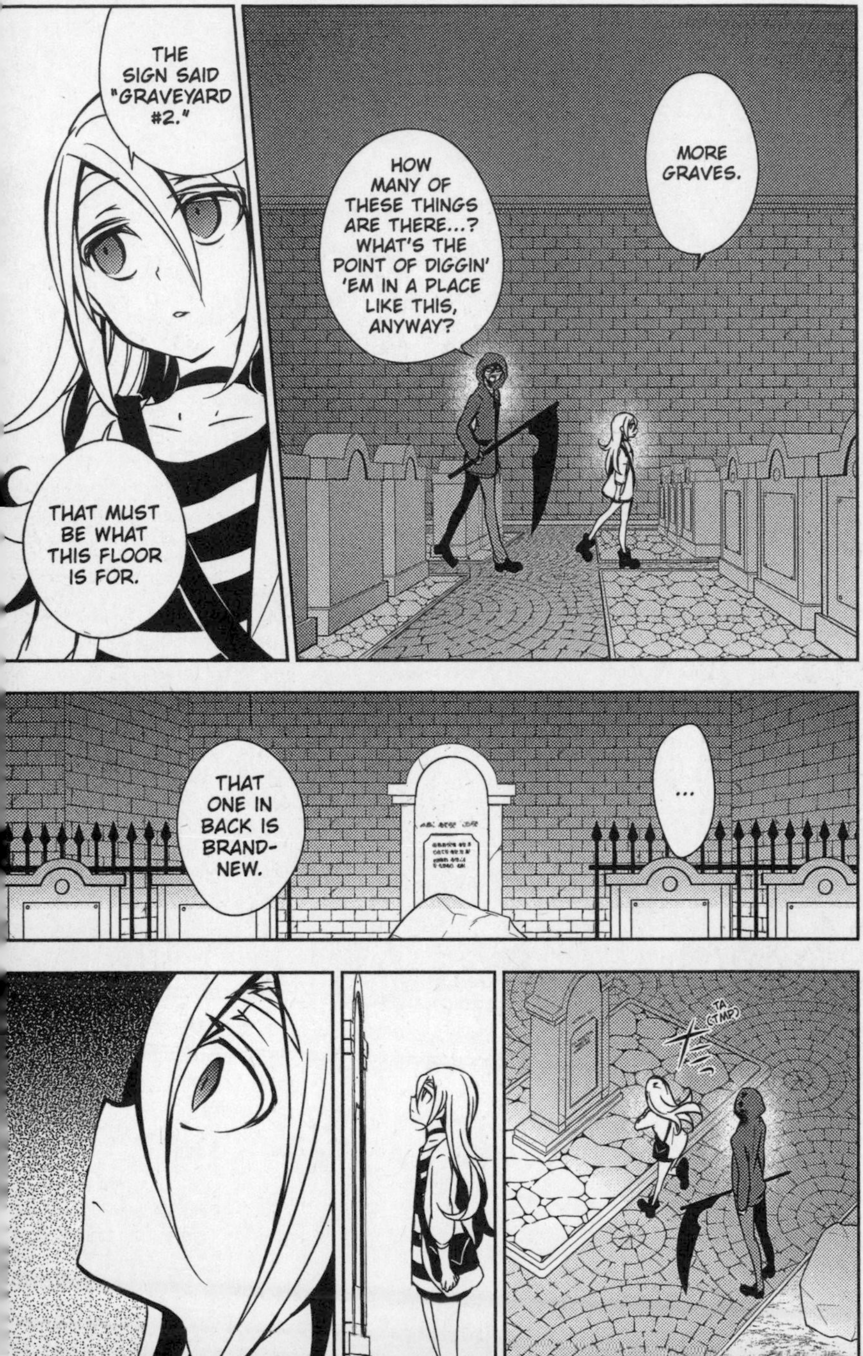
MORE GRAVES.
HOW MANY OF THESE THINGS ARE THERE...? WHAT'S THE POINT OF DIGGIN' 'EM IN A PLACE LIKE THIS, ANYWAY?
THE SIGN SAID "GRAVEYARD #2."
THAT MUST BE WHAT THIS FLOOR IS FOR.
...
THAT ONE IN BACK IS BRAND-NEW.
TA (STMP)

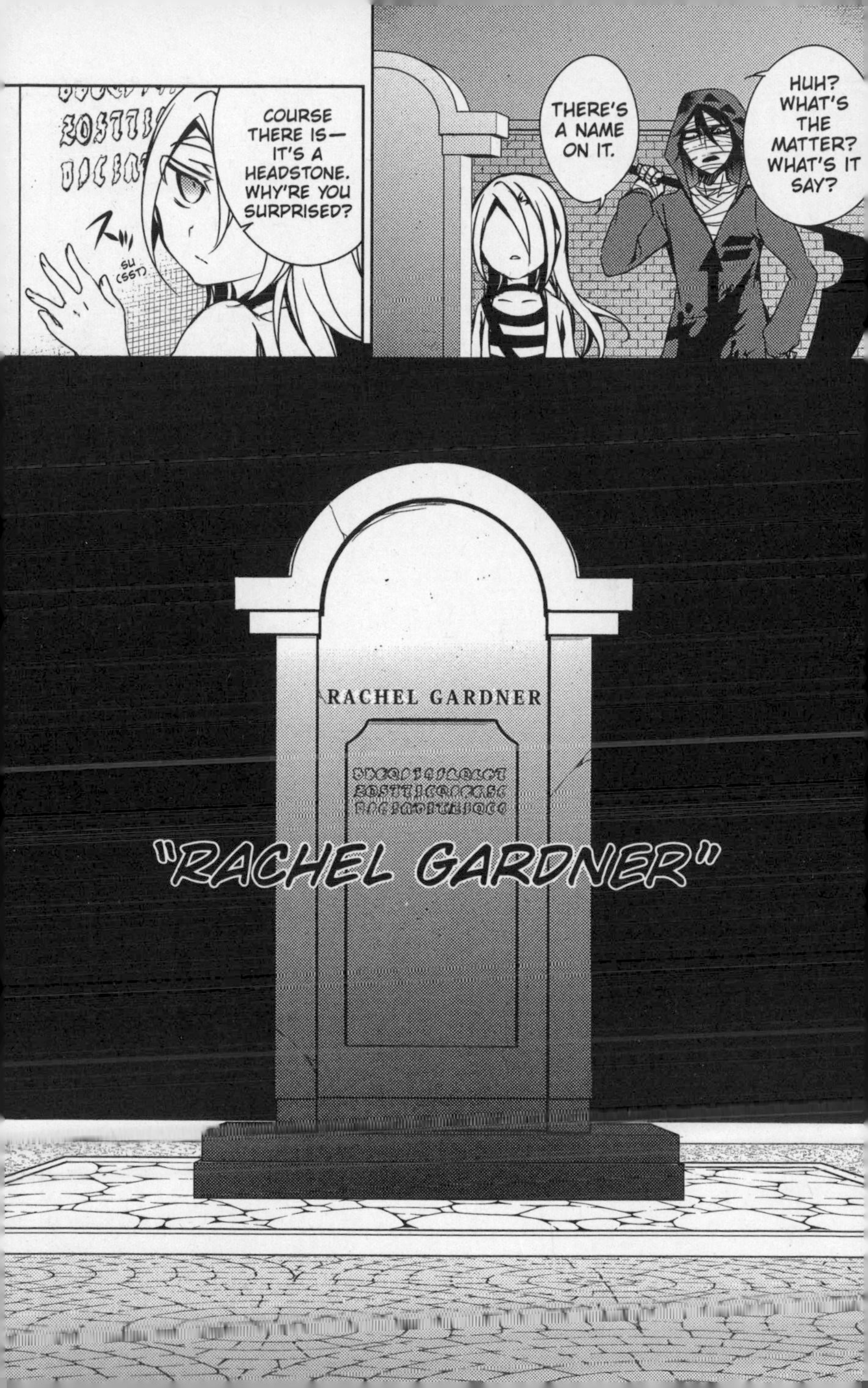
HUH? WHAT'S THE MATTER? WHAT'S IT SAY?
THERE'S A NAME ON IT.
COURSE THERE IS—IT'S A HEADSTONE. WHY'RE YOU SURPRISED?
SU (SST)
RACHEL GARDNER
"RACHEL GARDNER"

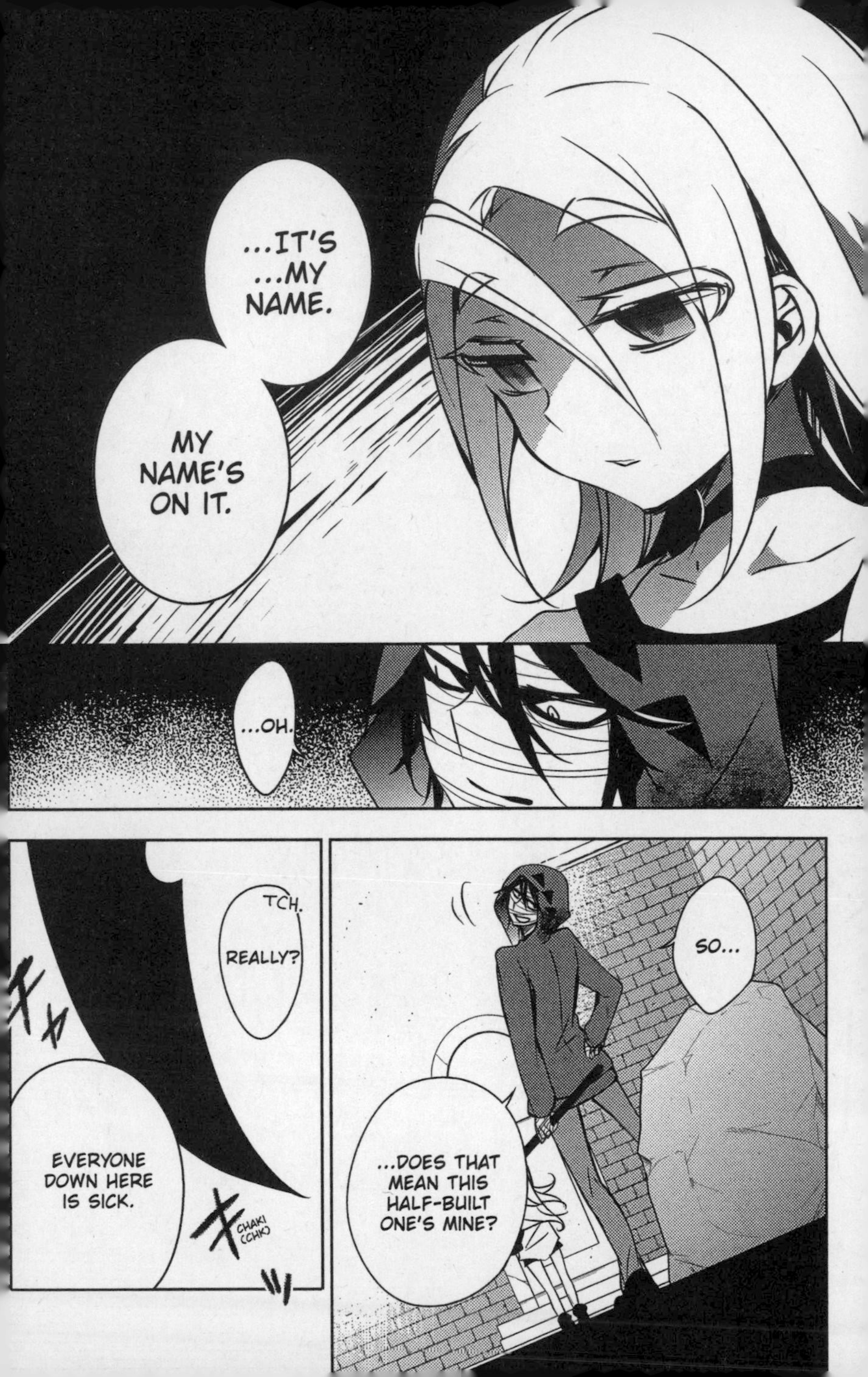
...IT'S ...MY NAME.
MY NAME'S ON IT.
...OH.
SO...
...DOES THAT MEAN THIS HALF-BUILT ONE'S MINE?
TCH.
REALLY?
CHAKI (CHK)
EVERYONE DOWN HERE IS SICK.

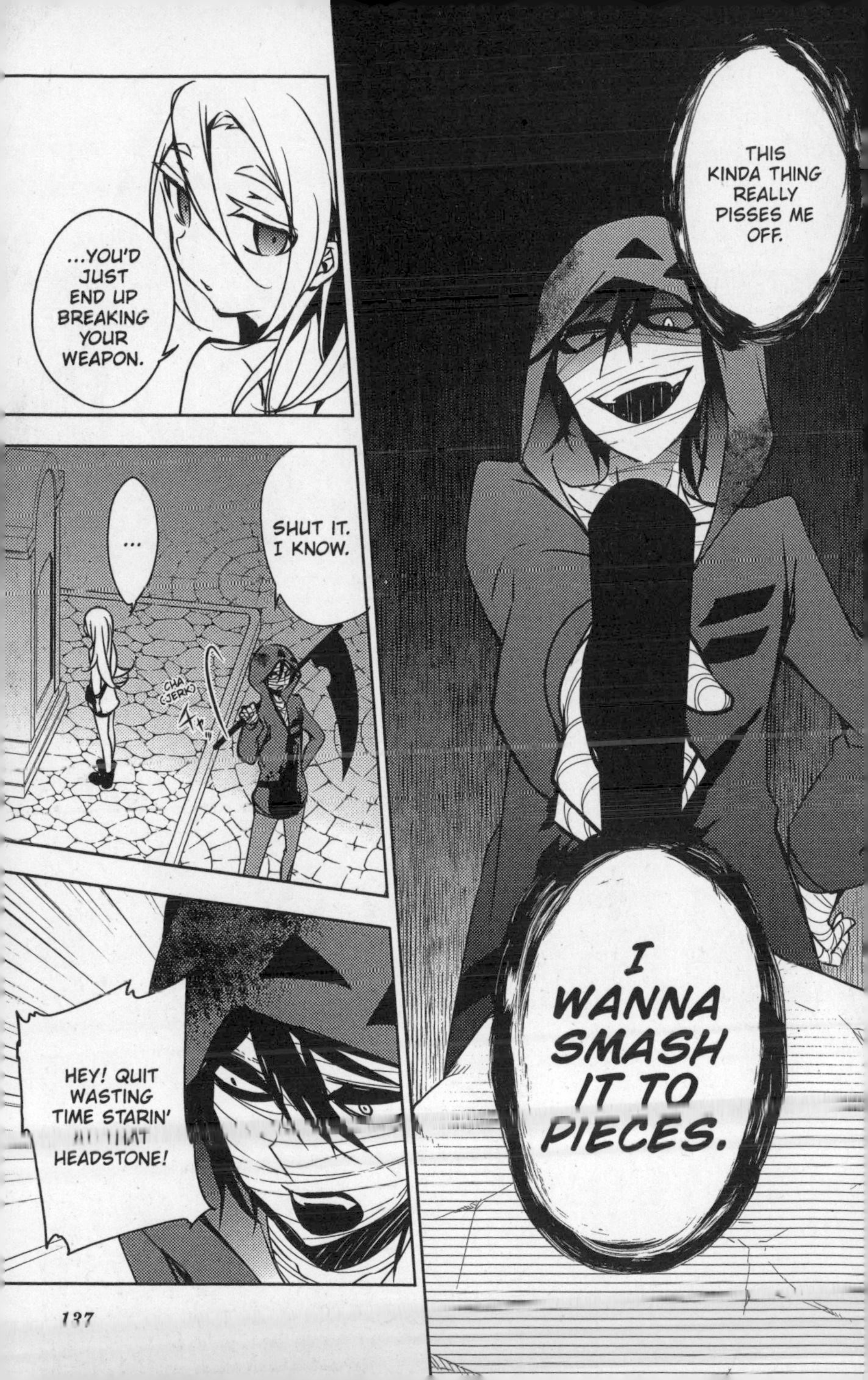
THIS KINDA THING REALLY PISSES ME OFF.
I WANNA SMASH IT TO PIECES.
...YOU'D JUST END UP BREAKING YOUR WEAPON.
SHUT IT. I KNOW.
...
CHA (JERK)
HEY! QUIT WASTING TIME STARIN' AT THAT HEADSTONE!

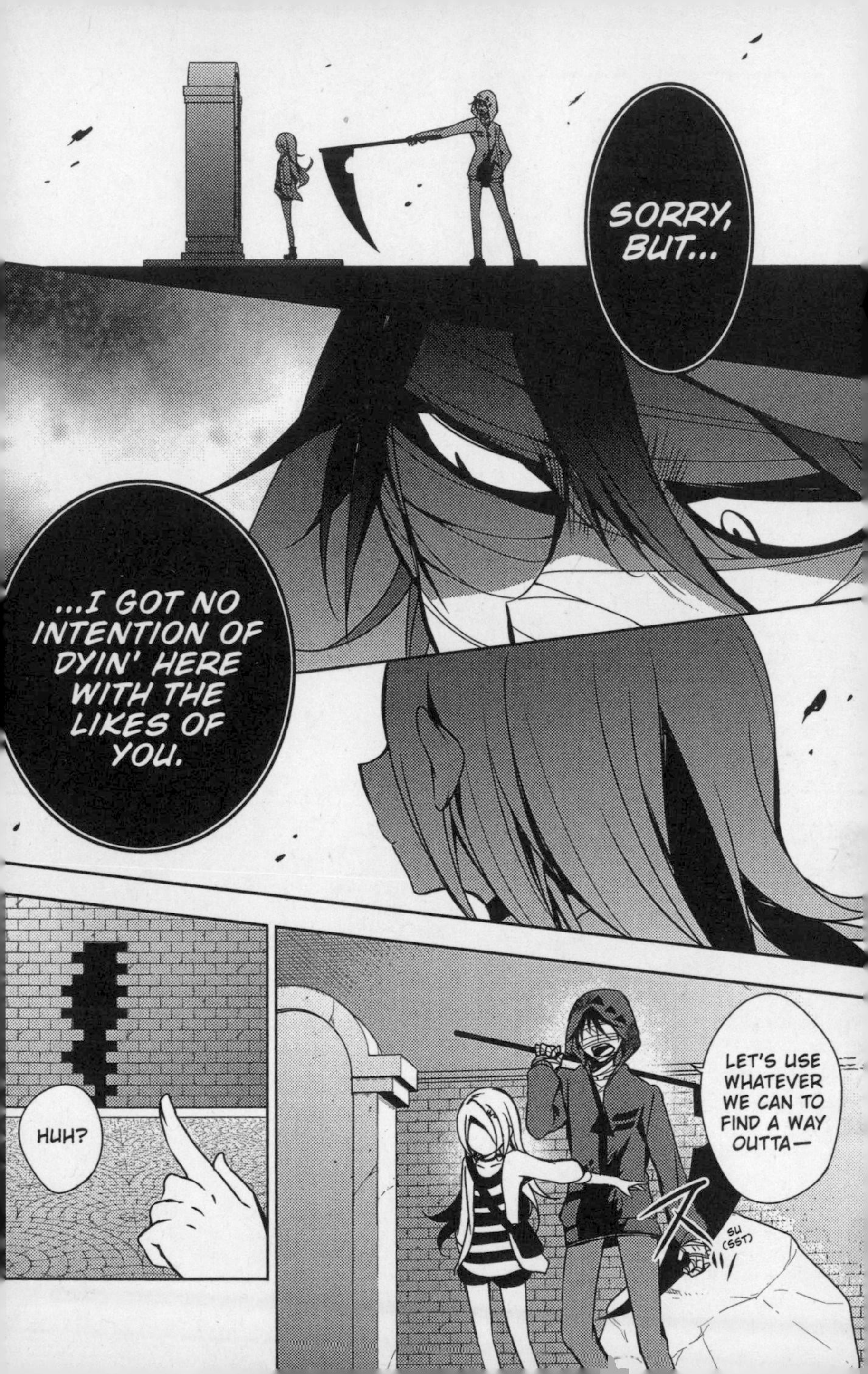
SORRY, BUT...
...I GOT NO INTENTION OF DYIN' HERE WITH THE LIKES OF YOU.
LET'S USE WHATEVER WE CAN TO FIND A WAY OUTTA—
SU (SST)
HUH?

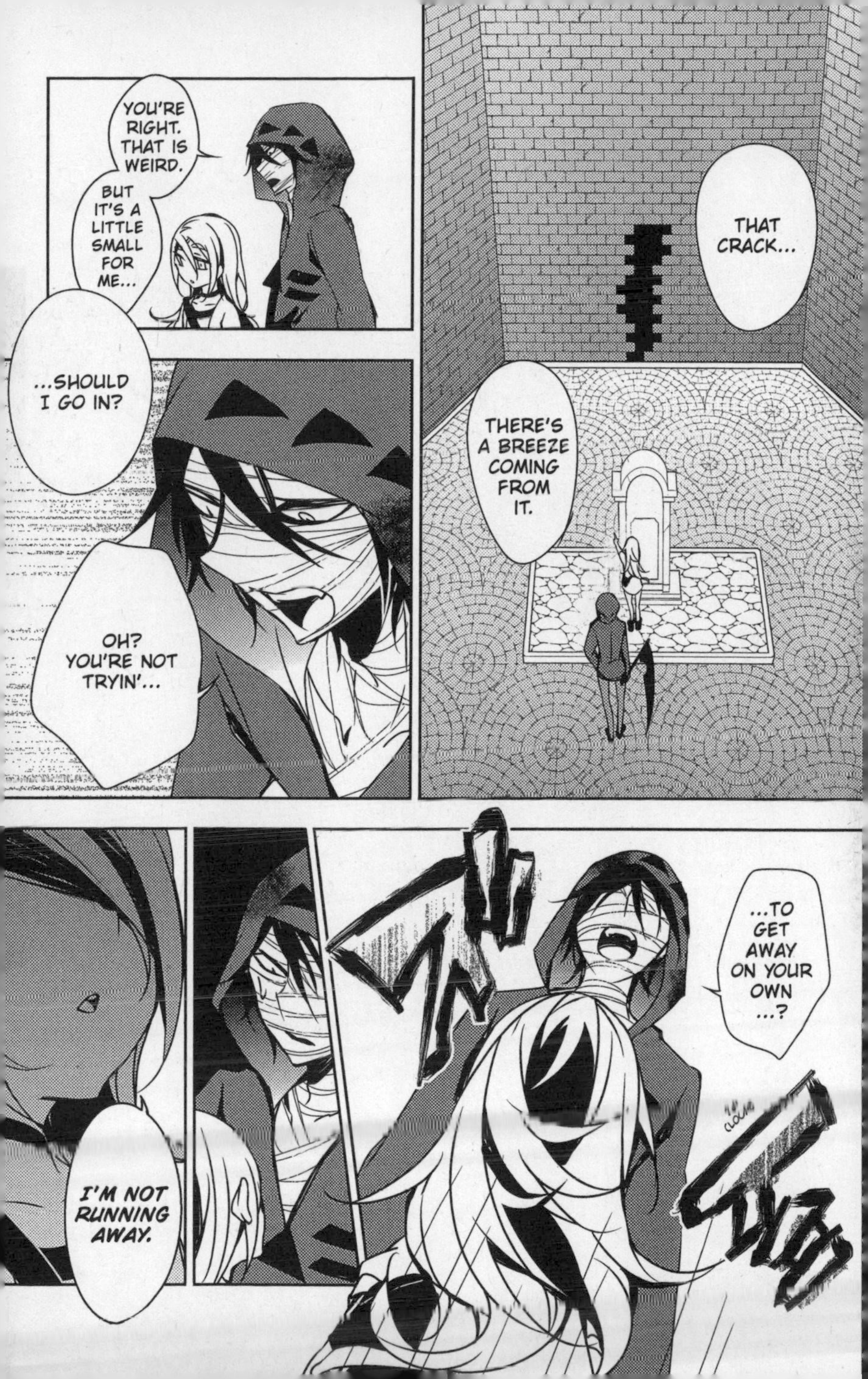
THAT CRACK...
THERE'S A BREEZE COMING FROM IT.
YOU'RE RIGHT. THAT IS WEIRD.
BUT IT'S A LITTLE SMALL FOR ME...
...SHOULD I GO IN?
OH? YOU'RE NOT TRYIN'...
...TO GET AWAY ON YOUR OWN ...?
I'M NOT RUNNING AWAY.

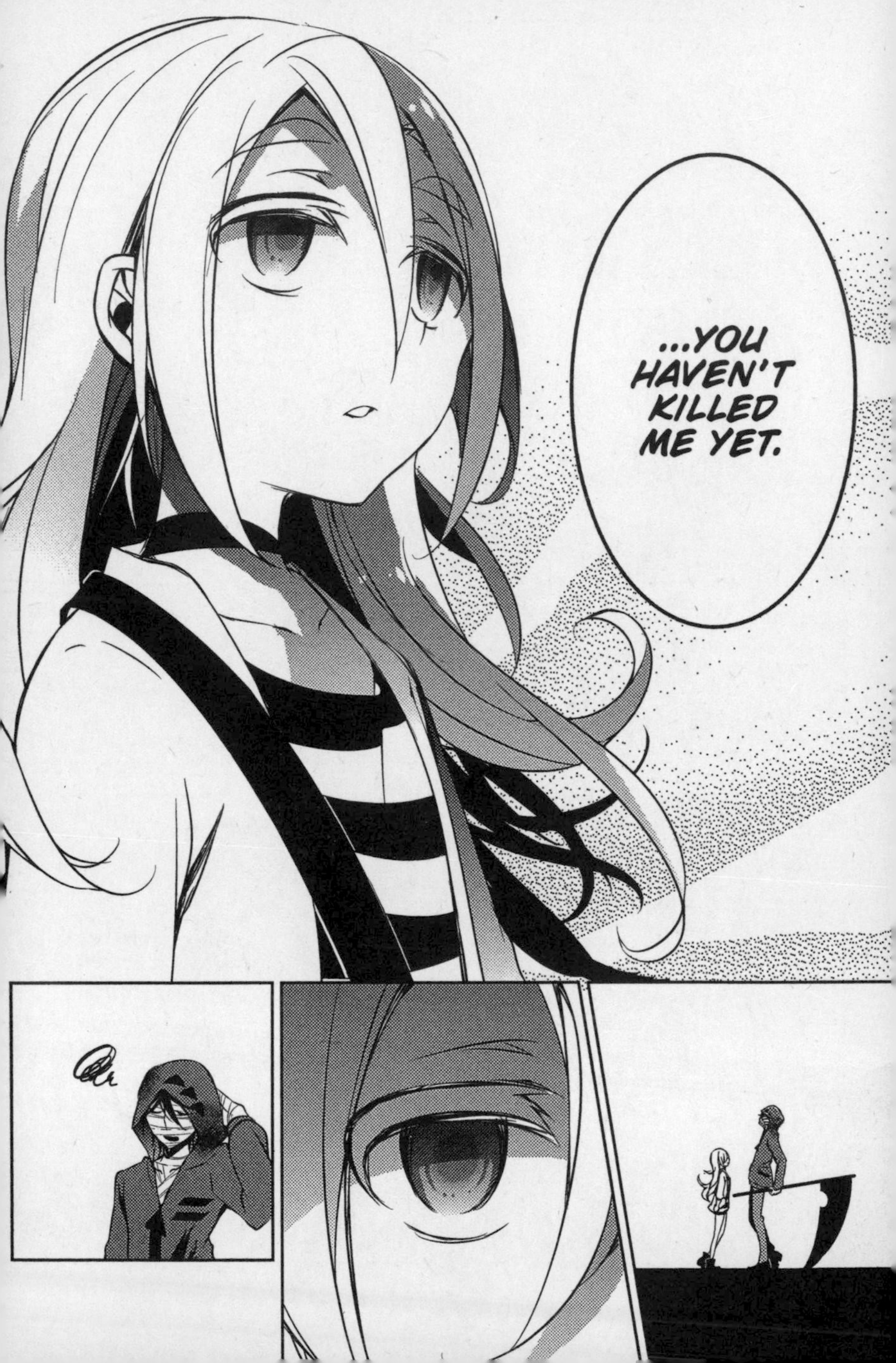
...YOU HAVEN'T KILLED ME YET.

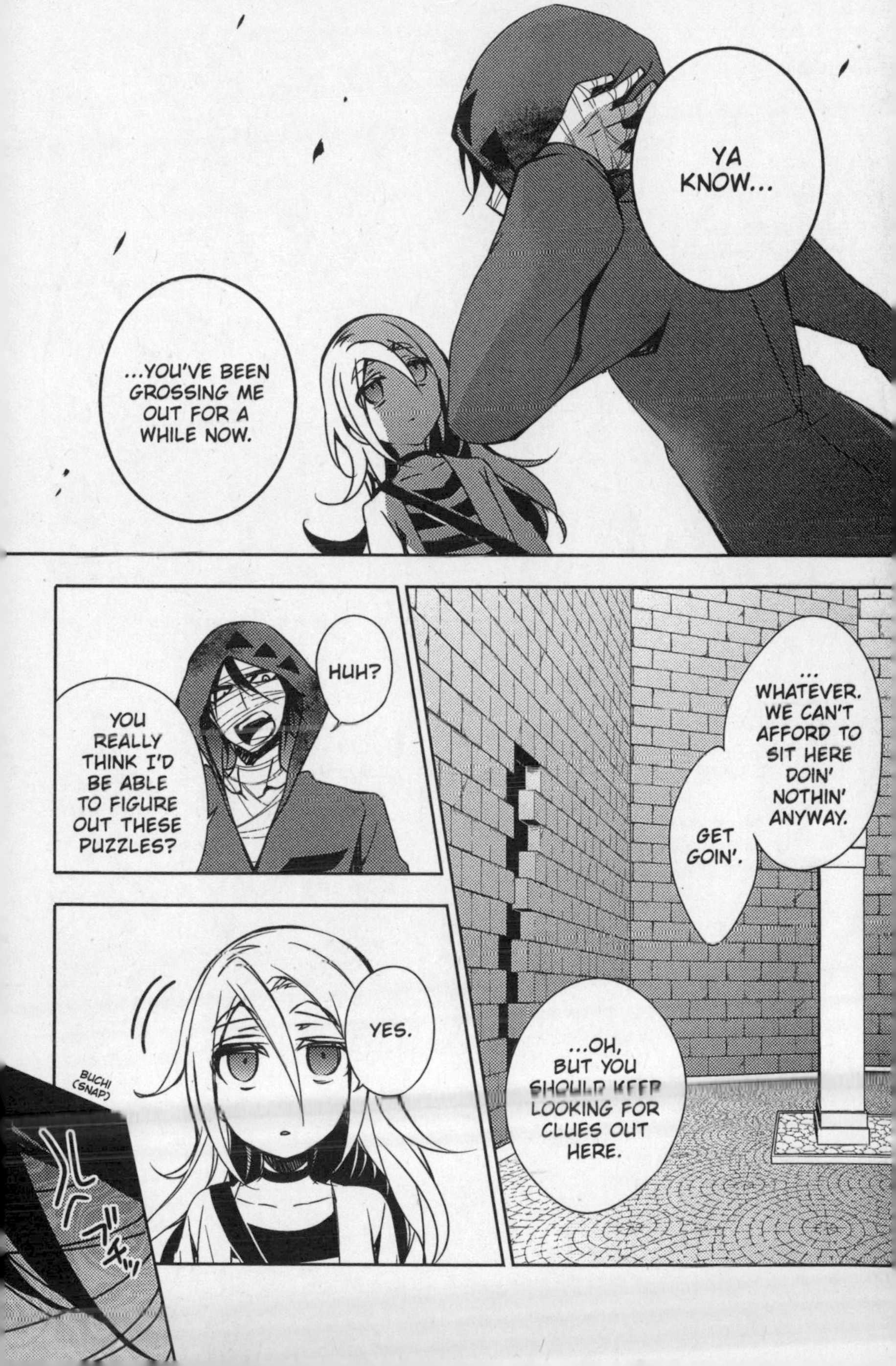
YA KNOW...
...YOU'VE BEEN GROSSING ME OUT FOR A WHILE NOW.
...WHATEVER. WE CAN'T AFFORD TO SIT HERE DOIN' NOTHIN' ANYWAY.
GET GOIN'.
...OH, BUT YOU SHOULD KEEP LOOKING FOR CLUES OUT HERE.
HUH?
YOU REALLY THINK I'D BE ABLE TO FIGURE OUT THESE PUZZLES?
YES.
BUCHI (SNAP)

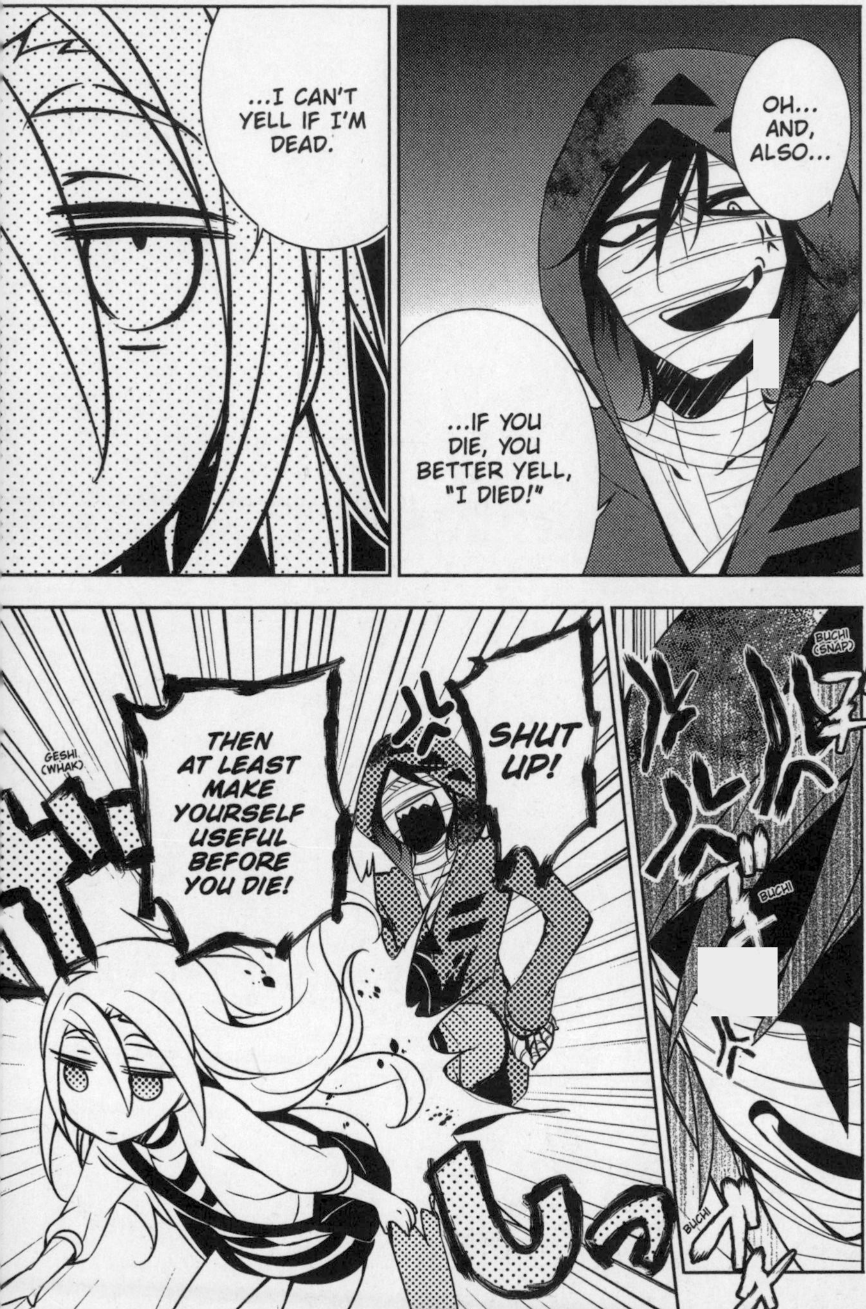
OH... AND, ALSO...
...IF YOU DIE, YOU BETTER YELL, "I DIED!"
...I CAN'T YELL IF I'M DEAD.
BUCHI (SNAP)
BUCHI
BUCHI
SHUT UP!
THEN AT LEAST MAKE YOURSELF USEFUL BEFORE YOU DIE!
GESHI (WHAK)

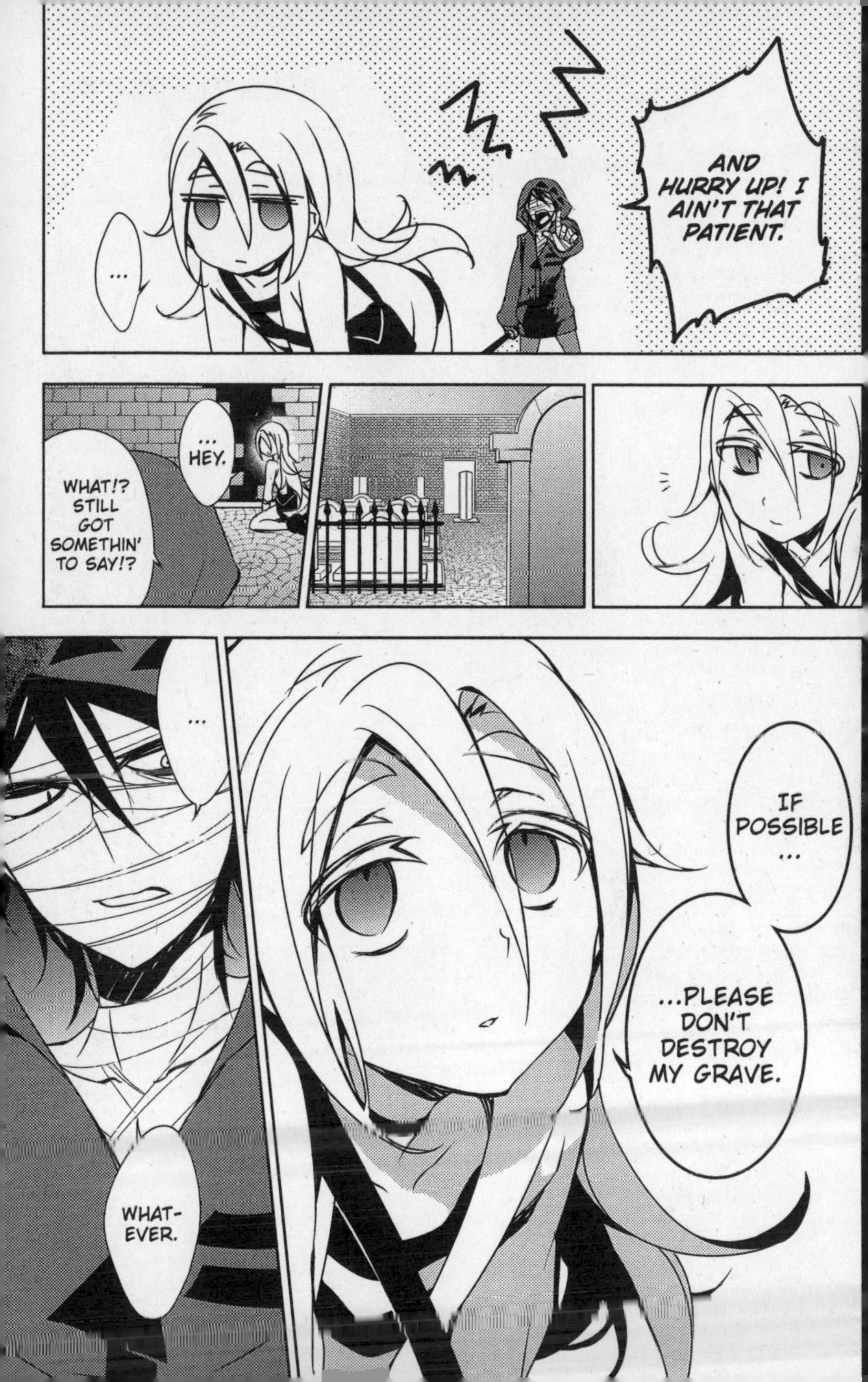
AND HURRY UP! I AIN'T THAT PATIENT.
...
... HEY.
WHAT!? STILL GOT SOMETHIN' TO SAY!?
IF POSSIBLE ...
...PLEASE DON'T DESTROY MY GRAVE.
...
WHAT-EVER.

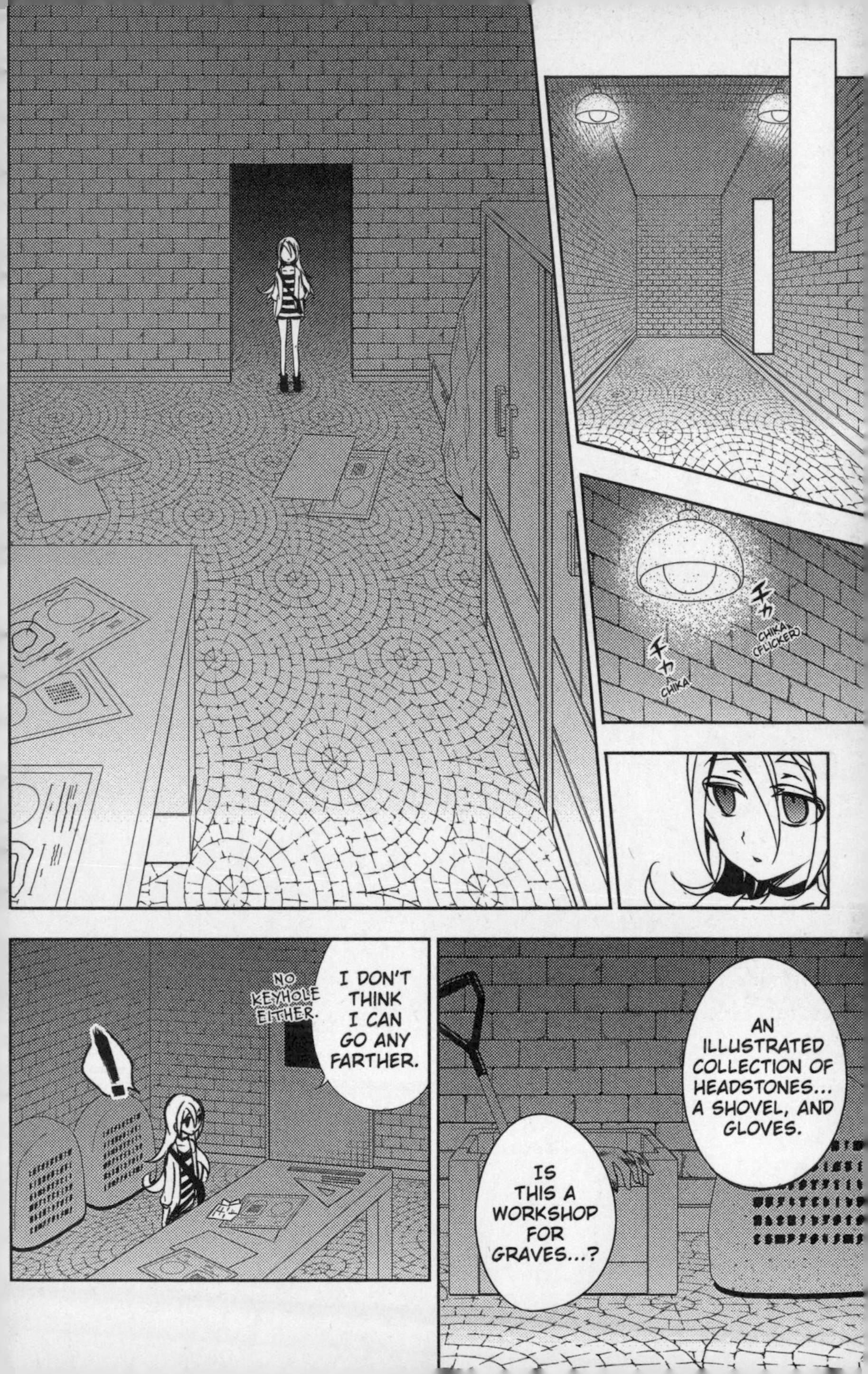
チカ
CHIKA (FLICKER)
チカ
CHIKA
AN ILLUSTRATED COLLECTION OF HEADSTONES... A SHOVEL, AND GLOVES.
IS THIS A WORKSHOP FOR GRAVES...?
I DON'T THINK I CAN GO ANY FARTHER.
NO KEYHOLE EITHER.
!

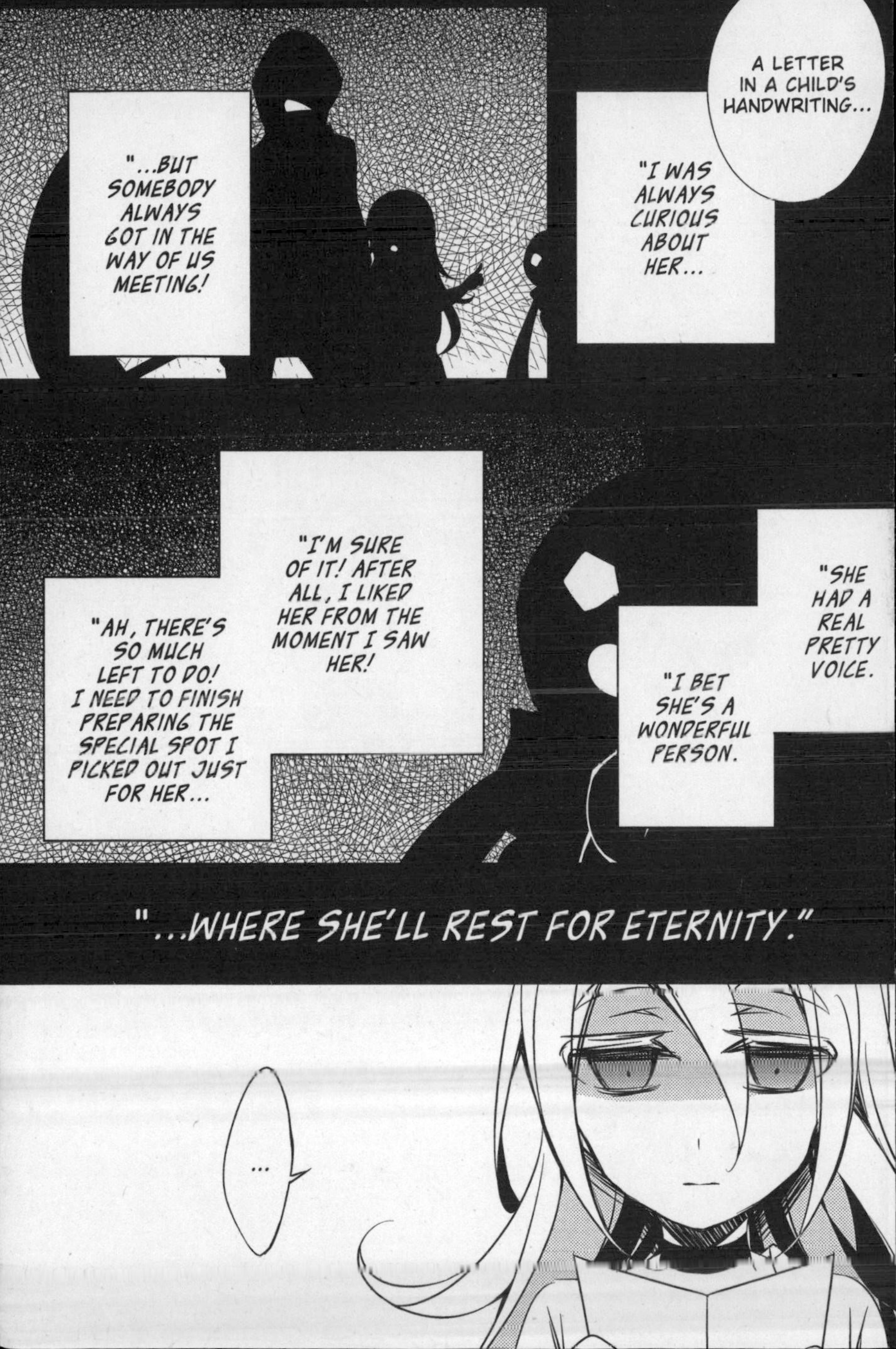
A LETTER IN A CHILD'S HANDWRITING...
"I WAS ALWAYS CURIOUS ABOUT HER...
"...BUT SOMEBODY ALWAYS GOT IN THE WAY OF US MEETING!
"SHE HAD A REAL PRETTY VOICE.
"I BET SHE'S A WONDERFUL PERSON.
"I'M SURE OF IT! AFTER ALL, I LIKED HER FROM THE MOMENT I SAW HER!
"AH, THERE'S SO MUCH LEFT TO DO! I NEED TO FINISH PREPARING THE SPECIAL SPOT I PICKED OUT JUST FOR HER...
"...WHERE SHE'LL REST FOR ETERNITY."
...

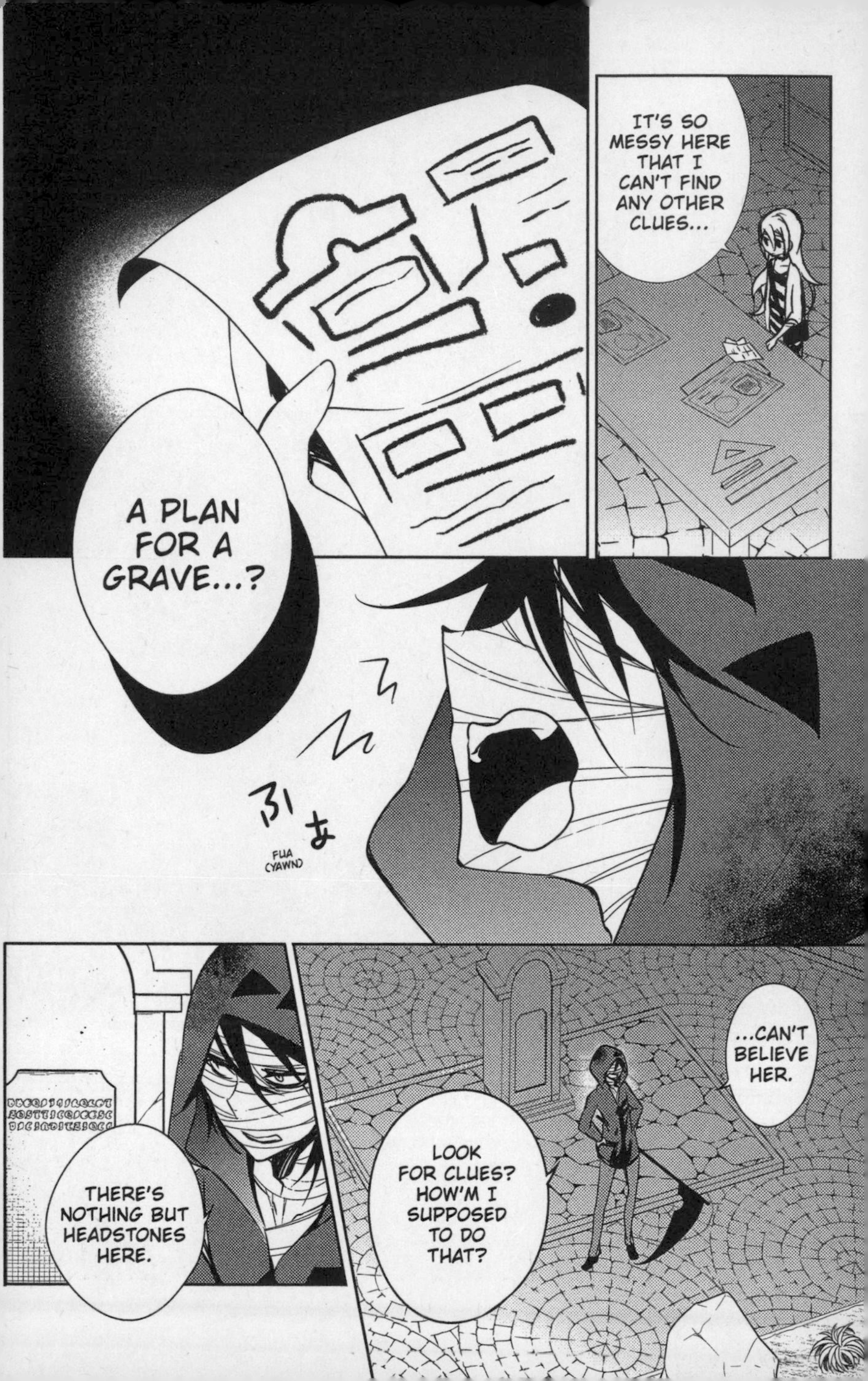
IT'S SO MESSY HERE THAT I CAN'T FIND ANY OTHER CLUES...
A PLAN FOR A GRAVE...?
ふあ
FUA (YAWN)
...CAN'T BELIEVE HER.
LOOK FOR CLUES? HOW'M I SUPPOSED TO DO THAT?
THERE'S NOTHING BUT HEADSTONES HERE.

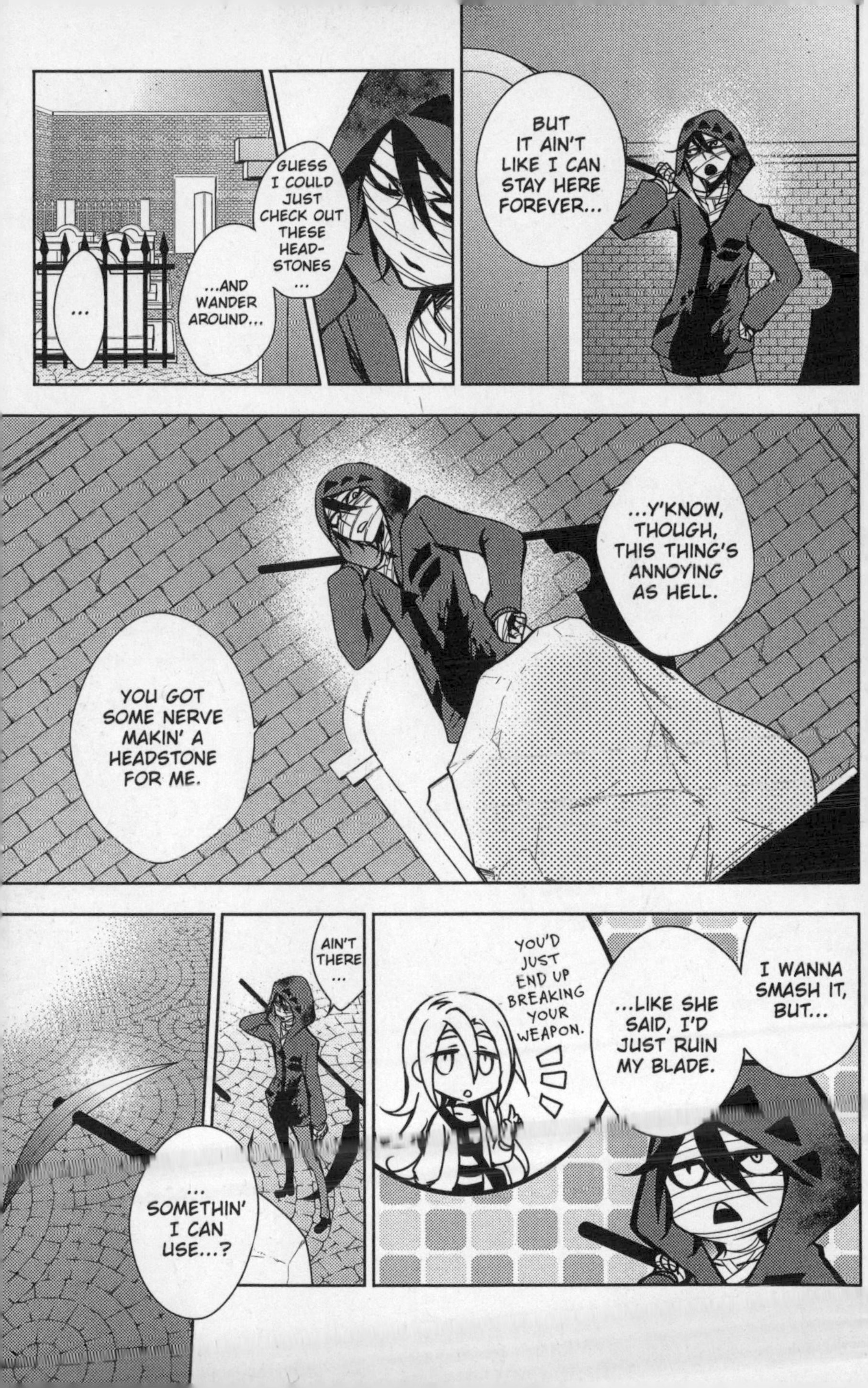
BUT IT AIN'T LIKE I CAN STAY HERE FOREVER...
GUESS I COULD JUST CHECK OUT THESE HEAD-STONES ...
...AND WANDER AROUND...
...
...Y'KNOW, THOUGH, THIS THING'S ANNOYING AS HELL.
YOU GOT SOME NERVE MAKIN' A HEADSTONE FOR ME.
I WANNA SMASH IT, BUT...
...LIKE SHE SAID, I'D JUST RUIN MY BLADE.
YOU'D JUST END UP BREAKING YOUR WEAPON.
AIN'T THERE ...
... SOMETHIN' I CAN USE...?

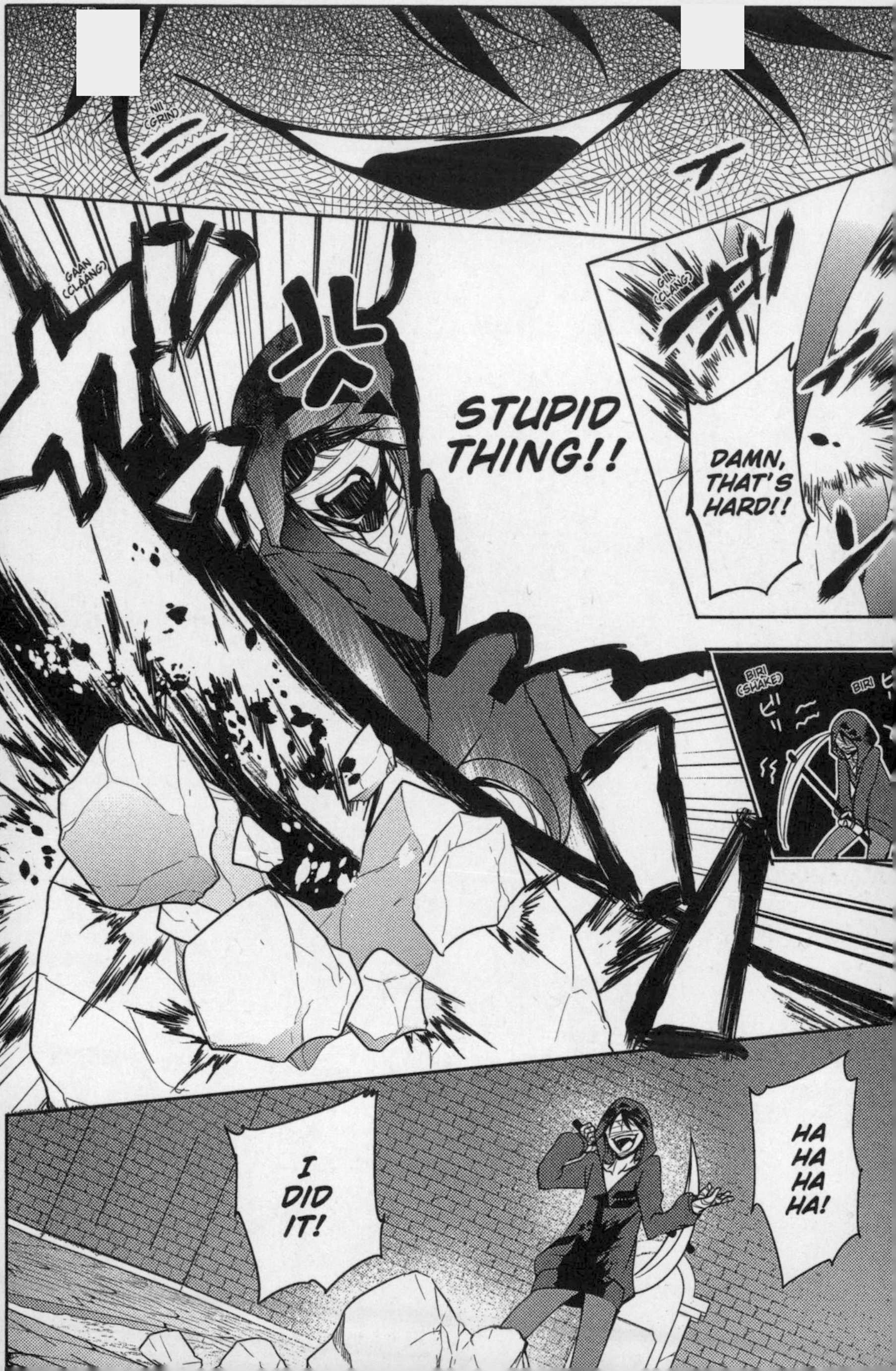
NII (GRIN)
GIN (CLANG)
DAMN, THAT'S HARD!!
BIRI (SHAKE)
BIRI
GAAN (CLAANG)
STUPID THING!!
HA HA HA HA!
I DID IT!

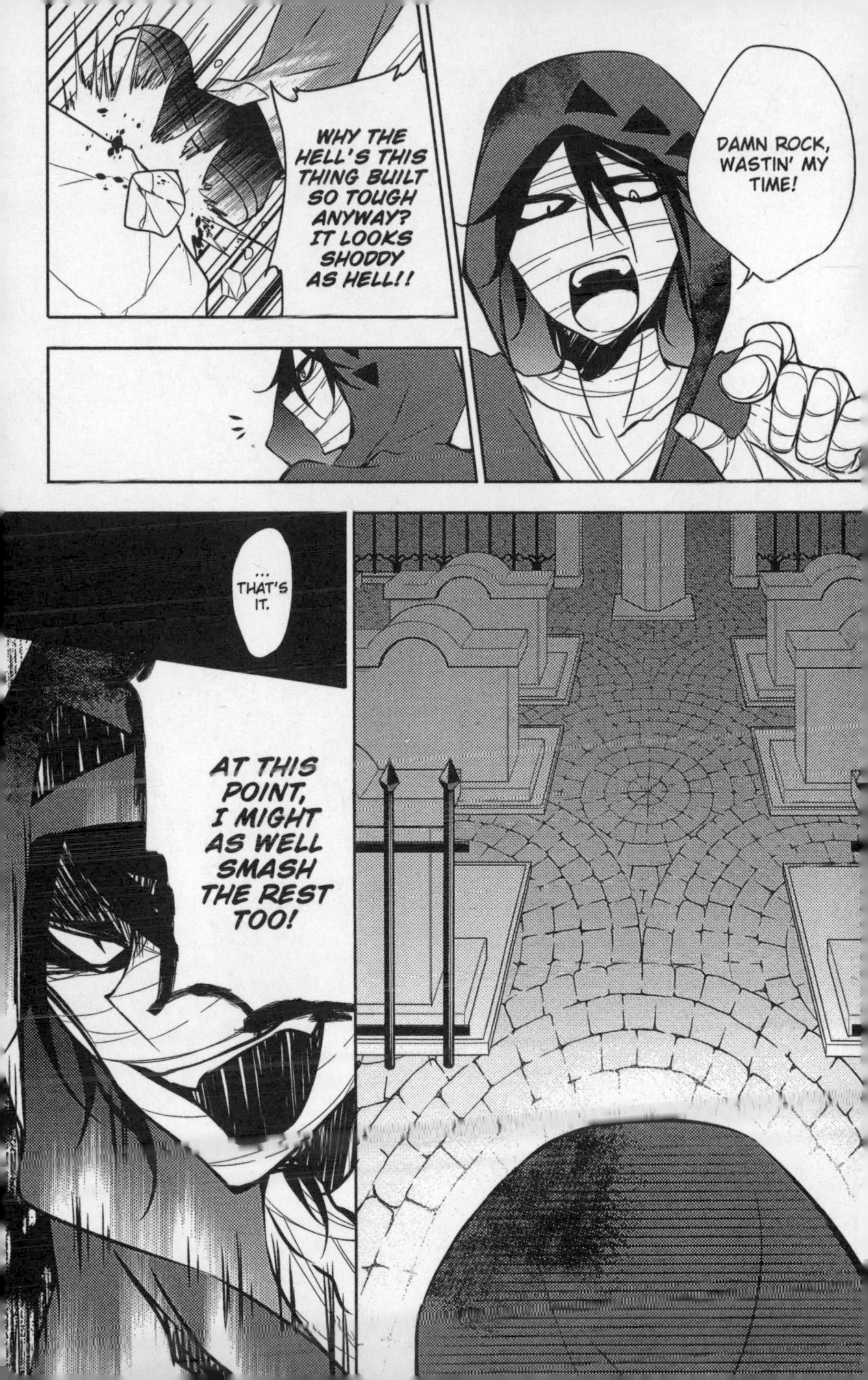
DAMN ROCK, WASTIN' MY TIME!
WHY THE HELL'S THIS THING BUILT SO TOUGH ANYWAY? IT LOOKS SHODDY AS HELL!!
... THAT'S IT.
AT THIS POINT, I MIGHT AS WELL SMASH THE REST TOO!

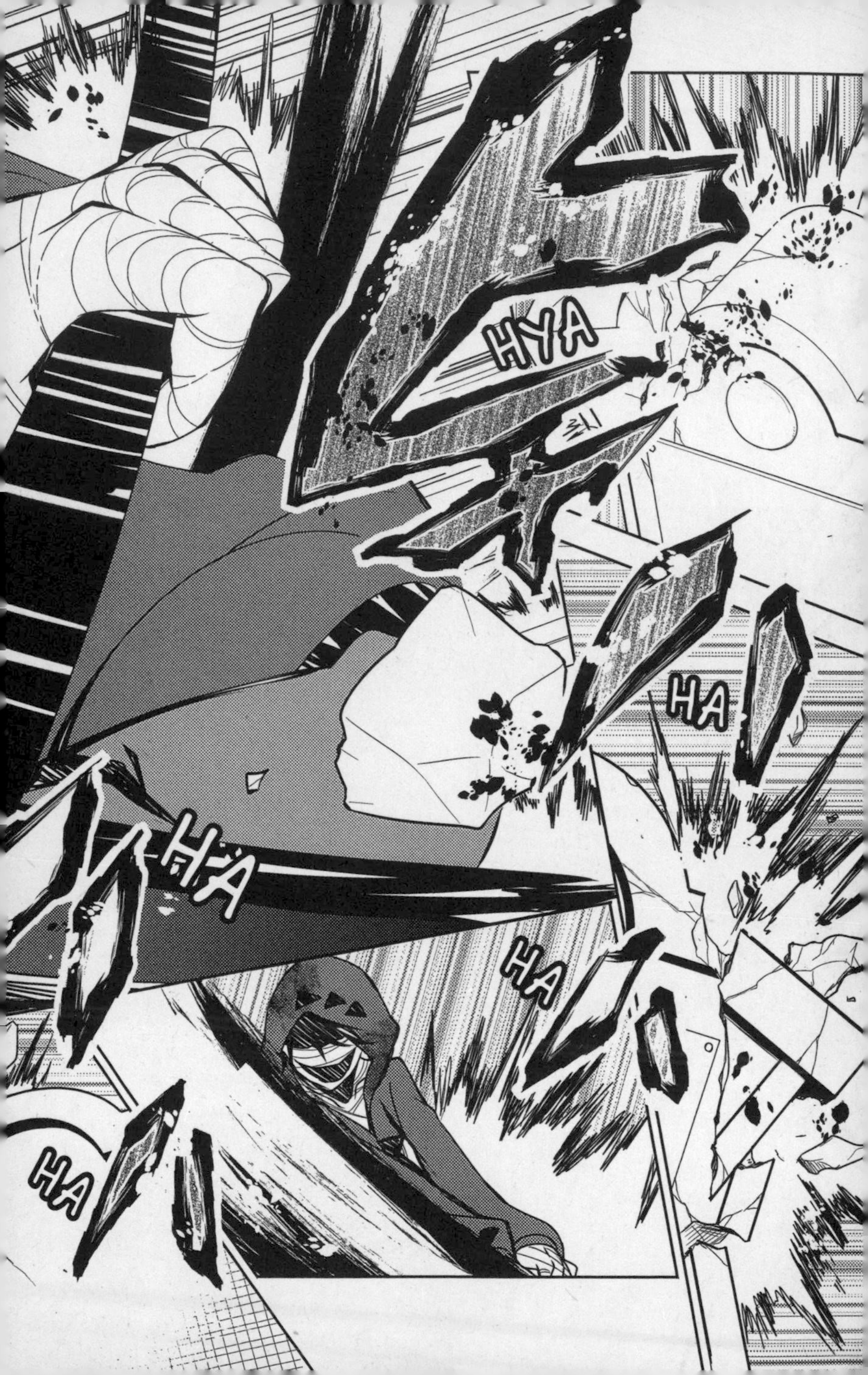
HYA
HA
HA
HA
HA

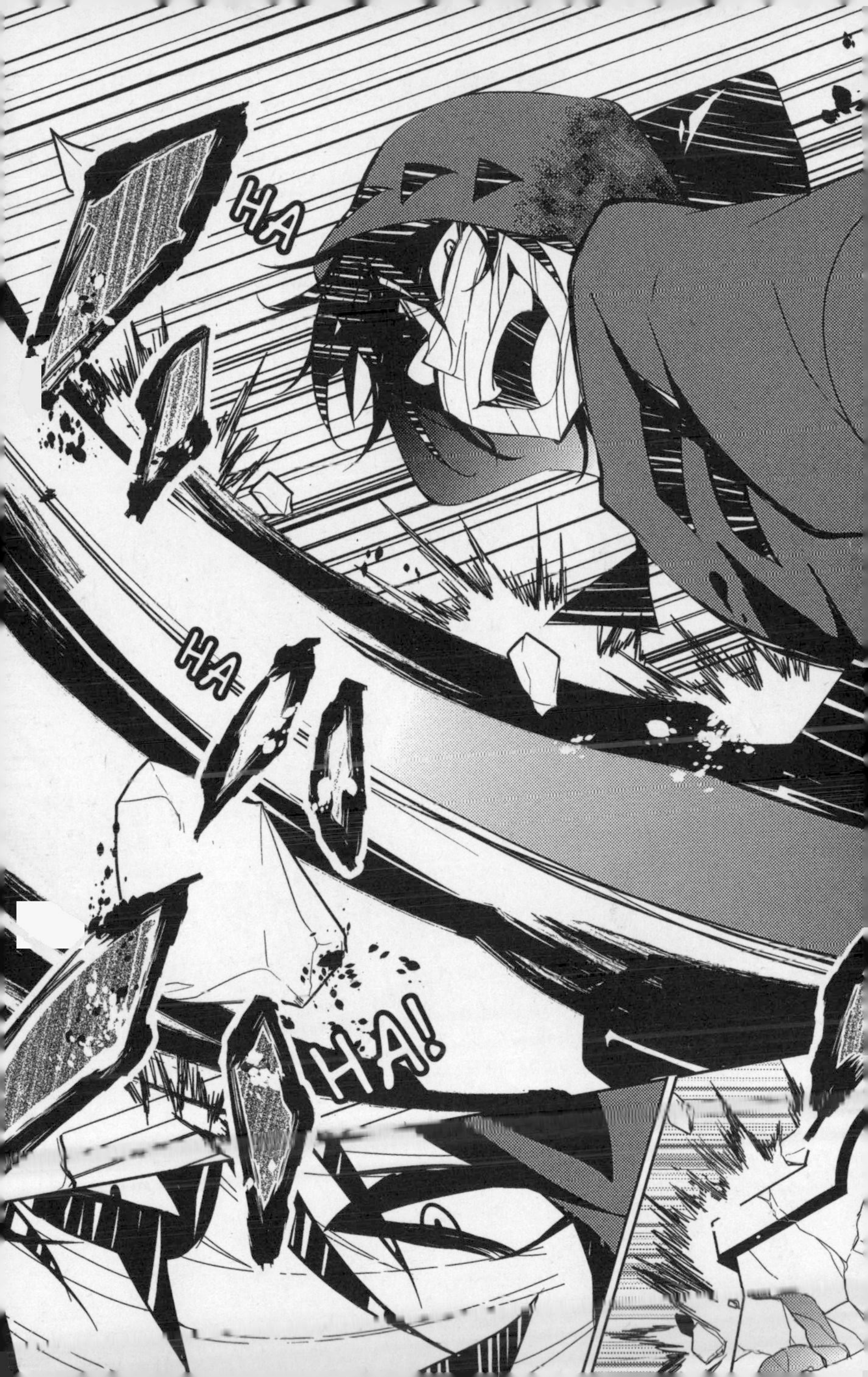
HA
HA
HA!

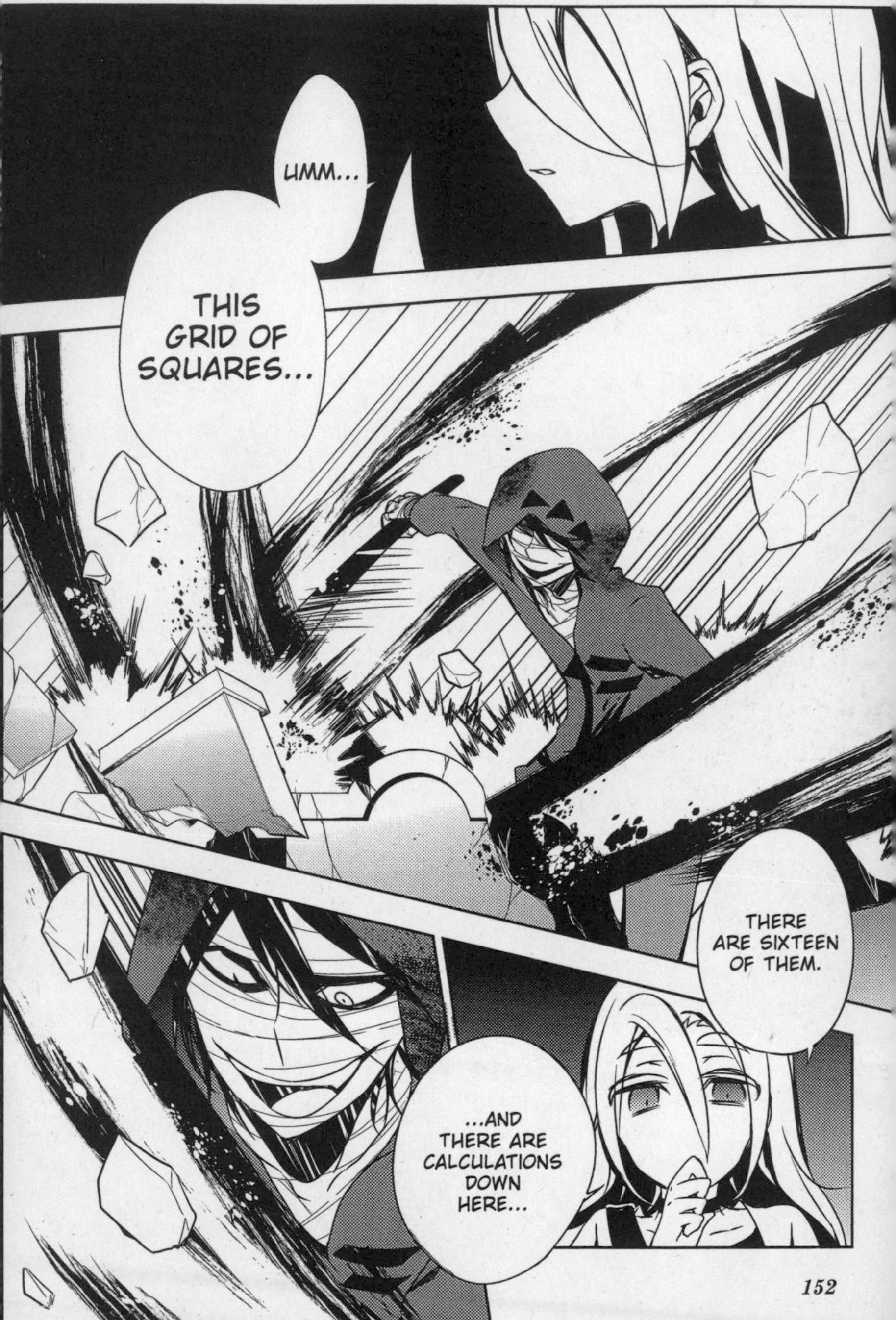
UMM...
THIS GRID OF SQUARES...
THERE ARE SIXTEEN OF THEM.
...AND THERE ARE CALCULATIONS DOWN HERE...

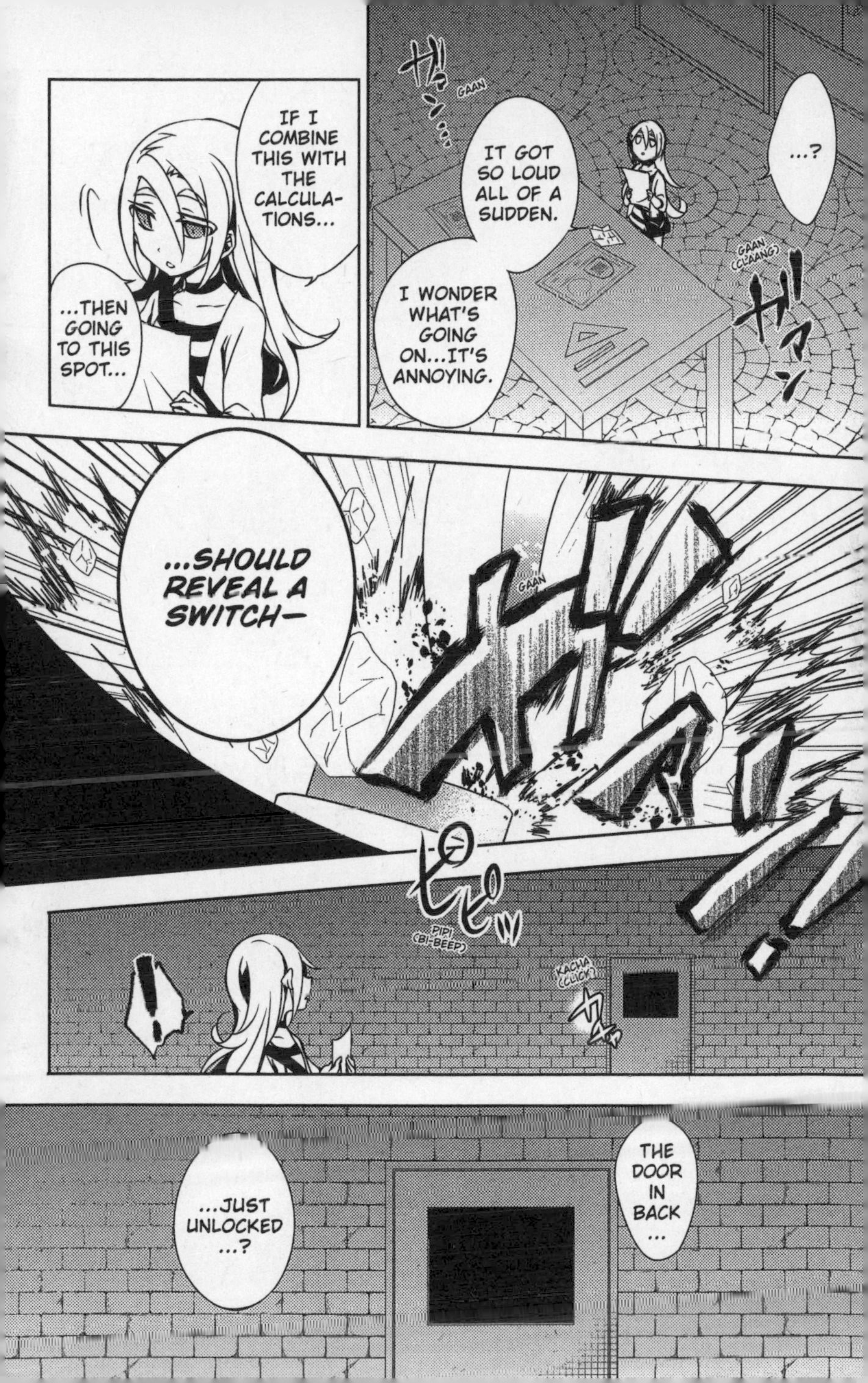
...?
GAAN (CLAANG)
GAAN
IT GOT SO LOUD ALL OF A SUDDEN.
I WONDER WHAT'S GOING ON...IT'S ANNOYING.
IF I COMBINE THIS WITH THE CALCULATIONS...
...THEN GOING TO THIS SPOT...
...SHOULD REVEAL A SWITCH—
GAAN
PIPI (BI-BEEP)
KACHA (CLICK)
THE DOOR IN BACK...
...JUST UNLOCKED...?

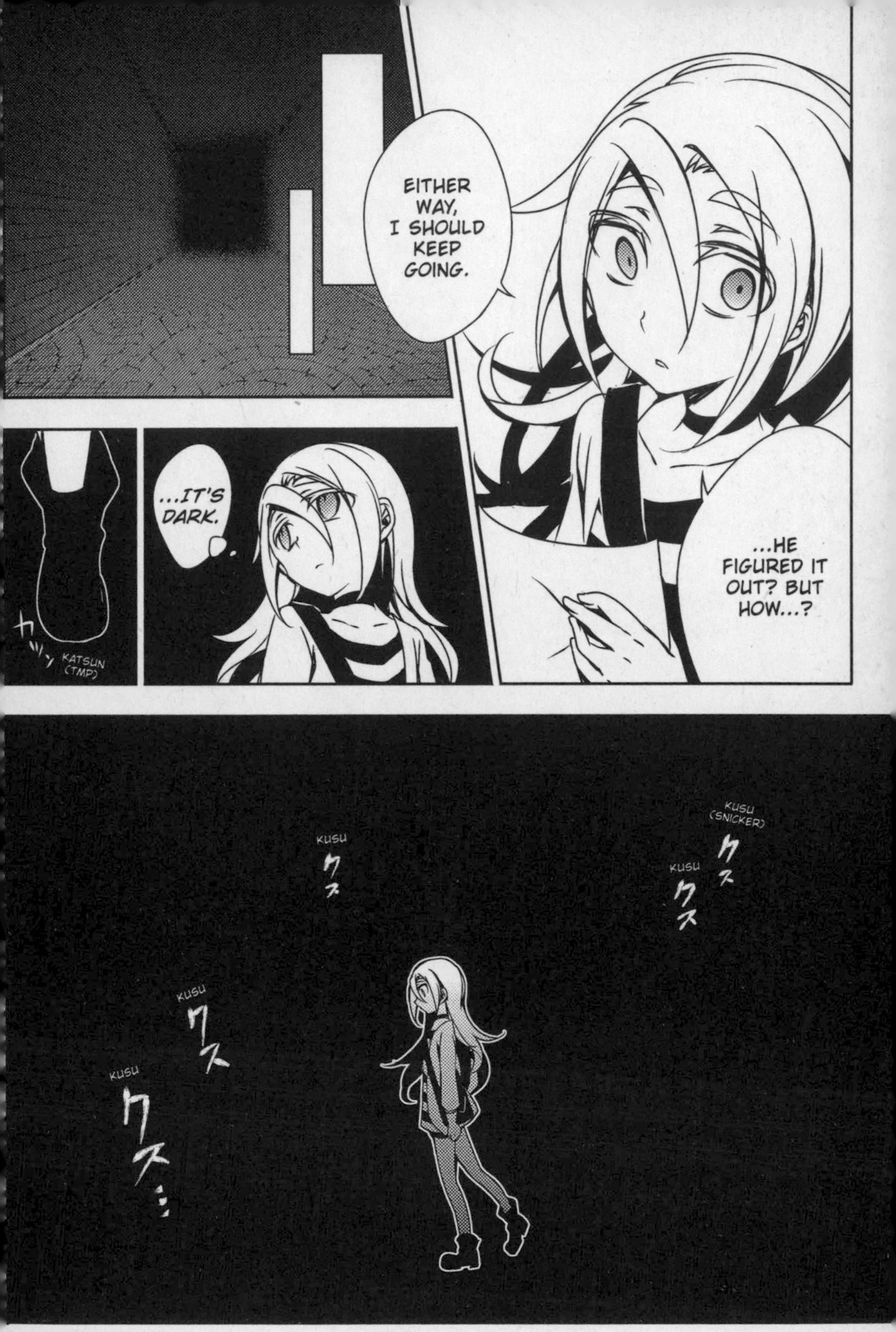
...HE FIGURED IT OUT? BUT HOW...?
EITHER WAY, I SHOULD KEEP GOING.
...IT'S DARK.
KATSUN (TMP)
KUSU (SNICKER)
KUSU
KUSU
KUSU
KUSU

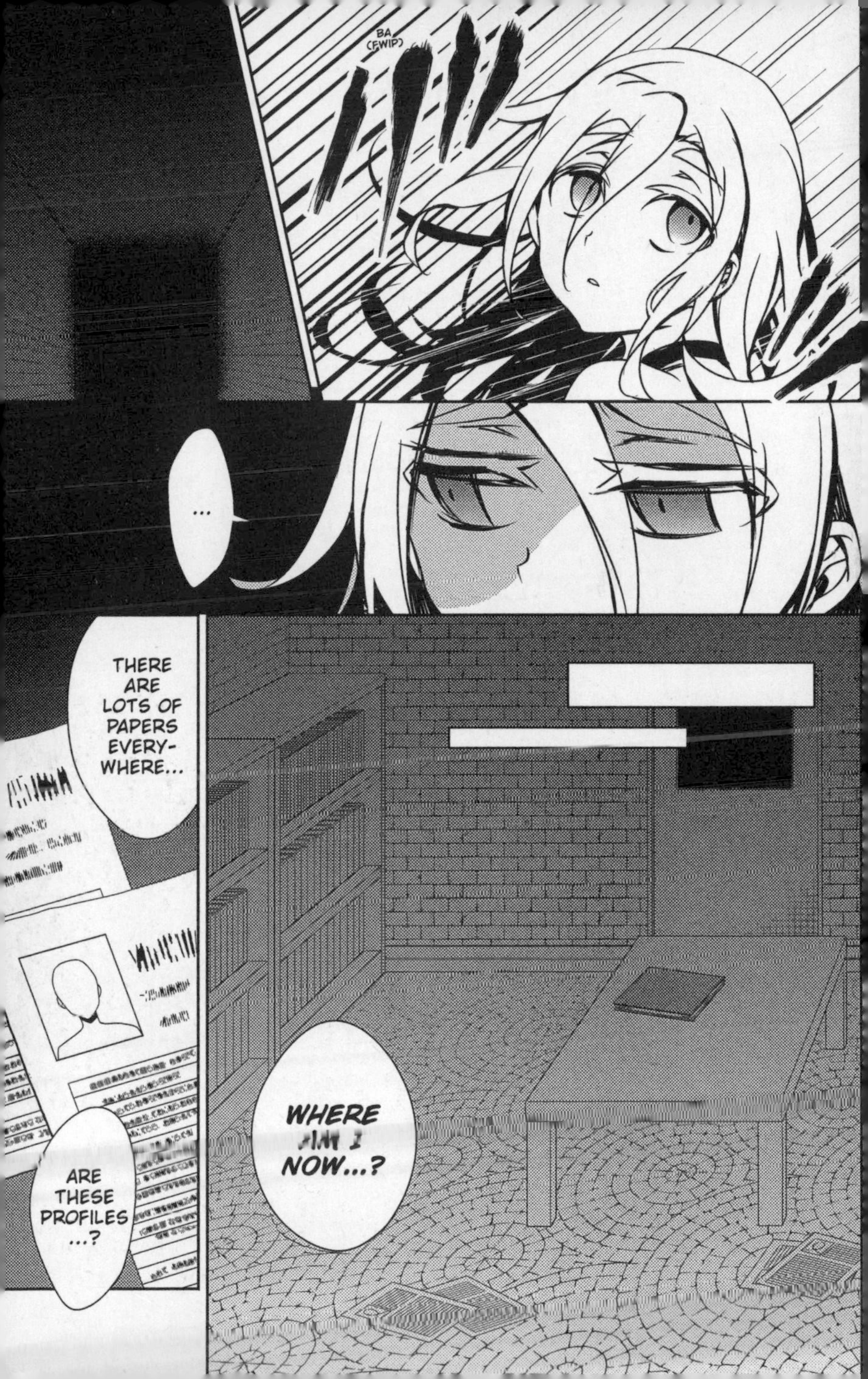
BA (FWIP)
...
WHERE AM I NOW...?
THERE ARE LOTS OF PAPERS EVERY-WHERE...
ARE THESE PROFILES ...?

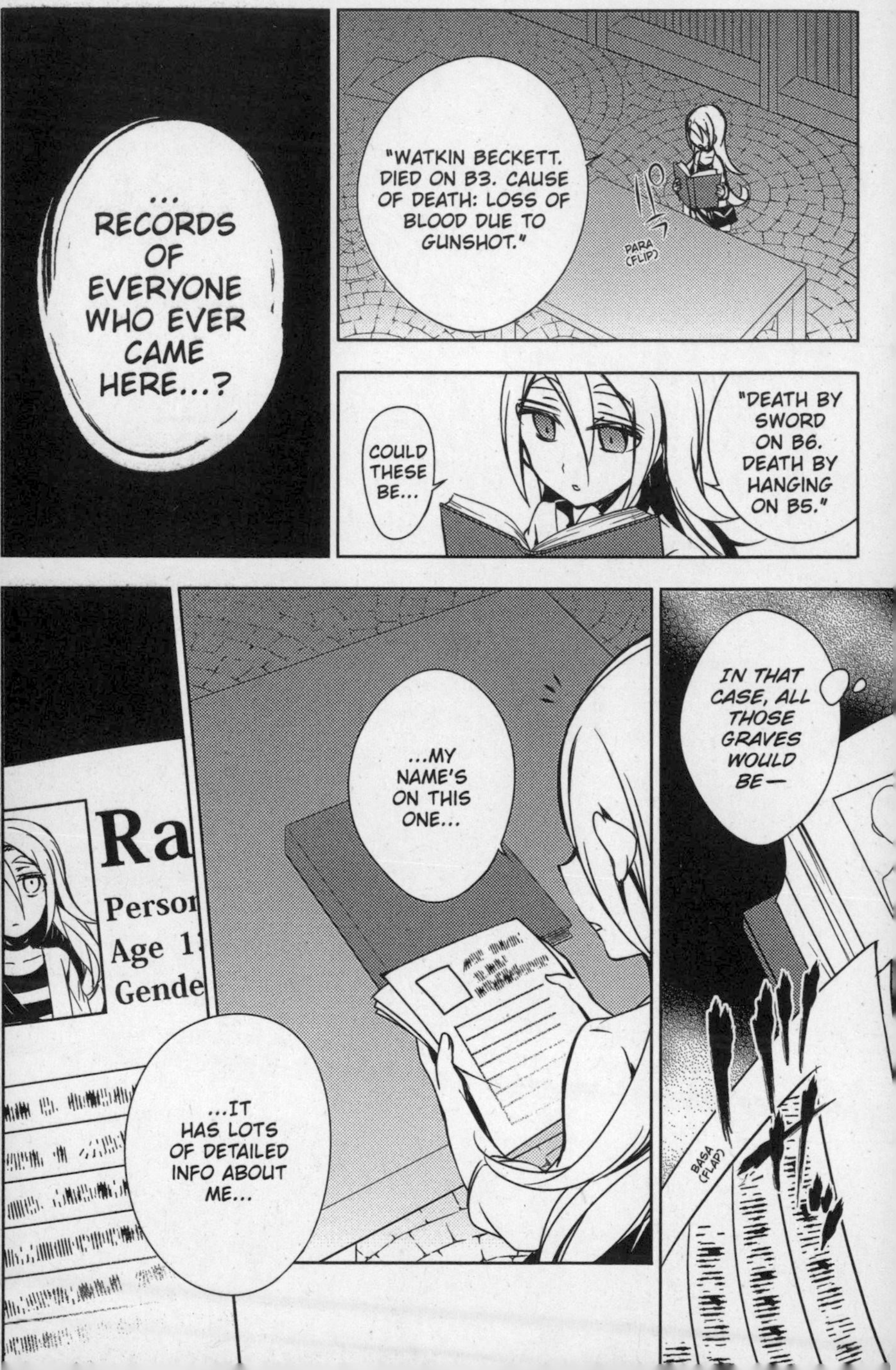

"WATKIN BECKETT. DIED ON B3. CAUSE OF DEATH: LOSS OF BLOOD DUE TO GUNSHOT."
PARA (FLIP)
"DEATH BY SWORD ON B6. DEATH BY HANGING ON B5."
COULD THESE BE...
... RECORDS OF EVERYONE WHO EVER CAME HERE...?
IN THAT CASE, ALL THOSE GRAVES WOULD BE—
BASA (FLAP)
...MY NAME'S ON THIS ONE...
Ra
Perso
Age 1
Gende
...IT HAS LOTS OF DETAILED INFO ABOUT ME...

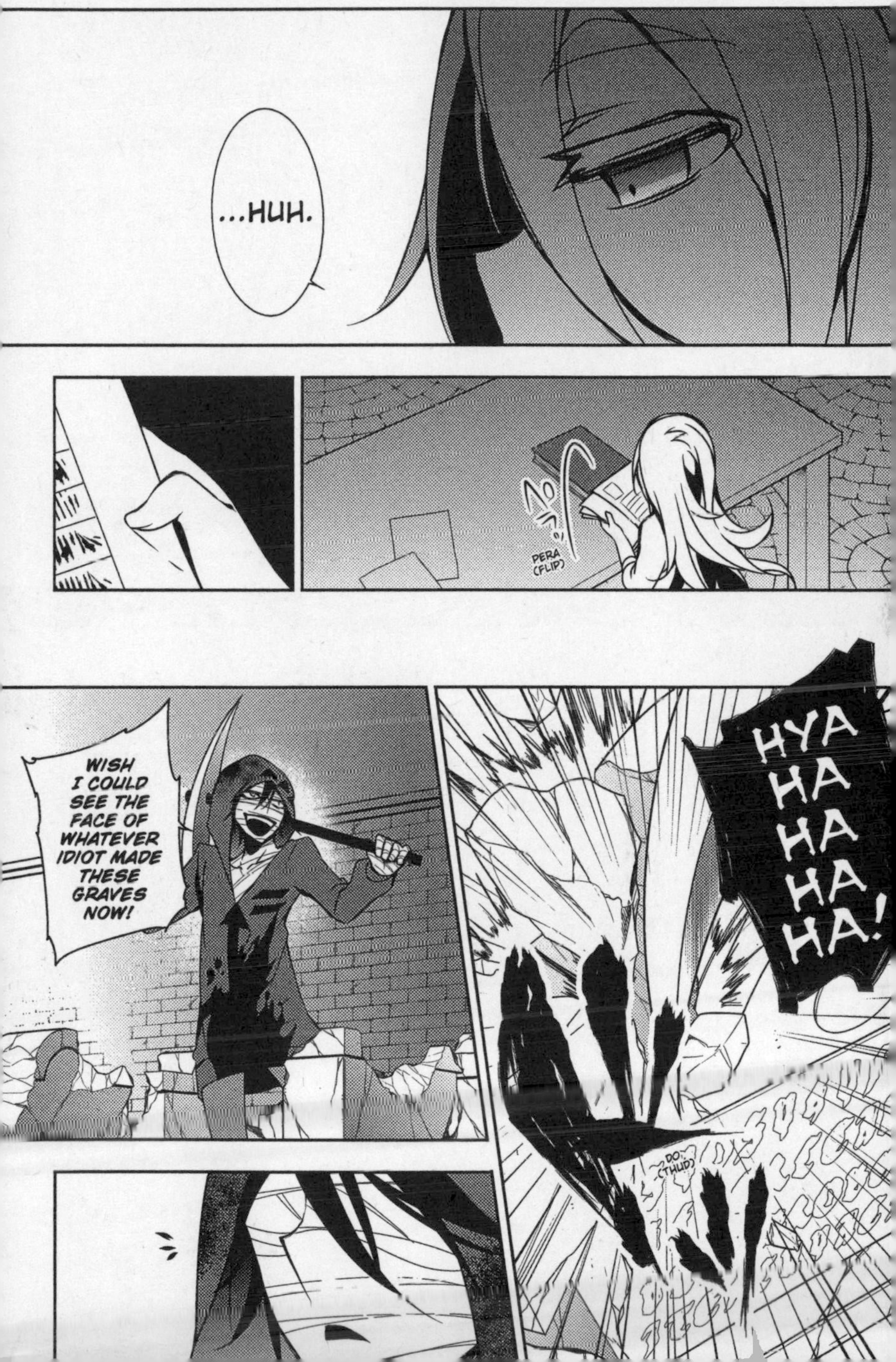
...HUH.
PERA (FLIP)
HYA HA HA HA HA HA!
DO (THUD)
WISH I COULD SEE THE FACE OF WHATEVER IDIOT MADE THESE GRAVES NOW!

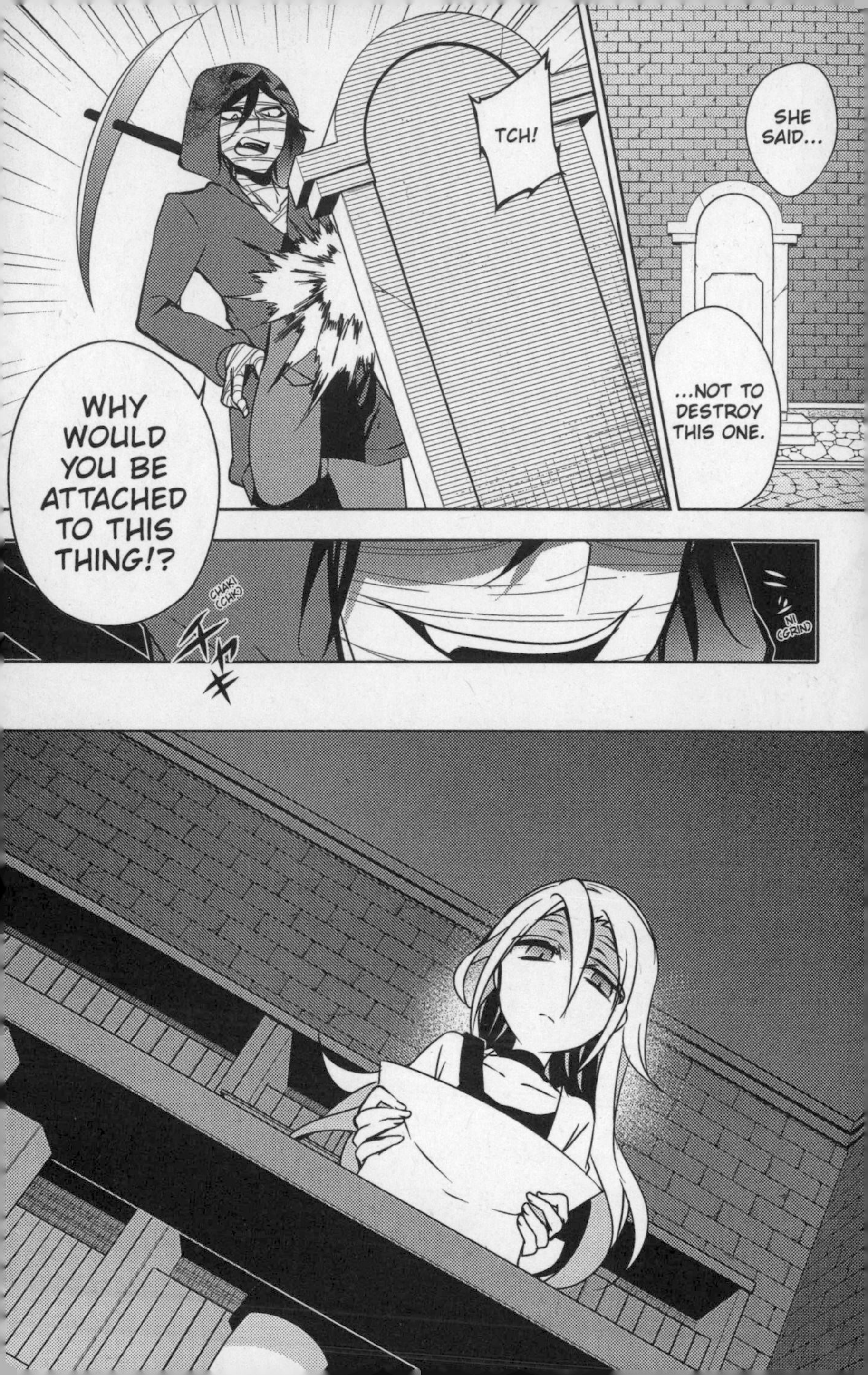
SHE SAID...
...NOT TO DESTROY THIS ONE.
TCH!
WHY WOULD YOU BE ATTACHED TO THIS THING!?
NI (GRIN)
CHAKI (CHK)

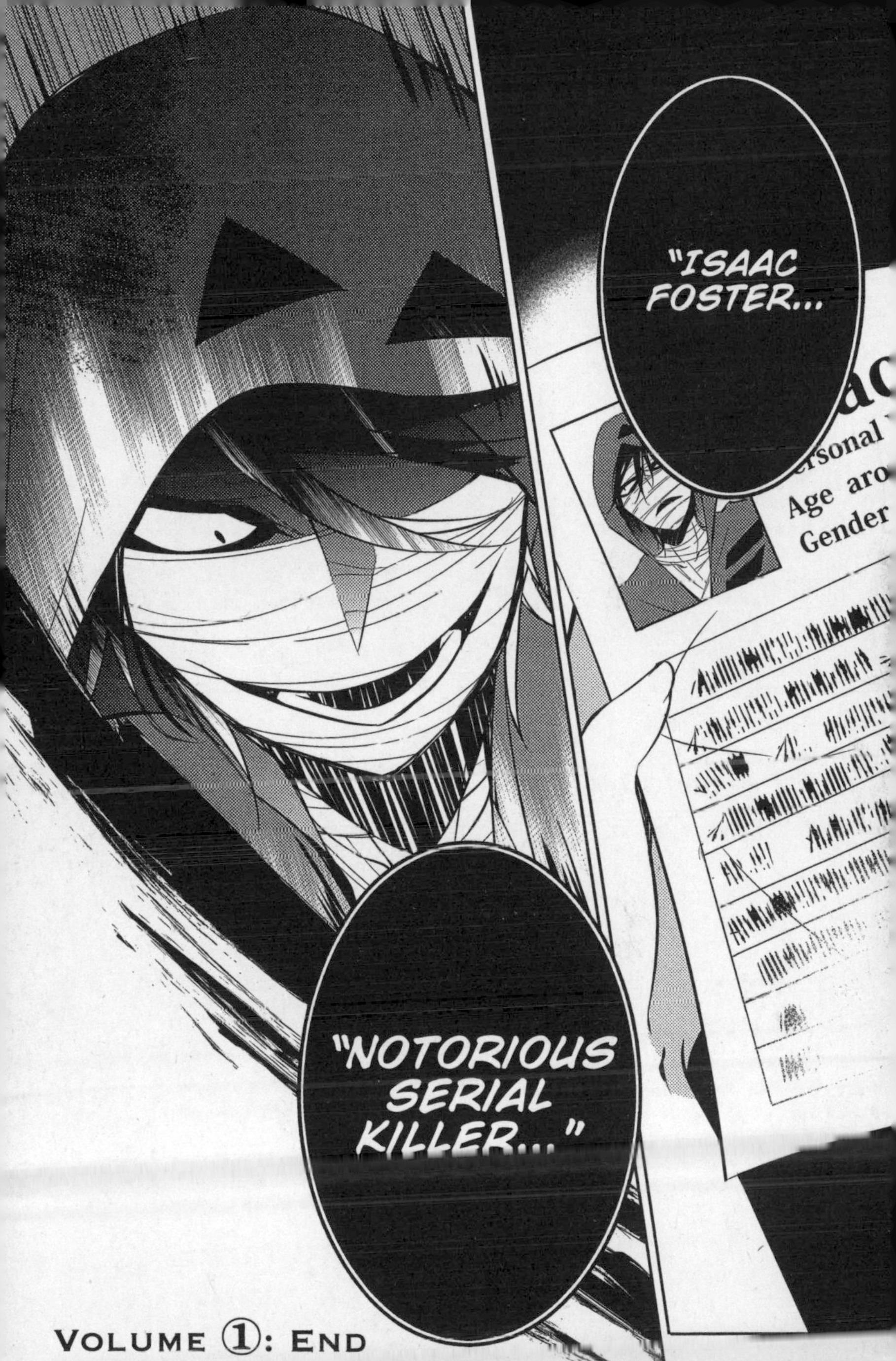
"ISAAC FOSTER...
"NOTORIOUS SERIAL KILLER..."
VOLUME ①: END

AFTERWORD

THANK YOU FOR PICKING UP VOLUME 1 OF *ANGELS OF DEATH*. I'M VERY HAPPY TO BE HANDLING THE MANGA ADAPTATION OF ANOTHER ONE OF MAKOTO SANADA'S WORKS FOLLOWING HIS PREVIOUS TITLE, *KIRISAME GA FURU MORI* (FOUR VOLUMES IN TOTAL). I CAN'T WAIT TO KEEP ON DRAWING RAY AND ZACK GOING THROUGH THE DIFFERENT WORLDS OF EACH FLOOR THAT CHANGE EVERY TIME THEY CLIMB UP ANOTHER LEVEL, MEETING THE EXTREMELY UNIQUE CHARACTERS FOUND ON EACH ONE, AND EXPLORING THE DEEPENING MYSTERY.
PLEASE LOOK FORWARD TO THE NEXT VOLUME!

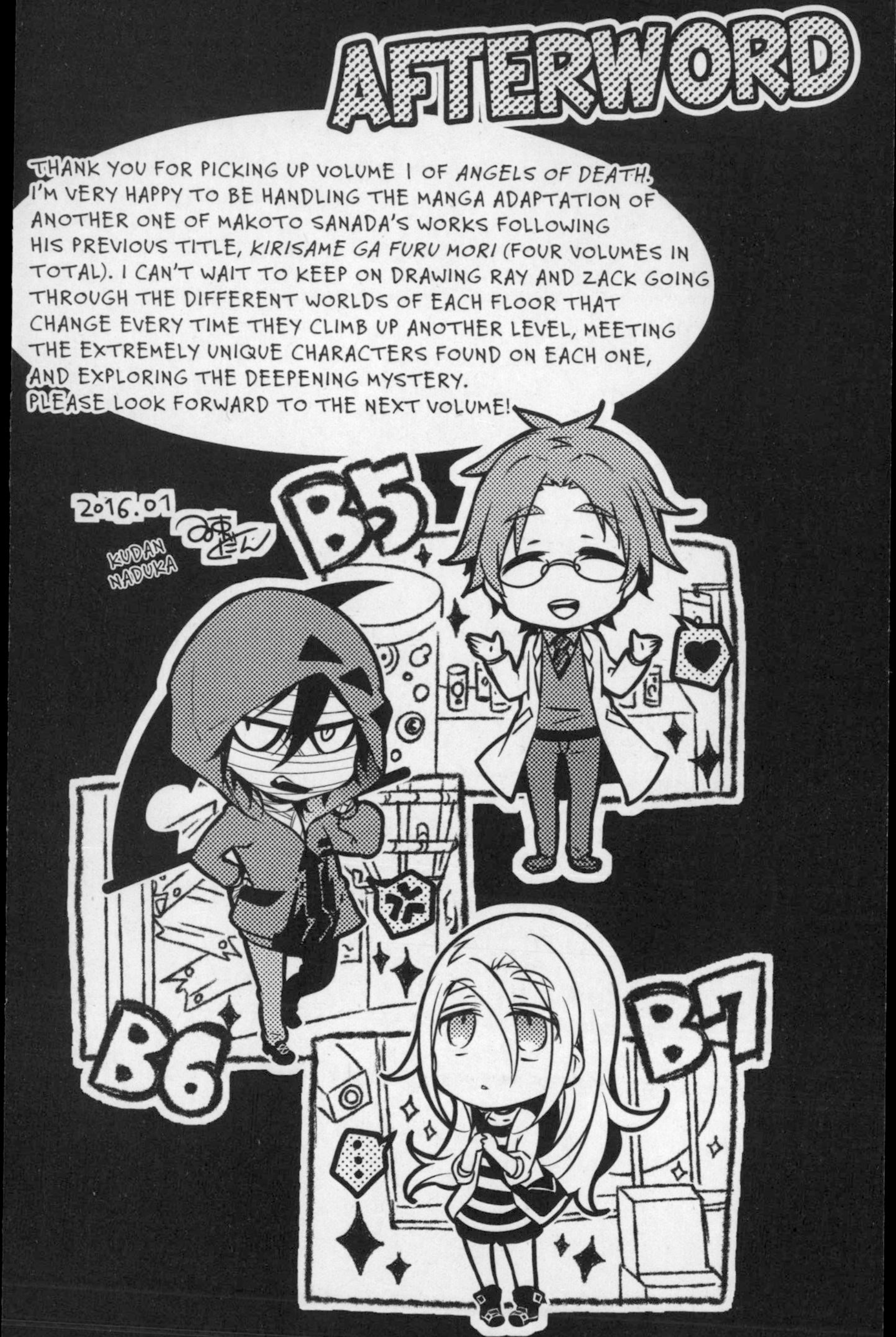
2016.01
KUDAN NADUKA
B5
B6
B7

[AFTERWORD]

Thank you very much for reading Volume 1 of *Angels of Death*'s manga adaptation. I'm very happy you decided to pick this book up.

I'm still shocked the decision was made to adapt my freeware game of the same name that was first released as a serialized title in *Niconico Game Magazine*. At the same time, I'm extremely grateful.

Kudan Naduka, who is working on this adaptation following our previous title, *Kirisame ga Furu Mori,* has depicted this work in an even more impactful way.

I hope you continue to enjoy watching Rachel and Zack as they move through the world of *Angels of Death* as it unfolds in manga form.

Makoto Sanada

Angels of DEATH 1

ART **KUDAN NADUKA**   ORIGINAL STORY **MAKOTO SANADA**

TRANSLATION: KO RANSOM

LETTERING: ANTHONY QUINTESSENZA

SATSURIKU NO TENSHI Volume 1 ©Kudan Naduka 2016, Makoto Sanada 2016. First published in Japan in 2016 by KADOKAWA CORPORATION, Tokyo. English translation rights arranged with KADOKAWA CORPORATION, Tokyo through Tuttle-Mori Agency, Inc.

English translation © 2017 by Yen Press, LLC

Yen Press
1290 Avenue of the Americas
New York, NY 10104

Visit us at yenpress.com
facebook.com/yenpress
twitter.com/yenpress
yenpress.tumblr.com
instagram.com/yenpress

First Yen Press Edition: December 2017

Yen Press is an imprint of Yen Press, LLC.
The Yen Press name and logo are trademarks of Yen Press, LLC.

Library of Congress Control Number: 2017949552

ISBN: 978-0-316-44176-6 (paperback)
978-0-316-44177-3 (ebook)

10 9 8 7 6 5 4 3 2 1

BVG

Printed in the United States of America